Shaq Impaq

Bruce Hunter

Bonus Books, Inc., Chicago

97   96   95   94   93   5   4   3   2   1

Library of Congress Catalog Card Number: 93-72144

International Standard Book Number: 1-56625-030-7

Bonus Books, Inc.
160 East Illinois Street
Chicago, Illinois 60611

Composition by Point West, Inc., Carol Stream, IL

Printed in the United States of America

Contents

Introduction

I was fortunate enough to meet Shaquille O'Neal in 1988 when he was a 16-year-old schoolboy, and I have covered his remarkable basketball career for the last five years. This is your chance to meet the real Shaquille, not the carefully packaged Shaq image you see on TV or at the arenas. You will get to know the tender-hearted, happy-go-lucky young man who's the rage of the NBA and marketing world as well as his selfish, occasionally violent side that makes league officials and his million-dollar sponsors shudder. In striving to present the complete picture of Shaq, I have interviewed and visited with hundreds of his friends, associates, family members, teammates and acquaintances. Wherever he's gone, Shaq has had a profound Impaq.

If you're one of the millions and millions of sports fans who loved every minute of his marvelous rookie season, then you'll understand how fortunate those of us are who knew Shaquille before he had worldwide appeal. We got to enjoy Shaq for his joking, fun-loving, smiling self before he got caught up in the draining, time-consuming world of pro sports and marketing. No athlete I've ever known could get a crowded room of hardened reporters to break out in laughter just by being himself. His long, crooked smile was contagious. He almost always made you forget whatever problems you had and just giggle a little. Some days, he would make up wild stories about completely changing his style of play. Other days, he would be routinely answering questions and then just crack up and cause everyone else to burst out laughing. Perhaps the best Shaq story was the time he arrived a few minutes late for an interview at LSU with magazine writer Ruth Laney. He discovered she had walked down the hall to the ladies' restroom and he proceeded to lock the door on her. He held back his laughter as Laney repeatedly banged on the door and yelled for help so she wouldn't miss her appointment with Shaq.

Everyone around him soon discovered that he was just a big kid, although much larger than most college students, who didn't allow the fame of being America's most heralded college player to affect him. Those who wondered how he could be such a level-headed young man with all the attention and hype he was getting needed only to check his past. His father and mother set high ethical and disciplinary standards in their home, and no child of theirs, even a 7-foot-1 All-World center, would get away with bending the rules.

Philip Harrison, who is said to be Shaq's real father despite the different last name, was a staff sergeant in the Army for 20 years and plans to retire in 1993. Though unfortunately best known for his frequent explosive outbursts, Harrison deserves credit for instilling an impenetrable sense of discipline, character and pride in his son. Anyone with children would have to admire the job he did in raising one of the finest young men you'll ever meet, aside from the explosive, egotistical traits that Shaq apparently acquired from his father. Harrison can also be charming and engaging as long as the conversation pleases him.

I found out the hard way that Harrison's temper flares easily. He attacked and threatened me after a routine interview in Orlando for this book. Actually, Shaq had to come to my aid, calming down his father and getting him to leave me alone. O'Neal had welcomed me to Orlando and introduced me to his teammates. Even though he was working on his own project, he did not object to my book. As always he was very cooperative, and simply told me, "Hey, you've got a job to do."

Lucille Harrison's motherly influence on Shaquille O'Neal is perhaps even more profound. She was the stabilizing force in the family. While Philip screamed at and "beat" his son, Lucille balanced it out with her tender, loving ways. Whenever Shaq is asked who's had the most influence on his life, he always says his mother. Perhaps that is why he continues to use her maiden name of O'Neal. Her gentle manner is reflected in Shaq's eagerness to share his good fortune with the homeless and underprivileged. Before he had any money, he gave of himself, regularly volunteering to speak to school children and youth groups in San Antonio and Baton Rouge.

It has been my privilege to watch Shaq progress from the class clown in high school to a college sensation who easily handled fame to a young pro superstar who leaped into the National Basketball Association with unprecedented style and grace.

While writing *Don't Count Me Out*, the story of a season inside Dale Brown's basketball program at LSU, I met a 6-foot-10 recruit by the name of Shaquille from San Antonio, Texas. Most college coaches were familiar with 16-year-old Shaq, but he certainly didn't have the tremendous credentials of his future LSU teammates Chris Jackson and Stanley Roberts. He immediately impressed me as a soft-spoken, humble youngster, who was obviously from a good home.

Later that spring, I flew with Brown to San Antonio to see Shaq again and meet his parents and siblings. Once again, I was impressed by the youngster and his family. The occasion was a banquet to honor Shaq's undefeated team. It gave me a chance to get to know him better.

But that was just the beginning. I covered all three of his college seasons, which provided one thrill after another. During his freshman year, he blocked a shot so hard that it went flying over my head at press row and landed 30 feet away on top of the head of a lady walking out to the concession area. I also got an up-close look at the Real Shaquille during more private moments, such as pickup games and off-court activities.

Once he got to Orlando to begin his NBA career, everyone who had followed his college career suddenly caught Magic fever. Sports bars and restaurants with satellite dishes were packed every time Shaq and Orlando played a game. But not even his most loyal fans anticipated the smashing success he immediately found in a league that isn't supposed to be dominated by a rookie. Of course, the nation quickly learned that O'Neal was no run-of-the-mill No. 1 pick. Some of his peers said he was already the NBA's toughest center to handle, due to his rare blend of size, power and athleticism.

Naturally, Shaq was showered with comparisons to the all-time greats: Wilt Chamberlain, Kareem Abdul-Jabbar, Bill Russell and some of the modern-day stars like Patrick Ewing, Hakeem Olajuwon and David Robinson. Chamberlain was quick to say that the new kid was "no Wilt." He was right.

When you look closely at O'Neal, you find a new breed of big man. He's a young guy who is 50 pounds heavier and much broader than Chamberlain was when he came into the league back in 1959. Former Magic coach and current v.p. Matt Guokas, who played with and against Wilt, says his new center is even quicker than his former teammate. Keep in mind that when Chamberlain ruled the NBA to the tune of 39 points a game as a rookie, he was playing against just one other seven-footer in the entire league. O'Neal, on the other hand, faces one or two every night.

Critics correctly point out that Shaq has all the physical tools to reach the elite level of basketball's all-time greats, but has a long way to go with his offensive repertoire.

What makes O'Neal so special is the way he blends his intimidating style of play with a warm, charming, easy-going manner away from the court. If it takes charisma to win the hearts of America, Shaq has enough to ensure himself a place as the game's most adored player, following in the footsteps of the retired Magic Johnson and Larry Bird and sharing the spotlight with the magnificent Michael Jordan.

Let me assure you, the Shaquille appeal is real and lasting. Yet when you put anyone under a magnifying glass for long enough, you will find flaws and short-comings. I've been observing this young man for almost five years. I spent the final stages of the 1992–93 NBA season in Orlando watching Shaq lead the Magic into playoff contention and ultimately lose out on a silly tie-breaker rule.

Shaquille O'Neal appears to be a carefree young man who's got the world at his feet. But what you see is not necessarily what you get. His father has been both a blessing and a hindrance in Shaq's life, providing the discipline to get to the top, but interfering with an overbearing, explosive personality that has exploded many times. Those who know Shaq well see a lot of his father in him.

O'Neal has a golden smile that radiates from a caring heart. But he is troubled by a fiery temper that caused him to beat up close friends and teammates at LSU. If he had not been protected by Dale Brown and other university officials, he could have faced criminal charges on at least one occasion, police records state. His temper has also come to light in Orlando, but for the most part, those tantrums have been confined to the privacy of the team's locker room, and he has yet to strike anyone. The only exception was the time he punched Detroit guard Alvin Robertson, who was trying to keep O'Neal from going after his teammate, Bill Laimbeer. And Shaq immediately said, "I'd do it again."

During my many years watching Shaq, I have come to understand and appreciate his strengths and weaknesses. I hope you will too.

Interestingly, when I interviewed Shaq for a *Sporting News* cover story for the 1990–91 college basketball preview magazine, he told me, "Man, my father really liked your book on Coach Brown. When are you going to write a book about me?"

Right now, Shaq.

Bruce Hunter
June 1993

one

Wunderkind

April 3, 1989

SAN ANTONIO, Texas—Shaquille O'Neal had grown two inches and put on 20 or 25 pounds from the first time I had met him on his official visit to LSU that previous fall. Without a doubt, he was the most impressive-looking high school athlete I had ever seen. The scary part was he already stood seven feet tall, weighed 270 pounds and had just celebrated his 17th birthday, so he was certain to keep growing and growing.

The remarkable teenager led Robert Cole High School to a perfect 36–0 season and the Texas Class AAA state championship. His next stop would be LSU, where he would join the much-celebrated duo of Chris Jackson, already one of the best players in college basketball, and Stanley Roberts, an offensively gifted seven-footer. Collectively, there seemed to be no stopping O'Neal, Jackson and Roberts.

O'Neal had the physique, strength and agility to bypass the college game completely and go right into the NBA. Moses Malone and Darryl Dawkins accomplished the feat of jumping right into the pro ranks out of high school. But even those giants didn't have the huge stature that O'Neal was blessed with at such a tender age. And where was the baby fat? None was to be found on this teen phenom.

But instead of some NBA team, Dale Brown and the LSU Tigers had the good fortune of a real commitment from O'Neal. Brown was in town to be the special speaker at the awards banquet to honor the Cole High team. It was Brown, though, who felt honored to be associated with O'Neal and his father, Army Sgt. Philip Harrison. Shaquille took his mother's maiden name—O'Neal—because he was born while his father was in Germany with the Army. He continued to use O'Neal because he would be the last one to bear that name. His legal name, however, is Shaquille O'Neal Harrison.

Brown, the controversial master motivator of college basketball, had a long-standing relationship with the Harrison family. He was particularly close to Philip Harrison, with whom he had the common bond of a rough, poverty-stricken upbringing. They also shared similar values of hard work and commitment to family.

A world traveler, Brown met O'Neal when he was just a 13-year-old Army brat living with his family in Wildeflecken, West Germany. Brown had been invited by a clergyman to conduct a basketball clinic for the soldiers. Shaquille inquired about drills that would help his jumping ability, and the coach gladly obliged.

"By the way, how long have you been in the service, soldier?" Brown asked his enthusiastic pupil.

"I'm not in the service," O'Neal grinned. "I'm only 13 years old."

"You're only 13!" Brown said, gawking at the 6-foot-8 lad. "What's your name, son?"

"Shaquille O'Neal, sir," he answered.

Glancing down at his enormous shoes, Brown asked, "What size shoes do you wear?"

"Seventeen, sir," he replied, still smiling.

"I'd like to meet your Dad," Brown said, now smiling himself.

O'Neal led Brown to the steam room where his father was. To the coach's surprise, Sgt. Harrison didn't seem at all interested in his son playing basketball for LSU or any other school.

"Coach, I really could care less about basketball," Harrison told him. "I want him to develop his intellect. I would like him to go on and be successful academically. I like sports. But my son is going to get an education. That's all I care about, thank you."

Brown, noted for his convincing ways, highlighted the advantages of going to college on a basketball scholarship and earning a degree from a major university. Soon Harrison became interested in what he had to say.

"Sergeant, we're going to be good friends," Brown said before leaving.

Thus began the recruiting process in which Brown would send some 2,000 letters to O'Neal and eventually get his recruit to sign with LSU in November 1988. Despite O'Neal's incredible size for his age, he was not wildly heralded, due to his late start in basketball. Great attention and acclaim, however, would soon come his way once he got the opportunity to play in national all-star games later that spring.

Although Brown had nothing but kind remarks for O'Neal, he saved his most glowing comments for his father. Brown described Harrison as a man of great character and integrity. Most importantly, Brown said the sergeant was honest in every regard, having told every coach visiting his son that he wanted no offers of money or any kind of help. In fact, Harrison made it clear that if there were offers, the offending coach and school would be barred from further talks with the family.

"I've never had a more enjoyable time recruiting a kid," Brown said on the flight to San Antonio to see the Harrison family again. "The sergeant is a truly great man. You don't have to play any games with him. All he wants for his son is an education and a chance to play basketball, in that order. Now that's the way every parent should be."

While it was not uncommon to have cooperative parents, it seemed Sgt. Harrison had gone beyond the call of duty.

When we arrived at the Fort Sam Houston Officers' Club, a tuxedo-clad Harrison was waiting at the door to direct us to a parking place. Brown was first to get out of the car and went right up to the sergeant and hugged him. LSU assistants Craig Carse and Jim Childers greeted him, and then I got a chance to shake his enormous hand. He reminded me more of an old Green Bay Packer linebacker than of a staff sergeant. He immediately huddled with Brown to talk about the banquet and other subjects, while the rest of us went inside to look for his eldest son.

There he was waiting in the hallway, towering above everyone else and, more impressively, taking up most of the hall. I could not believe my eyes. Stanley Roberts was enormous even as a freshman, even taller and thicker than Hakeem Olajuwon, whom I had covered as a player at the University of Houston. But neither came remotely close to the incredible physique standing before me in a dark tux. At an age when most kids are just beginning to mature physically, Shaquille was already a fully developed man, with a build that would have made him one of the largest centers in the NBA, much less the NCAA.

Shaquille wrapped his tree-trunk-size arms around his new coach. Actually, Harrison said Brown's new role would be that of a substitute father.

"He's your boy now," Harrison informed the coach.

Brown, who had no sons of his own, was only too happy to take this gargantuan lad under his wing for four years.

"Sergeant, I just want to say to you how much I admire the way you and your family have handled this," Brown said, putting his right arm around the big soldier. "You never played any games. Shaquille never played any games. There was never any deception. I really thank you for that. This has been the most enjoyable experience I've ever had in recruiting. Thank you."

Harrison nodded and beamed with pride.

Moments later, the honorees were called together for a press conference with a handful of local reporters. Taking a seat right next to his son, Sgt. Harrison did much of the talking, while Shaquille shied away from the attention, only occasionally offering a brief word. That would be typical of his reserved manner around the media for the next three years.

"I'm going to LSU to play for a championship team," O'Neal said several times.

This was the recruiting story of the decade. What were the odds that Brown, albeit a globe hopper, would be on a German military base at just the right time to meet a tall boy eager to learn about basketball because he was too big and awkward to do anything else? Throw in a father who didn't care that his son had the physical gifts to be the next Chamberlain, but merely wanted to find an educational opportunity for the boy. The sergeant immediately developed an infatuation with Brown. It was easy to picture Shaquille and Brown making annual trips to the Final Four and finally bringing home a national title to LSU, with the sergeant standing in the background cheering them on.

"We know Coach Brown is a man we can trust to be in charge of Shaquille," Harrison said.

"There's a special bond between us," Brown said. "It's something that I've never felt before with a family. You always try to get close to the player and his family and make them feel like part of our basketball family. That's very important to us. We've had some kids who didn't sign with us and years later, they'd call me or see me at a game and mention what a wonderful family atmosphere we have at LSU. But I never remember feeling so close to a recruit's family and seeing things eye to eye like the sergeant and I do."

Unfortunately, like most things that seem too good to be true, this relationship really was. Everything would change, some things more quickly than others.

In a matter of days, Shaquille would make his national-television debut in the Dapper Dan Roundball Classic and McDonald's All-American Classic. He would dominate both games in every possible way.

Overnight, the expectations would rise like a rocket. Shaquille would become a college superstar and be thrust into the national limelight. Many coaches and pro scouts were soon saying he would be the first player taken in the NBA draft whenever he wanted to come out. He would gain much acclaim not only for his great basketball performances, but for the way he handled fame. His father, unfortunately, would be consumed by it.

two

A Fighting Finale

March 13, 1992

BIRMINGHAM, Alabama—Shaquille O'Neal desperately desired to go out a champion. He had already earned all the individual acclaim that a college player could ever want—national Player of the Year, certain No. 1 pick in the NBA draft whenever he wanted to go pro. But when it came to championships, the mark of a truly great player, he had none. The closest thing was a co-championship of the Southeastern Conference in 1991. But that wasn't nearly enough to distinguish himself the way he wanted to. He had come to LSU with visions of Final Four appearances and national championships, just as Kareem Abdul-Jabbar, Bill Russell and Bill Walton had done. Those dreams had not been fulfilled and this, his junior year, would be his last shot, because he had already made up his mind to enter the NBA draft.

The SEC Tournament presented O'Neal with his best shot at winning at least one outright championship, even if it wasn't what he really craved. Shaq and the Tigers were considered the co-favorites, along with Arkansas, to win the title at the Birmingham-Jefferson Civic Center, and they were well on their way to an impressive start, pulling away from Tennessee in the early going and threatening to make it a rout. Arkansas had struggled earlier in the day and would be eliminated the next day by Alabama, leaving only center-less Kentucky and 'Bama in the path of LSU's title bid.

However, Shaq never made it to the semi-finals, even though his team did. With the Tigers pouring it on, to the tune of a 22-point lead with ten minutes left, O'Neal was inexplicably still in the ballgame. He got loose for another apparent dunk, but Tennessee center Carlus Groves decided not to permit it. He chased down the two-time SEC Player of the Year, grabbed the back of his jersey and tried to pull him down to prevent the easy slam. He did indeed prevent the basket, but his flagrant foul infuriated the temperamental O'Neal, who had been in fights with friends and foes alike throughout his three years at LSU. Without looking back, he threw his elbow in the direction of Groves's face, but fortunately for the Volunteer offender, the wild swing barely missed its target, and Groves's jaw was still in one piece.

Instantly, LSU coach Dale Brown exploded off the bench and led the charge of the Tigers, who were supposedly trying to protect the 7-1 O'Neal against the 6-8 Groves. Brown, who would later insist he merely intended to keep Groves away from his player, dashed right at the UT player and shoved him in the chest. Many reporters would call it a punch, but TV replays clearly showed that Brown had pushed Groves, who in turn took a swing at the LSU coach that appeared to graze his face. Brown, O'Neal and Groves were corralled by the game officials, but at least four other LSU players threw punches during the two-minute fracas, which ended only after Birmingham Police officers came onto the court.

When order was finally restored, police officers escorted Shaq off the court after his ejection from the game. Amazingly, the SEC officials at courtside did not eject Brown, even though everyone in the arena had seen him charge and make contact with the Tennessee player, which was clearly grounds for being tossed. The neutral crowd showered the Tigers and SEC officials with boos when the fans realized Brown would be able to continue coaching. Nonetheless, LSU went on to win the game easily with a makeshift lineup. Shaq, though, was suspended for the semifinal game against Kentucky, and the Tigers lost a close one.

"Some people were upset that I would stand up for a black man in the very city where they turned dogs and hoses on them a few years back," Brown said later. "My response is that I regret that I even did it, but I didn't do it with any intent of injuring anybody or hurting anybody. But enough was enough. I had brought the problem of Carlus Groves to the attention of the SEC. I had written a letter and sent a film to the SEC showing a flagrant foul that Groves had committed. There was no reply from the conference. If I had to do it again, I'd do the same thing again."

After the Tennessee game, Brown announced at a near-midnight press conference that he had met with Shaq and his father and advised his star center to turn pro. The LSU administration later reprimanded Brown for his actions in the Tennessee game and for encouraging a player to leave school before graduating.

"I'd do it again," Brown said. "The player's interests will always come first with me."

For Shaq, his inglorious college career came to a disappointing end in the NCAA West Regional in Boise, Idaho, where the Tigers opened tournament play with a routine win over Brigham Young, but blew another large lead in falling to Indiana in the second round.

O'Neal, who would wait two weeks before announcing his decision to leave LSU, closed out his college career with bitter dejection and left right in the middle of the spring semester, rendering all the previous educational rhetoric empty. In six postseason tournaments, he had failed to lead the Tigers past the second round. His personal record in SEC Tournament play was 1–3, and his NCAA mark was 2–3, a far cry from the records established by Jabbar, Russell and Walton.

Ironically, LSU had experienced much more success in the four seasons before Shaq's arrival, when the Tigers posted a 7–4 record in NCAA Tournament play, including one Final Four finish and one Final Eight showing, and had a 5–4 mark in the SEC Tournament, including one runner-up finish.

Interestingly, the year after his departure, Tigers were picked to finish last in the SEC West, but ended up winning more games without him than they did during his final college season.

Brown defended his former player, saying, "We tend to place a stigma on a big man. He's expected to win a lot of games and championships. If a big man doesn't make it to the Final Four or win a national championship, he's labeled a failure. Either that, or they say the coach is a failure. They say, 'You didn't win with the great center, so you can't coach.' That was really unfair to expect that of Shaquille."

In making his announcement to leave LSU early, O'Neal would repeat over and over that "it just wasn't fun anymore." Although he was not pushed on the issue of failing to win championships, it was clear to most that "fun" meant winning the big games and major titles. He was troubled by the sagging zone defenses that he faced every night, too.

Insiders say the relationship between Shaq and Brown, which had started with so much promise, became strained by the three years of poor postseason performances and the constant complaints from O'Neal's father. In fact, Shaq made his announcement to turn pro in San Antonio instead of in Baton Rouge.

Right from the very beginning of his son's playing days at LSU, Philip Harrison changed from the cooperative parent who just wanted his boy to get a good education and a rewarding basketball experience to an overbearing tyrant who demanded that his son be catered to and showcased in an offense that had other gifted players. Insiders say Harrison put Brown through three years of hell.

Brown was glad to bid farewell to his most celebrated player just to get rid of his burdensome father. In fact, other members of the LSU coaching staff say Brown was so fed up with Harrison that he made up his mind to ask O'Neal to turn pro after his sophomore season. Brown's wife, Vonnie, his constant counselor and confidant, finally talked him out of making a rash decision, and so he agreed not to approach O'Neal about giving up his last two years of eligibility.

Ironically, Shaq told teammates that he wanted to enter the NBA after his sophomore season concluded with two straight postseason losses and more disappointment. It was his father who talked him into remaining at LSU until his junior year.

Insiders say Shaq's father had interfered so much with the coaching staff—making as many as 10 collect phone calls a day—and alienated so many of Shaq's teammates by openly criticizing them in the stands, right in front of their parents, that many members of the LSU team were eager for O'Neal and his father to leave.

Harrison called Brown whenever he felt that Shaq wasn't getting the ball enough or the team wasn't doing something to his satisfaction. LSU players remember the sergeant phoning during team meetings, practices and even minutes before home games. His calls were equally divided between Brown and O'Neal. He would call to give his son advice or to wish him well, but he always had some demands for Brown. A former youth-league coach, Harrison thought he had all the answers to whatever problem the Tigers were having. He suggested new offenses, different drills and other strategies. Typically, it meant getting the ball more often to the center.

One time, he called and demanded that one of the team managers go get the head coach off the court during practice so he could come to the phone and answer his complaints. The unlucky manager said Brown seethed and refused to take the call, one of the few times he didn't hear Shaq's father out.

But the annoying phone calls were just the tip of the iceberg. When Harrison made his regular visits to LSU, he would barge into Brown's office or walk right into the offices of the assistant coaches and expect to get immediate attention. He even paraded into the office of Athletic Director Joe Dean when he didn't get satisfaction from Brown.

On game nights, Harrison thought he could go wherever he wanted in the Pete Maravich Assembly Center, security officials say. If a security guard or usher tried to stop him, he pushed his way past the official and proceeded on his way. At least twice he barged into the team's locker room area and was stopped from going there on several other occasions.

The sergeant's biggest blowup occurred during his son's final college season when LSU was battling for an SEC championship. Harrison was infuriated when he discovered the school was selling T-shirts with Shaq's picture on them. The university had received permission from the NCAA to market the Shaq shirts, but not from the sergeant. He bought one of the shirts and stormed past security personnel to get into the locker room, where only the players were gathered at the time. The sergeant screamed his objections to printing the shirts and criticized everyone from Dale Brown to Joe Dean. His tirade lasted several minutes and left the players in a stunned state as they prepared to play an important ballgame. LSU wound up losing to an average Georgia team and eventually lost the SEC title by a single game to Arkansas.

Sadly, those close to Shaq say Harrison's abusive behavior affected his son more than anyone else. He developed a harsh side that resembled his father's characteristics.

"Shaquille gets his combativeness from his father," said Herb More, who coached him at Cole High School in San Antonio. "Most people say he's just like his dad. But I think he's a lot like his mom, too. She was the strong, silent type and had a calming influence on Shaquille."

"At one time or another, Shaquille got in a fight with just about every player on the team," LSU assistant Jim Childers said. "He was just an emotional person, that's all. It was a heat of battle type thing. He'd say, 'Don't take what I say personally.' After it was over, he would really regret it. He'd apologize and say, 'Don't pay attention to that.' He never meant to hurt anyone."

His teammates say Shaq could be the most caring and thoughtful person one day, but the next, he would be cruel to his best friends.

Many members of the team pointed to Shaq as one of the chief reasons for the early departures of Chris Jackson and Stanley Roberts. Both C.J. and Roberts were soft-spoken and easy-going with fragile feelings. So when O'Neal criticized them for not passing enough to him or for not working hard enough, they became extremely rattled. After a year of that, they opted to play professional basketball.

O'Neal was particularly hard on Roberts, who possessed better offensive skills. Their rivalry started out as a friendly competition for the starting center job, but quickly developed into a strong disdain for one another. During pickup games, Shaq would throw elbows, forearms and hips at the usually passive Roberts. O'Neal's rough play would often lead to a shouting match and pushing. Several times they came to blows.

On one such occasion, Roberts had to grab a trash can to protect himself from a fierce attack by O'Neal. Teammates laughed at the sight of Roberts acting like a lion tamer in an effort to stop Shaq. LSU point guard Mike Hansen said Shaq was looking for some type of object to attack back with and get Stanley.

In addition to Roberts, O'Neal got into fights with other teammates, even some of his closest buddies, which Stan obviously was not. Vernel Singleton, one of the best-liked players on the team, bore the brunt of one such outburst by O'Neal. They locked up in an all-out fist fight. Singleton, a slim 6-6 forward, was actually getting the best of Shaq before teammates pulled them apart.

Surprisingly, Hansen was another. He shared the team's captains' quarters with Shaq and was one of his best pals at LSU. But Hansen had to hold on for dear life as O'Neal tried to throw him into a steel door during a dispute in the team's practice gym. Hansen, a foot shorter and 100 pounds lighter than his attacker, barely avoided a serious injury.

"Shaq definitely has a mean streak about him," Hansen said. "I think it's his character, having had all the accolades and wanting to fulfill his role of being a star. He was brought up in the military background. His father was really strict with him. I was brought up in the military, too, and there are lots of different kinds of people in military schools. There's a big racial and cultural mix. When you live in a foreign country, you're stuck on the base. It gets monotonous, so Shaq's Dad was very strict with him so he wouldn't get in serious trouble in the German community. I think that's where the meanness and toughness came from.

"I think the mean streak is something he got from his father. Shaq didn't trust many people and was always on the lookout. Whenever anything was on the line about his reputation or ability, that's when you would see his mean streak."

All of his fights with teammates occurred when the coaches were not around. But O'Neal had his share of scuffles and fights in public as well. During his freshman year, he was among several LSU players at the scene of a nightclub brawl. He was not arrested, although teammate Wayne Sims was. Two years later, Shaq could have been arrested, police officers say, for helping to instigate an all-out "riot situation" between LSU football and basketball players, but Brown arrived on the scene and persuaded the police not to arrest him. There was nothing Brown could do, however, to cover up Shaq's actions at the SEC Tournament.

After most fights or arguments, teammates say O'Neal would be extremely remorseful the next day and go apologize and hug his friend or fellow player. Most of his flareups involved competitive situations in pickup games.

When he wasn't intensely trying to beat someone, he was lots of fun to be around and one of the more popular players on the team.

Unfortunately, his temper troubles often left a lasting impression. Few people outside the LSU program realized there weren't many tears shed when Shaq left town.

three

Playoff Fury

April 24, 1993

ORLANDO, Florida—By now, Shaq was a four-letter word recognized and adored in virtually every home in America. In fact, surveys indicated young Americans considered Shaquille O'Neal the most prominent athlete in the nation. The whole country loved him, and every major corporation wanted him to be their endorser.

Shaq brought to professional basketball the charisma and marketing power of Michael Jordan, the impact and importance of Magic Johnson and Larry Bird, and the dominating ability of Wilt Chamberlain and Kareem Abdul-Jabbar. Many NBA executives said there had never been a player to add so much to the league so soon. NBA Commissioner David Stern simply said, "He's going to be terrific."

The $42 million man of the Orlando Magic had just

finished a heralded rookie season by leading his team to its biggest win in franchise history. It was an occasion when 21-year-old Shaq should have been on top of the world. He had completed a Rookie of the Year season and put his team into position to make the NBA playoffs for the first time. Yet instead of going out to celebrate with family, friends and fans, Shaq was chasing down his father to try to keep him out of trouble again.

Many close to O'Neal fear the only thing that can stop him from being the greatest—and the richest—player ever to grace the NBA is his own Dad, Army Sgt. Philip Harrison.

Shaq and the Magic simply destroyed Dominique Wilkins and the playoff-bound Atlanta Hawks, 105–86. It was the final game of the regular season, and playoff fever created a new level of excitement in a city renowned world-wide for its entertainment. Anybody could drive down the interstate and pay $35 to see Mickey Mouse at Disney World, but a ticket to Shaq's House, the Orlando Arena, was a priceless commodity. Ticket seekers lined the streets more than two hours before a Magic home game in the O-(Neal)Rena.

With Shaq's help, the Magic improved 20 games to finish 41–41 and moved into position to make the playoffs. O'Neal was obviously the reason for Orlando's turn-around, and many players and coaches in the league were already calling him the most powerful, dominant player in the game. "As far as I'm concerned, he's the most dominant center in the NBA, bar none," Cleveland's Brad Daugherty said. Now Shaq and the Magic just needed the rival Miami Heat to hold on for a win over Indiana to earn a playoff berth.

No reporter complained when Shaq cut short his locker room interviews and said, "That's it, fellas. Gotta go now. I've got a date."

Shaq deserved a night of celebration after providing so many thrills to the Magic faithful and a world of basketball fans, who had already reserved a throne for young O'Neal—the Air Apparent to Michael Jordan as the game's most popular player. In fact, Shaq had already surpassed Jordan as the most sought-after athlete in the world for endorsements. NBA officials couldn't have been more ecstatic about finding a fresh superstar to replace Johnson and Bird.

"Nobody could have anticipated what Shaquille did as a rookie," said LSU coach Dale Brown. "I certainly couldn't have envisioned this kind of success so soon. No one could have. This is the most phenomenal happening in the NBA since Wilt Chamberlain hit the league. It may be even bigger, because Shaquille is a wonderful, special young man. He loves people. He was genuinely good with kids and all the fans. And I know money isn't going to change him one bit. He has a very simplistic approach to life. He smiles all the time. Shaquille is really just a big kid, who everybody loves."

Unfortunately, Shaq wasn't able to go enjoy himself right away as he had planned. Waiting for him was his father, who had already instigated one scrap that night and was about to start another. While most of his teammates watched the final minutes of the Indiana-Miami game that would determine their playoff fate, O'Neal had to assist his fuming father, angered this time by an interview with a writer. This time, I was the unfortunate victim of his temper, and I had to be literally rescued by Shaq.

O'Neal, a 7-foot-1 giant of a man with an asset value approaching $120 million, had everything going for him that a person could possibly have, except he remained haunted by a troublesome father. Associates say he pleaded with his father not to move to Orlando, which led to his first heated argument with his father over the objection to the family's planned move from San Antonio to Orlando in September.

Why wouldn't he want his own father around? The sergeant had been a disruptive influence on Shaq's college career at LSU and it continued with the Magic. During one stretch, the Magic were 0–8 at home when Harrison was visiting his son and the team went 0–10 on the road with Shaq's Dad in the stands, according to team officials. Finally, the sergeant relented and said he would not attend many of the Magic's games once he moved to Orlando with the rest of the family. Insiders say Shaq reluctantly accepted those terms.

Soon after arriving at the last game of the Magic's season, Harrison erupted into a rage over seeing one uninvited guest enter *his* hospitality room, which was set up by Reebok officials for the Harrison family and their guests. Reebok had endured numerous problems with Harrison since signing his son to a four-year contract worth $20 million. The ShaqAttaq commercials with Shaq, Wilt Chamberlain, Bill Walton, Kareem Abdul-Jabbar and Bill Russell had received rave reviews, and the ShaqAttaq shoes officially hit the market in March. However, Pete Robey, the original Reebok official assigned to O'Neal, told friends in Baton Rouge that he desperately wanted to get off the account because of the ongoing problems with Shaq's father, who was also shown in one of the ShaqAttaq commercials, saying, "And what is more, my son, you will be a man." Unfortunately, Harrison wouldn't let Shaq be his own man.

Actually, Reebok might not even have signed O'Neal if industry leader Nike had not pulled out of the running. Nike president Phil Knight told LSU officials that he wanted to sign Shaq, but pulled his company out of the bidding after Harrison put on a display of crudeness and vulgarity at a meeting between Shaq and Nike executives. With Jordan already in its fold, Nike chose to pass on O'Neal, despite his obvious talent and potential to ascend to the top of the basketball and marketing world.

Reebok vice president Tom Carmody was the latest victim of Harrison's tantrum, which was witnessed by many Orlando fans, team officials and reporters. The sergeant screamed profanities at Carmody, waved his arms in the air and shook his index finger at him. The shouting continued off and on for about 20 minutes before the Magic-Hawks game.

"It happens all the time," Carmody later told a reporter.

Orlando Magic director of public relations Alex Martins came by to try to solve the problem and calm down Harrison, but he proceeded to shout at Martins as well. The sergeant also demanded to be given more of the special Shaquille medallions minted by Pepsi that were handed out to Magic fans as part of Fan Appreciation Night. He shouted complaints at Shaq's agent, Leonard Armato, and sent Shaq's publicist, Dennis Tracey, running to the pass gate to give tickets to two more of the sergeant's guests. I followed Tracey there and asked if I could interview Harrison. He smiled and replied, "You can try."

Tampa Tribune reporter Martin Fennelly asked Martins to introduce him to the sergeant so that he could get an interview. They walked together toward the hospitality room and Martins attempted to make the introduction. But the sergeant was so incensed at the Reebok official that he didn't stop screaming long enough for Martins to get his attention. Fennelly overheard the sergeant yelling, "You're fuckin' right. This ain't no fuckin' joke."

This was just another in a long line of explosive rages from the father of the Magic's superstar. The club's unofficial policy was to turn their heads and let Harrison do what he wanted. NBA officials took a slightly stronger stance when he blew up at the All-Star Game. NBA Director of Media Relations Terry Lyons happened to be attending the Magic's final game and told Fennelly that the NBA had to send its director of security to talk with Harrison at the All-Star Game in Salt Lake City, but to little avail. He caused a wild scene that was reported all over the country.

Ironically, the Magic's package of press clips on Shaq includes a report on his father's unruly behavior at the All-Star Game, almost as if the team is trying to warn people about him. The headline reads: "Shaq's Dad is harder to stop than his son." The story reported that Harrison was "barging past security officers like a fullback sweeping around right end" and "ignoring pleas by security officers to stay out of areas off limits to the public."

On this occasion, Harrison was in a rage over being given just 13 tickets for the All-Star Game. He had 14 guests and was incensed that NBA officials didn't automatically give in to his demands. The sergeant pushed his way past security guards until he found Leonard Armato, who was holding an extra ticket.

But before Harrison had gotten his way, the arena security officers heard their walkie-talkies screeching with several all-points bulletins to be on the alert for the rampaging sergeant. League officials simply advised security officers to handle him with kid gloves.

"We don't want a confrontation with him," said one senior security officer.

The *Orlando Sentinel* reported, "Harrison is powerfully built and nearly as big as his son. He's 6 feet 5 and weighs 250 pounds, which may be another reason guards made only halfhearted attempts to stop him as he paraded through checkpoints. Suffice it to say that not all fathers of NBA players are afforded such leeway. His son has been a pro player for only half a season, yet NBA officials already know almost as much about Shaq's Dad as they do about Shaq. But Harrison doesn't mind that some people feel he pushes his aggressiveness to the point of being a bully, that he rushes past security officers because he knows he can get away with it. After all, he is Shaq's Dad, and Shaq is the best young superstar to enter the NBA since Michael Jordan in 1985. The NBA needs Shaq, so it tolerates Shaq's Dad."

When a copy of the *Sentinel* story was sent to LSU coach Dale Brown, he just shook his head and breathed a sigh of relief that the sergeant was no longer his problem. Brown sent a copy of the story to Armato, who was now shackled with Shaq's Dad.

After reading the story, Armato wrote a letter to Brown, saying, "The truth eventually comes out, however slowly."

Harrison readily admitted to living out his childhood dreams through his son. But unfortunately, his overbearing manner often hindered Shaq from enjoying his own life.

Even more regrettably, Harrison's intimidating ways have rubbed off on O'Neal, who is otherwise a funloving, caring young man willing to share his fame and fortune with teammates, family, friends and the needy. Publicly, Shaq is the fulfillment of the NBA's dream for a superstar with talent and charisma.

"He's got it all," Magic Johnson said, describing his successor to superstardom. "He's got the smile and the talent and the charisma. And he's sure got the money, too."

But simply from playing pickup games against O'Neal, Johnson detected another side to him. "Shaquille, the best part about him is that he's mean," Magic remarked after enduring a physical beating from the rookie.

That same mean streak helped Michael Jordan literally command the Chicago Bulls to three straight NBA titles in 1991, 1992 and 1993. As documented in the bestseller *The Jordan Rules*, the Bulls' superstar overruled decisions by Coach Phil Jackson and dictated to his teammates how to get him more shots. O'Neal did exactly the same thing at LSU and immediately took the same approach as a rookie with the Magic.

Friends and associates say Shaq's only flaws stem from his father's insistence that he establish himself as the toughest, most dominating player in the game and demand that his teammates cooperate. If they don't fall in line, he bullies them. He has a mean streak that has come to life during low points at LSU and Orlando. Shaq the Superstar can turn into Shaq the Intimidator whenever he's not satisfied with his teammates' performance or they challenge his place of pre-eminence.

"Shaquille is like Dr. Jekyll and Mr. Hyde," said an LSU team member. "He is great to be around most of the time, but he has a certain meanness about him."

In his rookie season, Magic players learned to take cover when Shaq was disappointed about something. He would use the privacy of the locker room to berate teammates for getting out of "the offense." Magic coaches Matt Guokas and Brian Hill scrapped their motion offense to accommodate Shaq with a post-oriented scheme.

"About 60 to 70 percent of our plays are designed to get the ball to Shaq," Hill admitted. However, perimeter players Scott Skiles, Nick Anderson and Dennis Scott would often take the large majority of the shots, to the dismay of O'Neal, who would respond with locker room tantrums like those of his father.

"Shaquille knows how to be an asshole," Magic forward Donald Royal said. "He's a lot like Michael Jordan. To be a superstar, in a sense, you have to be an asshole. You have to demand certain things of your teammates to win. Shaq is very good at it. He knows he's the focal point of the team, and he speaks up when things aren't going right. He points fingers at people and gets mad at them. But sometimes that has to be done to get a team going. Michael has taken a lot of flak because he gets on his teammates, but he's got two rings [now three] to show for it. That's what it's all about. Believe me, Shaq is good at it."

During a late-season game at Miami, O'Neal made his first six shots in the opening quarter, but didn't see the ball much the rest of the game. He finished with just 18 points and was furious by the time he hit the locker room. "He was so mad at us," Royal said. "He went off. Man, he went off at us. But it was something he had to do. I've never seen a player that mad."

Not only was Shaq prone to condemn his teammates, they say his ego was hard to deal with as well. Magic point guard Litterial Green laughed about Shaq always calling himself Mandingo and saying, "I'm big and I'm bad, and I've come over here on a boat from Africa."

"I've got a beautiful smile, and it comes in three versions: the $1 million smile, the $2 million smile and the $3 million smile," O'Neal often told teammates and reporters. "I'm a very marketable player. Tall, dark and handsome, and a pretty good player."

Royal, his teammate and friend, even took heat from O'Neal for trying to stop him from fighting Detroit guard Alvin Robertson. The much-publicized incident started when Shaq was fouled hard by NBA hatchet man Bill Laimbeer. O'Neal turned to go after him, but was held back by Robertson, a scrappy player himself.

"After being cracked like that, the last thing you want is to have someone holding you," Royal said. "Shaq told Robertson, 'Let go of me!' But Alvin never let him go. I tried to pull Shaq away from Alvin. But when he threw that punch, there was no way I could stop him. He threw me and the punch. Afterwards, Shaq got mad at me for trying to hold him back. Man, was he mad! But that's just Shaq."

O'Neal was by no means the only player in the league to hit someone during a fight-marred season. But he shocked the league and marketing world by saying, "And I'd do the same thing again." His panic-stricken sponsors began issuing press releases stating their companies were certain this would not be an ongoing problem with O'Neal, while they hoped that they had not hooked up with a thug.

After realizing he might have tarnished his image, O'Neal came up with the excuse that Robertson had struck him in the groin. However, the TV replay showed Robertson's arms wrapped around Shaq's chest. O'Neal was criticized throughout the country for trying to justify his striking another player, particularly a bystander like Robertson, who was trying to be a peacemaker.

While O'Neal was playing at LSU, the local media never wrote a single story about the sergeant's tirades and his ongoing feud with Brown. There was an unwritten rule that if you reported what Harrison was actually like, you would be shut off from interviewing his son. Of course, there was nothing reported about Shaq's fights, either, except the two times the police had to be called in.

The same standard was adopted by the Florida media during Shaq's rookie season. The article by the *Sentinel* on the All-Star Game fracas was the lone exception to the rule, and it was reported by Barry Cooper, who had befriended the sergeant and took a sympathetic approach in writing about his uncontrolled antics.

"We all know about his Dad, but we kind of overlook it," another Orlando reporter said.

A writer from another Florida city remarked, "If you want to keep talking to Shaq, you don't write about his Dad. And if you can't talk to Shaq, you might as well get out of town because you can't do your job. Shaq is the show in Orlando."

The biggest game in Magic history provided the local heroes with a chance to clinch their first non-losing season in four years as an expansion team and, more importantly, to stay alive in the race for the eighth and final spot in the Eastern Conference playoffs. Orlando and Indiana were tied for the magical eighth position, both at 40–41. But the Pacers held the tie-breaker advantage, meaning that the Magic's only chance was to beat Atlanta and hope Indiana would lose later that night to Miami. However, the Pacers were huge favorites playing the injury-ridden Heat on their home court. The Magic's game tipped off at 7:30 p.m., while the Pacers would tip off a thousand miles away in Market Square Arena at 8:30.

The Hawks, which had a shot to earn the fifth playoff spot in the East, came out with the hot hand to start the game and jumped to an early 12–2 lead. But Orlando coach Matt Guokas called a timeout and settled his team down. Led by Shaq, the Magic began to take over the inside and thoroughly dominate Atlanta's Jon (Kontract) Koncak. Incredibly, Orlando took a 26–17 lead at the end of the first quarter with Shaq contributing 11 points and 11 rebounds.

After hitting just five of 23 field-goal attempts in the opening quarter, Atlanta made a late run in the second quarter to slice away at the Magic's lead, which had increased to as many as 17 points. Wilkins, the only player in the NBA other than Jordan to average 30 points or more for most of the season, finished out the half with 15 points and helped pull the Hawks within 48–37 at intermission. Shaq, meanwhile, showed 17 points, 13 rebounds, three assists and one blocked shot for his first-half performance.

During the halftime break, Martin Fennelly finally got his interview with Harrison. I noticed them talking in the portal where the Magic enter the arena. I walked over to introduce myself and request an interview.

"Excuse me, sergeant," I said, looking up to the rugged, sturdy man, who is built like Shaq, only half a foot shorter. "I'm Bruce Hunter. I met you and your family four years ago at the high school banquet in San Antonio and then I covered Shaquille at LSU." I could tell he didn't remember me, so I asked, "Can I get an interview with you for a book I'm doing on Shaquille?"

Before he could answer, someone called to him and he started to turn away. I quickly asked, "How about after the game?"

"Sure, after the game," Harrison replied and walked off.

In the second half, Orlando turned it into a rout behind Shaq, Nick Anderson and Dennis Scott—nicknamed "The Young Guns" by O'Neal himself. Anderson's running one-hander put the Magic ahead by 15, and just minutes later, Scott drained a baseline jumper to boost the margin to 20, igniting a wild celebration in the rockin' O-Rena.

No doubt the place would have gone berserk had Shaq managed to bring down another basket like the one he had destroyed the previous night in the Meadowlands. In trying to rekindle the Magic's fading playoff hopes (Orlando had to win its last two games and Indiana had to lose its last two), Shaq had almost injured himself when his thunderous dunk ripped down the entire basketball standard. The shot clock came crashing down and gave Shaq a glancing blow to the head. After a 46-minute delay, the Magic found a way to Nick the Nets (Anderson scored a career-high 50 points), and Detroit cooperated by knocking off Indiana.

Shaq seemed to be headed for an encore performance in the season finale at home, where he had yet to break a rim, backboard or complete basket standard. His fourth of five dunks on the night came ever so close. He picked up a long rebound and broke free of the pack for an easy slam. But as usual, he brought his 303-pound force field crashing onto the rim. The rim bent almost straight down, the backboard swayed, and the basket standard shook. However, Shaq had to settle for a breakaway dunk instead of a shattering slam. It still gave the Magic a 72–52 lead with 2:42 left in the third quarter, and the club waltzed home to a 19-point victory that kept its playoff hopes alive.

Right after the game, I began looking for Harrison, but there was a long post-game celebration. All of the Magic players were called back on the court to give away their game jerseys to lucky fans. Shaq's was the last one to be given away. A little boy romped excitedly to midcourt to shake the hand of an obliging but clearly exhausted O'Neal, who handed off the jersey and walked off the court without so much as a smile.

Harrison and his guests remained in the arena watching a laser show and a Magic highlight video. I walked over to the team locker room, where at least 30 reporters had congregated outside the door waiting for admittance. Finally, the door opened and everyone struggled to get through the doorway, knowing that the first ones to enter would be able to get closest to O'Neal and get his post-game comments on tape. You had to be within an arm's length to hear his whispered replies.

Someone yelled, "Shaq's in the shower."

Nonetheless, most of the reporters hovered around his locker and started waiting for him. Seated next to Shaq's locker was Dennis Scott, and a few of the reporters asked him about the game and his thoughts on the possibility of playing the Knicks in the playoffs.

After a few minutes, Shaq emerged from the shower area with one towel wrapped around his waist and another one draped over his head, as if he wanted to hide from yet another barrage of questions. He worked his way to his locker and sat down, ready to begin fielding questions from a crowd of about 30 television, radio and newspaper reporters jammed into an area of about 15 square feet. Microphones and cameras were everywhere.

This was a scene that was all too familiar to O'Neal, besieged by interview requests ever since he burst into national prominence as a freshman at LSU. He developed a playful rapport with the local media, but when surrounded by a large gathering of unfamiliar reporters, he was very soft-spoken and reserved. One-sentence responses were his trademark, although he had improved through the help of an interview training program at LSU and later from lots of tips from the Magic staff and Armato. But while his comments were often brief, there was a certain charm about his mannerisms and remarks. He had already become one of the more popular players for interviews in the NBA.

"Shaquille, what do you think about the possibility of playing against Patrick Ewing and the Knicks in the playoffs?" asked a TV reporter from a local station.

That question was bound to come up. But of course, Miami had to beat Indiana to make the Ewing-O'Neal matchup reality rather than speculation. Naturally, everyone connected to the NBA would have loved to see the great rookie go up against the Olympic Dream Team center. They had already met in four heated regular-season showdowns with Shaq and the Magic winning twice and Ewing helping the Knicks win the other two. Even though the Knicks were the top seed in the East, many thought O'Neal and company could make it interesting in a five-game series.

Earlier in the evening, Hawks assistant coach Bob Weinhauer wondered out loud if the NBA had instructed the game's three referees to help the Magic get into the playoffs. Weinhauer felt the Magic were getting all the calls, so he yelled at the NBA's Terry Lyons, "It looks like you guys are going to make sure you get O'Neal against Ewing."

Even though O'Neal wasn't going to say so publicly, he told teammates and friends that he could already do what he wanted against Ewing, who, surprisingly, had great difficulty handling Shaq's power game inside. Shaq would often say the only NBA centers who could play at his level were Hakeem Olajuwon and David Robinson. Both of those Western Conference centers had to rely on superior quickness to get past him, though. Shaq also had great disdain for Charlotte center Alonzo Mourning, his only rival for Rookie of the Year honors. He made up rap songs about how 'Zo was just the second pick and second-best newcomer in the league.

Much of the O'Neal-Ewing controversy was caused by Knicks coach Pat Riley, who coached the two big men in the All-Star Game. First, Riley complained when the fans voted Shaq to the first team ahead of Ewing, making him the first rookie since Jordan to start in the All-Star Game. Then in the actual game, O'Neal outperformed Ewing until late in the third quarter when Riley put the

Magic man on the bench and went with his own player.

O'Neal realized the rivalry with Ewing would last as long as they were both in the league, so he was careful not to say much publicly about his true feelings. After their first meeting in New York, Shaq said, "I think I did pretty good against him [he outscored Ewing 18–15 and outrebounded him 17–9]. It was a good show. Pat's a great player. I'm a pretty good player."

On the eve of what could be their first playoff encounter, O'Neal was once again guarded in his response.

"We've got a lot of respect for the Knicks. They're a great team," Shaq said. "Sure, we'd like to have a chance to play them. It's always a challenge for me to play against Patrick. He's one of the best players in the league."

"Are you playing well enough right now to beat the Knicks?" the TV reporter asked.

"I don't know," Shaq answered cautiously. "We need to work on our offense. We haven't been playing that well lately."

Actually, the Magic had pulled out of a mid-April tailspin during which it lost to lowly Milwaukee and Philadelphia and dropped three of four games in a seven-day stretch. In the final week of the season, Orlando beat playoff-bound Boston, New Jersey and Atlanta and routed Washington for the fourth time while losing only to the Celtics in the Garden.

Due mainly to Shaq, the Magic finished as the most improved team in the NBA. The club's 20-game improvement was significantly better than the league's second-most improved team, Houston, which won 13 more games than it had the previous year.

The Magic had basically the same players who combined to win only 21 games in the 1991–92 season. The only difference was that O'Neal had taken over at center for former LSU teammate Stanley Roberts, who was dealt away to the Los Angeles Clippers in a three-team deal that brought two first-round draft picks into the Magic coffers. Orlando went into the 1993 draft with two first-round picks and will have the same luxury in 1994. Although Pat Williams won't admit it publicly, Shaq influenced his decision to unload the highly popular Stanley Roberts, whom Shaq didn't get along with in college and didn't want to play with again.

Shaq led Orlando in virtually every key statistic: scoring (23.4 points), rebounding (13.9), field-goal percentage (.562) and blocked shots (3.53). He was the main focus of the ballclub on the offensive and defensive ends. The Magic's supporting cast for O'Neal needed to get better, and it certainly did when the club got the No. 1 pick in the 1993 draft as well. Nick Anderson, the first player ever drafted by Orlando in 1989, and Dennis Scott, the fourth player taken in the 1990 draft, were adequate swing men. Anderson, a 6-6 shooting guard, averaged 19.6 points and 6.2 rebounds, but shot just 44 percent from the field. An even more streaky shooter, Scott hit as many as nine three-point baskets in one game and averaged 16.3 points, but the 6-8 small forward shot just 43 percent from the field and averaged a mere 3.4 rebounds. Scott played only 68 games in the last two seasons at an annual salary of $2.4 million.

Journeyman point guard Scott Skiles had a career-high 9.4 assists average, due mainly to Shaq's presence. But his inconsistency (3.5 turnovers per game) plagued the offense. And it didn't help that starting power forward Terry Catledge broke his right hand in the opening game and later a knee injury sidelined him for most of the season. The Magic picked up Tom Tolbert, who was waived by Golden State, but he provided just 8.3 points and 5.6 rebounds as the new starting power forward. Backup power forward Brian Williams was also injury-prone.

The Magic did get some solid performances from reserves Donald Royal, Anthony Bowie, Jeff Turner, Greg Kite and Litterial Green. The talented Green, a rookie who played against O'Neal while at Georgia, was being groomed to be the starting point guard unless the Magic get a better player through the draft.

Despite the deficient supporting cast, O'Neal did not complain publicly. His only complaints to teammates came when he didn't get enough shots. But several Magic players say it's only a matter of time before Shaq starts dictating personnel moves to management as Michael Jordan has done throughout his years in Chicago.

On the subject of the Magic's final game, one reporter wanted to know what the team had done differently after falling behind 12–2.

"You had a 36–6 run or something like that at one point," the reporter said. "You must have been doing something different."

O'Neal shrugged and said, "We just started to run our offense the way it's supposed to be run."

Of course, that means getting the ball to O'Neal. The franchise center had a good night of recognizing double teams and passing the ball back out to Anderson, Scott or Skiles. The Magic had done an excellent job of reversing the ball in order to find Scott or Anderson for the wide-open jump shot, while still getting O'Neal enough shots to keep him happy. He finished with game highs of 31 points (12 of 16 FGs) and 18 rebounds. Anderson complemented him with 27 points and Scott had 14.

"You guys did a good job on Dominique, didn't you?" asked another reporter.

"Dominique is a great player," said Shaq, who helped keep Wilkins (nine of 23, 27 points) from getting many good shots inside, although Anderson was primarily assigned to him. "Great players are going to get their points."

"Shaquille, talk about the season that this team has had," the same reporter requested.

"We should have won a few more games," he answered. "It was a good year for us, but we could have done better."

"How about your year? You like percentages, what would you rate your season?" asked another reporter.

"Oh, it was about 72.2 percent," Shaq said and grinned his big boyish smile.

"What are you going to do this summer?" the reporter followed up.

"I'm going to be in a movie with Nick Nolte, I'm going to shoot some commercials, some rap videos, and I'm going to work on my game," he quickly replied. He didn't mention that he planned to attend the Pete Newell camp for centers, which he had done the previous summer as well.

It was interesting that Shaq put basketball last on his list of priorities for the summer. The Magic coaching staff and executives were very concerned about his unbelievably demanding schedule. Head coach Matt Guokas had asked him throughout the season if there were too many interviews set up for him, not to mention the innumerable appearances and appointments scheduled through Leonard Armato and Dennis Tracey.

"Sometimes we just have to tell the sponsors he can't do it," Tracey said. "They want him all the time, but we have to draw the line. We have to let them know who's the boss."

Guokas and many of O'Neal's teammates worry that he won't have the time or the incentive to develop his skills as other players do. In the final week of the season, Shaq told *Orlando Sentinel* columnist Brian Schmitz that he was going to shoot 1,000 jump shots a day during the summer. When that comment came out in the paper, it gave some of his teammates something to laugh about. One said he doubted the big guy would have time to shoot 1,000 jump shots all summer.

At LSU, Shaq was notorious for his lack of interest in improving his skills. While teammates would urge him to come practice with them, he'd smile and say, "If you've got talent and heart, you don't need to practice."

"We'll have to sit down with his people and work out some kind of schedule," Guokas said two days before the season ended. "Certainly, he won't have to work out eight hours a day. But there are a lot of things he needs to work on. He'll be working with our shooting coach [Buzz Braman]. He obviously needs to improve on his free throw shooting. He needs to work on his turnaround jumper. And maybe he needs to add one or two more moves."

The real question is: Will Shaq be on the move too much to attend to his basketball weaknesses?

Some of his Magic teammates question whether Shaq has the desire to become one of the all-time greats.

Others suggest he might want to be the best player in the game, but they doubt he really cares about being on a championship team.

Greg Kite, a nine-year veteran who played on two world championship teams at Boston, said Shaq does not seem to have the same hunger for a title that he saw in his ex-teammate Larry Bird and former foe Magic Johnson. When asked if O'Neal is willing to take some occasional advice, Kite just laughed out loud. Insiders say Shaq rarely takes advice from anyone on the team.

"The thing that set Larry apart was all he talked about was winning," Kite said. "Throughout his career, Larry stayed hungry. He wanted to win a championship every year. You could see the same hunger in Magic Johnson. Larry and Magic were great competitors and they made their teammates better. Michael Jordan does the same thing. But you really don't see that from Shaq. He plays hard, but he doesn't talk about winning. I don't see the hunger there."

Even Guokas admitted that O'Neal, as a rookie, did not show the great desire of a champion. Guokas said there is a marked difference between his former teammate, Chamberlain, who played on world championship teams in Philadelphia and Los Angeles, and his current star.

"The difference with Wilt was he was such a tremendously competitive person," Guokas said. "He was always competitive on the court and off the court. Every time. He would bet on a shot in practice. He would bet you in cards. We played cards together all the time. Wilt loved to win. He loved to win, no matter what we were doing.

"The true mark of a great player in this league is making everyone around you better," Guokas continued. "To this point, Shaq really hasn't been able to make his teammates better. The team overall is obviously better, but he's got to work on getting everyone else more involved. He's got to learn how to make everyone else better. If he's doubled and he can't score, then he's got to learn how to get other players some good shots. It's a learning process for him."

When O'Neal first joined the Magic, he didn't even know how to set an effective pick and had no idea how to run a good pick-and-roll. And those were just the basic fundamentals of the pro game he had to learn.

Actually, the many roles of Shaq were not yet clearly defined. Shaq the player always fulfilled his obligations to the Magic as far as practices, meetings, shoot-arounds, film sessions and games. But at the same time, Shaq the Media Megastar and Shaq the Marketing Sensation had to be factored into the equation, and these roles demanded more time than he had to give.

By the middle of the season, O'Neal had already become the hottest sports commodity in the world. A survey of Fortune 500 companies showed Shaq was the most sought-after player for endorsements, having surpassed Michael Jordan. While the rookie sensation wasn't making $36 million a year in gross income like Jordan, he was certainly headed in that direction and his portfolio of endorsements was soaring beyond the great Michael's.

In addition to the $20-million Reebok deal for his own shoes, O'Neal signed promotional contracts with Spalding for his own basketball, Kenner Toys for his own action figures and Classic Trading Cards for his own sport card. The last of his major deals was choosing Pepsi over Coke.

All of these agreements, along with his record-breaking $42-million deal for seven years with the Magic, will bring an estimated $120 million into the O'Neal coffers. All of it was orchestrated by Leonard Armato, who handled Kareem Abdul-Jabbar and currently works with Hakeem Olajuwon.

The difference between O'Neal and his predecessors (Jabbar, Chamberlain and Russell) is image. The previous great centers in the league possessed all of the physical tools to excel on the court, but had no charm or charisma to go with it. They were practically unmarketable.

Shaq, on the other hand, has a carefully guarded image of a Goliath with a grin on his face and a heart as big as a basketball. While Wilt, Bill and Kareem grimaced when they had to be interviewed or meet the public, Shaq jumps for the opportunity and acts as if he has never before had the chance to meet fans or talk to a network reporter. Those close to him say Smilin' Shaq is often an act.

Back on the night of the Magic's final game, O'Neal finished his interviews in about 10 minutes, announced his plans to leave for a date, and oddly enough, took off without bothering to watch the rest of the Indiana-Miami game that would determine the Magic's postseason fate. Most of the other players took their time showering and dressing because they planned to stay in the locker room for about half an hour to watch the rest of the Pacer-Heat game. Some wondered if Shaq was even interested in whether or not his team made the playoffs.

I left the locker room hoping to find Philip Harrison. As I headed to the portal, the post-game hoopla was still going on. I began to look around for Harrison, and after a few minutes, I spotted him walking back toward the hospitality room. "Can I get that interview now?" I inquired.

"Go ahead," the sergeant answered.

Wishing to get him talking candidly, I decided to begin with a positive, open-ended question. I turned on my tape recorder and reached up with my left arm to get it near his mouth and asked, "What are you most proud of concerning Shaquille?"

"Everything," he said. "The whole thing. I'm proud of everything he's done. What do you mean? Be specific."

"All right, let's start with this: Away from basketball, what makes you most proud of Shaquille?" I asked, rephrasing the original question.

"The way he handles himself. That comes from the way he was raised," Harrison said proudly. "We taught him how to conduct himself. We taught him the right way and the wrong way. Shaquille had discipline in his life. If he did something wrong, he got punished for it and he learned not to do it anymore."

Ironically, the next question that I had written down in my notebook was about how Shaquille was raised. As I glanced around, a small crowd of Harrison's guests and Magic fans had gathered around him to listen to his remarks. He was clearly enjoying the attention, speaking more emphatically, almost grandstanding.

"What basically is your philosophy on raising children?" I asked, seeking more details.

"Too many parents give their kids everything they ask for," Harrison responded. "We don't believe in spoiling our kids. We believe in discipline. When Shaquille was young, he did some things he wasn't supposed to do. He didn't like all the moving around in the military. He wasn't happy being in Germany, so he did some things he knew he shouldn't do. When I found out about it, I beat him. Man, he got some beatings. I beat him every day."

Like most writers who had talked to Shaq about his childhood, I had already heard the stories of his wayward behavior as a boy. Shaq said he was headed toward being a juvenile delinquent until his father straightened him out, or beat it out of him.

"When did Shaq get his worst punishment?" I asked.

"The fire alarm," Harrison immediately replied. "He set off the fire alarm in our apartment building. When I came home, I asked Shaquille if he had done it, but he shook his head no. Then I looked at his hand and he had that green stuff on there that you get when you pull a fire alarm. When I saw that, I beat him and beat him. He never did that again."

Looking down my list of questions, I realized the sergeant's responses were taking longer than expected and I wanted to make sure I had the chance to ask the most important questions. The next one was about Shaquille's quick rise to stardom in the NBA.

"Sure, I knew it was going to happen," Harrison said. "Of course, I knew he was going to do this. I've always known Shaquille was going to be the greatest player in basketball. That's the way I taught him to play. I told him to let everyone know that it's his court and his game. Nobody is going to stop Shaquille. He was the best player in college. Sure, I knew he was going to be the best player in the pros."

At this point, we started to get some crowd participation from Harrison's entourage, all wearing black Shaq shirts and hats.

"Hey, man, Shaq would have won a national championship in college if it hadn't been for Dale Brown," shouted a man who was dressed just like Harrison and had similar facial features, though his stature was not quite as imposing. "Shaquille should have won three national championships. He's always been the best. Dale Brown just didn't coach him right."

"Yeah, Dale Brown can't coach," added a younger member of the Harrison clan. "He never used Shaquille right."

Several other derogatory comments were made about Brown, so I waited for Harrison to offer his own thoughts on the controversial LSU coach. I waited and waited. But Harrison only smiled, preferring to let his family do the talking. I decided to save the questions about Brown for the end of the interview.

"Do you still critique his performance?" I questioned.

Once again, Harrison hesitated before responding. It seemed he wanted to say, "Sure, I still coach him." But he didn't.

"If he asks me, I tell him," Harrison finally replied. "But I don't tell him anything unless he asks for my advice."

"You've told reporters you are fulfilling your dreams through Shaquille. Is that fair to him?" I asked.

"Of course I'm doing that," he retorted. "I didn't get the opportunity that Shaquille has. I made some mistakes. I had a chance, but I messed up. I didn't listen to my father. I wanted to make sure that Shaquille didn't mess up, that he took advantage of his opportunity. And now I'm enjoying it, too."

Not knowing how much longer he would talk to me, I decided it was time to jump into the more sensitive matters, particularly his feelings about Dale Brown and his thoughts on Shaq's resistance to the sergeant moving to Orlando.

"What about Dale Brown? Have you mended the relationship with him?" I inquired.

Of course, everyone was aware of the Brown-Harrison feud stemming from a public argument over whether or not Brown interfered with Shaq's negotiations with Reebok.

"What do you mean by mending our relationship?" Harrison shot back. "What's wrong with our relationship?"

For the first time, the sergeant's temper began to show, so I tried to pose a neutral question: "Describe your relationship with Dale Brown."

Harrison waited for what seemed like a minute or more before giving a reply. He seemed very unsure of what to say, but finally answered, "There's nothing wrong with Dale Brown. I never had a problem with Dale Brown. It's that damn media's fault."

At first I thought he was blaming me somehow for the fallout between him and Brown.

"I don't mean you," Harrison said. "I'm talking about the media people who wrote that stuff about Coach Brown. He didn't even say what they wrote he said. I have no problem with Coach Brown."

What Harrison wasn't saying was that Brown had cornered the sergeant in a Los Angeles hotel room and demanded a public apology. Harrison, who seemed very intimidated by the mention of Brown's name, had indeed apologized publicly and never said another bad word about Brown to the press.

It was through LSU team members that I learned about the subject of my final questions concerning Shaq's reluctance to have his father around when he's playing basketball. In fact, insiders say Dennis Tracey was shocked when Shaq had his first shouting match with his father over the family's proposed move to Orlando. O'Neal clearly wanted to be left alone, but the sergeant argued that he should have his family around him. An apparent compromise was reached when Shaq agreed to let the family move to Orlando if his father didn't come to many of the home games.

"Do you still plan to move your family to Orlando in September?" I asked the sergeant.

"Of course we're moving to Orlando. We're family,"

Harrison said, beginning to raise his voice. "Family sticks together. We're coming here. Now, I don't plan to come to all the games."

"Why won't you come to all the home games if you're going to be living here?" I asked.

"I'm not going to come to all the games," he reiterated. "I've got other things that I'll be doing. I've got other children. I'll be coaching some basketball. No, I'm not coming to all the games."

Finally, I decided to ask the toughest question. It was also the last on my list.

"Is Shaquille agreeable to you moving here?" I asked.

"What do you mean? Of course he is," Harrison said. "What are you talking about?"

"Somebody had told me that Shaq might not be in favor of it," I told the sergeant.

"Who the hell is somebody?" he shouted. "Who the hell is somebody?"

"I can't really say," I replied.

Although Harrison was clearly angry at the line of questioning, he was not at all in a rage as he had been earlier in the evening when he lambasted the poor Reebok official. Perhaps he held back because there was a crowd of people watching him. I certainly had no reason to think he was mad at me personally. After all, I was just asking questions that any journalist would ask.

After glaring at me briefly, Harrison continued, "Do you have any more questions?"

"No, that's it," I said and thanked him for the interview.

I assumed that I had seen the last of the sergeant and returned to the Magic locker room to try to get some more interviews. Shaq was dressed now in his own unique style. He was wearing a black bucket cap, black shirt, black pants and a shiny multi-colored vest trimmed with gold. He and Dennis Scott made their way out the side door of the locker room.

Only a handful of players and about a dozen reporters remained in the room. Magic Director of Player

Personnel John Gabriel and several other team officials stopped by to congratulate the players and watch the final minutes of the Miami-Indiana game. It was in the fourth quarter and Indiana had come from behind to take the lead. The Heat, however, was within striking distance, so there was still hope that the Magic might make the playoffs for the first time.

I decided to watch the rest of the Indiana game in the locker room with Martin Fennelly. Steve Smith hit a three-point shot to pull Miami within three points with 1:30 left. Just then, Scott Skiles came out of the shower area and anxiously asked for an update on the game. He stood next to me and frowned as Indiana scored to stretch the lead to five.

At the entrance to the locker room, Shaquille appeared. I was surprised to see him again after he said he was leaving. But I kept watching the Indiana game and talking to Fennelly, who later said he saw Shaq pointing me out to his father. Sgt. Harrison came right into the locker room and walked past Fennelly and me. I kept watching the game, and the sergeant just stood there. Finally, he said, "I need to talk to you."

Assuming that he wanted to expound on our earlier interview, I said fine. Actually, he had placed an arm around my shoulders and was trying to lead me out of the locker room anyway. I thought his behavior was odd, but not out of character for someone like him. I was not yet aware he wanted to do anything but continue to chat.

With his arm still around my shoulders, we walked into the office of Matt Guokas's secretary. Harrison ordered one of the secretaries to get out, leaving us alone. Then he abruptly closed the two doors to the office and got right in my face. I quickly realized he had no intention of being interviewed.

"What the hell are you doing writing about my family without my permission!" he screamed and began hitting me in the chest with an open fist. His blows weren't hard enough to knock me down, just enough to push me around and intimidate me. His stature alone did that. The sergeant stands 6-5 and must weigh 250 pounds. I'm 5-11 and 155 pounds and certainly not foolish enough to take him on.

Harrison shoved me up against a desk and hollered even louder, "You're trying to make money off us. We're not going to make anything off this. You're writing this unauthorized book and you're just using my son!"

"Wait, sergeant," I said, trying to explain that Shaquille had not objected to the book. I wanted to tell him books like this are often written about star athletes and celebrities.

But the sergeant didn't give me an opportunity to talk. He just kept poking me in the chest. I noticed his hands were shaking and his face was quivering. At that point, I felt certain that he was going to hit me if I tried to stop him from pushing me in the chest, so I tried to remain calm and let him vent his fury.

"What the hell are you doing asking me about my family and talking to me about Dale Brown? If you want to know about Dale Brown, go talk to Dale Brown," Harrison shouted.

My mind flashed back to the words of an LSU coach, who said, right before I left to go to Orlando, "The sergeant is going to have a breakdown and hurt himself, hurt someone else or kill someone." Since I didn't want to be that person, I froze.

After a brief pause, he demanded, "I want that tape. I want you to erase that interview. No, I'm taking the tape recorder." Before I could protect my tape recorder, he had grabbed it out of my hand. Then he threw it down on the desk, causing it to break open. The batteries went flying out of the back, and other parts of the tape recorder scattered.

Later, the secretaries in the basketball office found one of the batteries on the floor and I found the other one. The tape was never recovered, so the sergeant obviously took it with him. He also planned to take the recorder and my notebook, which he jerked out of my hand.

Stunned by his fury, I did not attempt to stop him from taking the recorder and notebook. But I did say, "Sergeant, I'll be glad to erase your interview, but there are other interviews on the tape that I need."

I also asked him to return my notebook, but he refused and became even more angry. He began poking me in the chest again and screaming as only an Army sergeant can.

"You'd better not write anything about my son!" Harrison fumed. "If you write a book about my son, I'm coming after you!"

His message was clear to me. He was threatening to beat me up or worse. In almost 20 years as a writer, I had been yelled at many times, but this was the first time anyone had ever shoved me around, taken away the tools of my trade and threatened to come after me. It was a chilling thought, especially coming from a man the size of the sergeant and with his reputation for unstable behavior.

At this point, I could think only of getting out of the room without being further assaulted. The tape recorder, tape and notebook were important to doing the job that I was hired by Bonus Books to do, but my physical well-being was more important.

The only thing I could think to do was apologize. I wasn't sure what I was apologizing for, but I hoped it would save me.

"I'm sorry, sergeant," I said. "I apologize. I didn't know you were opposed to the book."

My words did little to ease the anger on the sergeant's face. He seemed ready to hit me at any moment.

Outside, Martin Fennelly could hear Harrison's shouting and feared that he was going to injure me seriously. Fennelly also heard the sergeant's threat, "I'm going to come after you." The Tampa writer attempted to come to my aid, but as he reached out to open the door, Shaq's 6-foot-2 mother stopped him.

"This is a private conversation," Lucille Harrison said. "You can't go in there."

Fennelly did not enter. Later, he told me, "I felt like saying, 'How can it be a private conversation? Everyone in the arena can hear him yelling.'"

I'm convinced the only thing that saved me was Shaquille. After the sergeant had raged on for about five minutes—Fennelly said it was closer to 10—Shaq slowly entered the room with his mother right behind him.

Never had I been so glad to see a friendly face. In this case, embarrassment was written all over Shaq's face. I immediately felt pity for O'Neal, knowing this was not the first time he had been terribly embarrassed by his own father.

Once Shaq and his mother entered, the sergeant refrained from striking me again. However, the shouting continued for about another minute. Harrison took a closer look at my notebook.

"What have you been writing about my family?" he demanded. As he attempted to read my notes, I thought to myself that I was glad I had developed my own form of shorthand, which nobody else can decipher.

"What the hell does this say?" the sergeant shouted.

"It's just notes about the game," I replied.

Finally, to my great relief, Shaq moved toward his father and took the tape recorder out of his hands. Then he took the notebook away from his father, who did not try to stop him.

Angry as ever, the sergeant stormed out of the room, followed by his wife. Shaq just shook his head, handed the tape recorder and notebook back to me, and turned to walk slowly out the door.

For several seconds, I stood absolutely still as if frozen by fear. When I had collected myself, I began to pick up the pieces of my tape recorder. I was so relieved the attack was over that I didn't leave the room right away. Besides, I wanted to make sure the sergeant had left the basketball office and wouldn't come after me again.

As I walked out of the secretaries room, I looked down the hallway toward the locker room and saw Fennelly standing there. He came right up to me with a worried look.

"Are you all right?" he asked. "Did he hurt you?"

My first reaction was to downplay the attack. I didn't want to seem like a wimpy reporter, even though I felt like one at that point.

"I'm OK. He pushed me around and kept yelling at me," I said wearily. "I'll be all right."

But the more I thought about it, the more I realized I wasn't all right. I had been attacked for no reason.
My equipment had been broken and my tape had been
taken away. What bothered me most was the threat the
sergeant had made.

"Are you sure you're all right," Fennelly kept asking. It was obvious that I was shaken up, but I didn't want
to become the story myself. My job was to write about
Shaquille O'Neal and his family.

Fennelly wanted to know all the details of the incident. He also told me about trying to come my aid. "I
thought he was going to beat you up," he said. "I can't believe somebody would come after you like that. You're just
an unassuming guy. This will go great in my story."

My philosophy has always been to keep the writer
out of the story. But in this case, Harrison had forced me
right into the heart of it.

I saw Shaq standing at one end of the hall, so I
went up to talk to him. I felt bad for him as he was still
embarrassed by the ugly incident. I looked up at him and
said, "Shaq, I never would have talked to your father if I
had known he was going to get so mad."

Shaq just kept looking down and said, "Man, that's
OK."

I turned to walk away and saw Alex Martins
standing further down the hall, so I decided the Magic administration needed to be aware of what happened. Martins was watching the final seconds of the Miami-Indiana
game as the Pacers wrapped up the victory and the final
playoff spot in the East. He asked me to wait until the
game ended, which it did in just a couple of minutes.

It took me only a few minutes to cover the events of
the interview with the sergeant and subsequent attack in
the locker room. Martins looked concerned, but took no action.

"Hey, I'm sorry," Martins said. "Thanks for telling
me."

After that, I walked with Fennelly next door to the
media work room, where we talked some more about the
whole matter. Fennelly continued to ask me if I was all

right, and my answer was always yes. However, I was actually very much afraid that I had not seen the last of the sergeant. I remained in the media room for about 20 minutes, trying to decide what I would do if the sergeant were waiting for me in the hall and wondering if I should go directly to the police station to file a complaint.

At about 11:30, I made up my mind to leave the arena. Fennelly walked out with me, but his car was parked on the other side of the building. I decided to request a security officer to go with me.

The main hallway in the lower level of the arena was almost cleared out by the time I walked toward the exit next to the security station. I still planned to ask a security guard to go with me to my car, but when I got to the security office, there was only one security officer on hand, and he was on the telephone.

Instead of waiting, I opened the door and looked all around the area where Shaq parks his customized Chevrolet Suburban. The souped-up Chevy was gone, and I hoped that meant the sergeant was out of the area as well.

About a dozen fans were still lined up by the gate waiting for one more autograph. I carefully scanned their faces to make sure the sergeant wasn't waiting for me. To my relief, there was no one that large and imposing around.

I walked slowly through the players' parking area next to the arena and looked to my left where my Chevy Lumina was parked about 200 feet away in the general parking area. The only people still in the lot were an older man and woman sitting in a pickup truck.

Hurriedly, I walked to my car, opened the door and got in. I immediately pushed the power locks, started the engine and drove away.

Since I didn't know the location of the police station and didn't want to stop to ask anyone, I headed west on I-4 toward Kissimmee, where my wife and two young sons were waiting for me at our hotel room.

It was shortly after midnight when I arrived back at the hotel. My wife was waiting up for me, and the boys were sound asleep.

"You'll never believe what happened to me tonight," I said. Then I told her all the details of the most alarming night of my life. She was even more upset than I was when I told her of the attack and the threat. Right away, I got the phone book out and began trying to get through to the Orlando Police. It took three calls and about 20 minutes before I finally got in touch with information officer Barbara Straka, who said I could come to the station or give my complaint over the phone. Since I was already exhausted, I gave her the complaint over the phone.

"What's his problem? Why did he act like that?" Straka asked after taking down the details.

I couldn't give her an answer. I certainly did not anticipate Harrison's attack and threat. All I wanted to do was give him a chance to state his feelings about his son. It was a basic interview like any of the thousands that I had conducted in the past. But it turned out to be one I'll never forget.

Shaq would later tell the *Orlando Sentinel,* "He [Harrison] was just upset. He thought the guy was just out to make money off us. He was yelling. My Dad doesn't know that anyone can write a book about a celebrity to make money off him. My Dad didn't know the rules. He didn't think it was right."

Harrison would not comment on the incident.

Later that weekend, a complaint was filed with the Orange County Sheriff's Department that Harrison had knocked down a tourist at Disney World. Charges were yet to be filed in that case.

four

Sunday Afternoon Chat with Shaq

On a beautiful April afternoon, the Orlando Magic beat the Boston Celtics for only the third time in franchise history. Naturally, there had been a full house of 15,151 in the O-Rena to watch the important late-season game. But that exuberant crowd had filed out and gone home hours ago.

Then out of nowhere, thousands of kids, in all shapes and sizes, came bouncing down the stairs of the arena, racing as fast as their little feet would carry them. Some were trailed by a winded Mom or Dad. Others seemed to come by themselves. All appeared near hysteria as they made a mad-dash effort to get as close to courtside as possible. Before long, four or five thousand kids and parents had scrambled into a seat.

A Michael Jackson concert? No. Perhaps a circus? Not that, either. It was all for one basketball player who had already performed that day on the same court.

The Shaq Attaq Basketball Exhibition was set up

by Pepsi to show off its newest celebrity and give Shaquille O'Neal a chance to do some public relations work with the kids of the Orlando community. To get into the event all you had to do was present the paper carton from a 12-pack of Pepsi or Mountain Dew. Obviously, the local convenience stores and supermarkets had been forewarned to expect a rush for these drinks.

Indicative of Shaq's mass appeal, there were youngsters and adults in the audience of every imaginable age, race and economic status. For the most part, though, it appeared to be a middle-class happening with lots of casually dressed folks taking their children to the event of the year. Every one of the kids hoped to be selected to go out on the court with Shaq.

The boisterous crowd settled in right on schedule at 4:30, but Shaq was nowhere to be found. Actually, he had told a local magazine writer after the game, "Man, I'm going home to sleep."

"But you've got that clinic in about an hour," the writer reminded him.

"Yeah, but I can still catch a couple hours' sleep," Shaq grinned.

Sure enough, O'Neal was still back at his huge Colonial style home in the most exclusive estate in the Orlando area. Magic coach Matt Guokas's wife, Barbara, happened to be the real estate agent who helped Shaq pick out his beautiful home in the Isleworth section.

Since the Shaq Attaq promotions staff handling the clinic knew that O'Neal was in no hurry to get back to the arena, they arranged for some advance entertainment. Stuff, the big green dragon mascot of the Magic, did a little dancing and a lot of shaking hands and mingling with the crowd. The TV 18 Magic basketball team got the young fans stirred up by giving them a chance to throw a small plastic ball out of the stands and into a mini-basket attached to the back of one of the team members.

Magic players Litterial Green, Jeff Turner and Anthony Bowie took positions on the upper concourse, where they signed autographs for almost an hour. The Magic Dancers did their part as well by putting on several dance routines. Of course, there were plenty of Shaq and team highlight videos to be shown on the big screen.

But the sideshow wasn't what these thousands of children had begged their parents to come see. They wanted the Real Deal, and he was still not available.

After more than an hour's wait, many of the spectators were beginning to verbalize their agitation. The clinic organizers made the mistake of showing the same highlight video more than once. That caused one young boy near the court to yell, "Tell the truth, Shaquille isn't here."

Others started shouting in unison, "We want Shaq! We want Shaq! We want Shaq!"

"Where the hell is Shaq?" screamed an unhappy teenager.

Finally, after the fans had been kept waiting for an hour and 15 minutes, a cage was wheeled out onto the court. The TV 18 basketball crew grabbed a man dressed up like an NBA ref, placed him in the cage and put a cover over the cage. Magically, a huge basketball began to inflate inside the cage, and out of the basketball popped Shaquille O'Neal.

By then, Shaq received a lukewarm ovation from the tired crowd. But things quickly picked up.

Wearing a Pepsi-Shaq Attaq shirt, Magic practice shorts and his trademark Reebok shoes, O'Neal paraded around the court waving to his fans. A young handicapped boy was led onto the court in a wheelchair, and Shaq introduced Walter Young as his special guest. After a long conversation with O'Neal, the boy was wheeled to a position right on the sidelines where he could get a perfect view of the events to come.

The fun began with the Kids Dribbling Relay Race. To make it more challenging, the boys and girls had to wear Shaq-size 20 Reeboks. It was a hilarious scene as the boys and girls tripped and stumbled their way up and down the court. Shaq went around helping them back to their feet. When one little boy had trouble making a layup while wearing the gigantic shoes, Shaq pitched in and lifted the boy over his shoulders for an easy dunk.

Next, Magic assistant coach Brian Hill conducted a 15-minute clinic using O'Neal, Green and Turner to explain the team's three-man offensive set. They showed how the post offense was designed to get the ball to Shaq, who then had the option of executing a drop step, spinning into the lane or taking a fallaway jump shot. Another part of the offensive plan had O'Neal passing to Turner for a jump shot on the wing or passing back out to Green at the point.

Playful as ever, Shaq refused to dunk the ball for the first half of the exhibition. Each time he would drive to the basket, he would simply finger-roll the ball through the net, "Come on, Shaq, dunk it," the boys and girls called out. He just grinned more and more each time.

Finally, after much encouragement, O'Neal started to slam a few. But since his ankles weren't taped and he hadn't warmed up properly, he didn't put on any power dunks. The crowd didn't mind. They just wanted to see Shaq slam it through the goal.

As part of the exhibition, Hill invited some of the boys and girls to come out and play defense against Shaq, Turner and Green. A little blonde girl named Amber tugged on Shaq's shirt and held him up from going to the basket. Gladly obliging, the huge center let the little girl pull him down to the floor. It brought a roar of laughter from the delighted audience.

The crowd pleaser was saved for last. It was the fans' chance to ask Shaquille any questions they wanted. The boys and girls quickly lined up at four stations in the stands where microphones were set up.

A little boy with a squeaky voice asked the first question, "Do you try to play better against players like Patrick Ewing and David Robinson?"

The crowd loved it. Fun-loving Shaquille laughed, too.

"Those are great players," Shaq finally answered. "But I try to play the same way every night. No matter who I'm playing against, I want to go out there and show them everything is mine."

There was prolonged cheering from the crowd. They were enjoying the interaction with their superstar.

Every time he answered a question, they cheered him on.

"What are you going to do during the off-season?" another boy asked.

"I'm going to rest," O'Neal said immediately.

After further contemplation, he added, "I've got to do a movie. I've got to do a couple commercials. I've got to do a couple videos. But I'll still be working and I'll be practicing."

One of the older boys got the next question and asked how old Shaq was when he started playing basketball.

"I was nine years old," Shaq replied. "When I was 14 or 15, I knew basketball would be my game."

A teenage girl then drew the most laughter of the afternoon when she asked for Shaq's phone number.

"It's 694-beep, beep, beep, beep," he teased.

Stepping up to the microphone, a young boy asked what O'Neal liked best about the NBA.

"I just like to go on the court and dominate," he said, pausing before adding, "The best thing that has happened to me is I worked hard, I listened to my parents, I stayed off drugs, and I stayed in school. That's why I'm out here today."

Before he could finish, Shaq was showered with applause, particularly from the parents and grandparents. That was the message they wanted their youngsters to hear from the Magic star.

Back to the questions, another boy wanted to know which center "gives you the most trouble?"

"Patrick Ewing and David Robinson are really tough," Shaq said. "But [Hakeem] Olajuwon gives me the most trouble, because he's quick and he's a scorer."

A tall boy inquired about Shaq's thoughts on the 1996 Olympics. He answered, "I don't know what they're going to do about the Olympic team. If they pick me, I'll go. But if they don't, I'll wait until 2000."

"Do you enjoy playing for the Orlando Magic?" a tiny girl asked.

"Yes, I do," O'Neal answered matter-of-factly, bringing on more applause.

"What was your most embarrassing moment in the NBA?" another girl asked.

O'Neal shrugged and said, "I don't know."

A small boy asked if Shaq is scared when he breaks the basket.

"Am I scared? A little bit," he said. "I don't want the glass to mess up my pretty face."

The next two questions were a little touchy, but O'Neal answered them without hesitation.

"Which player in the NBA don't you like?" asked a girl.

"Probably Alonzo Mourning," Shaq said, drawing approval from the Magic fans, who also don't care for the trash-talking center of the Charlotte Hornets.

When asked about which team he likes to play against most, O'Neal shot back, "The Knicks." The crowd loved that answer, too.

Another good question came from a very young boy: "Do you regret hitting that guy [Alvin Robertson of the Detroit Pistons]?"

"I didn't really hit him hard. I was just stretching and my hand hit him," answered O'Neal, who received a $10,000 fine and a one-game suspension, keeping him out of an important game that the Magic lost to Mourning and the Hornets.

After the cheers subsided, Shaq got more serious with his remarks: "Fighting is not good. Fighting does not solve anything. It just happened. Maybe it was wrong. Maybe it was right."

The next question concerned his plans after his seven-year contract with the Magic expires in 1999.

"I'll probably just retire," he said, straight-faced.

As the boos showered down, he added, "No, I'm just kidding."

Another tyke stepped up to the mike and asked, "How old were you when you first slam-dunked the ball?"

"I was 17 and I was 6-11," Shaq answered. "I couldn't dunk until I was 6-11."

A young fan inquired about O'Neal's much-publicized feat in Phoenix where he buckled the backboard.

"It felt pretty good," Shaq grinned. "But again I was kind of scared. I thought it might mess up my pretty face."

"What do you need to improve on most?" asked the next youngster.

"Free throws, free throws," smiled Shaq. "I need to work on my jump shot and some other things. But I'm going to be all right."

The first parent got a turn to question O'Neal and asked about his meeting with Wilt Chamberlain and Bill Russell to film the much-acclaimed Reebok commercial.

"It was kind of fun meeting those guys," Shaq said. "People don't get to meet those guys very often. I went there and took care of business. It was a lot of fun. I forgot to get their autographs, though."

When asked about the NBA player he likes to dunk against most, O'Neal surprised the crowd. "Manute Bol," he said, "because he's 7-7 and it's fun to dunk over him."

A grandmother got a turn and asked him about his thoughts on Detroit center Bill Laimbeer. As soon as she mentioned Laimbeer, the arena was filled with boos.

A smiling Shaq answered, "My mother always taught me if you don't have anything nice to say about a person, don't say anything at all. I don't have anything to say about Bill Laimbeer."

After the applause subsided, a teenage boy asked, "Who do you look up to?"

"My parents," Shaq answered. "Everyone should listen to your parents."

Once again, the parents in the audience clapped and cheered loudly. Shaq's wise advice was greatly appreciated.

When one fan wanted to know about the Magic's draft plans, O'Neal shrugged and asked for some help from Brian Hill, who said the club would probably pick in the 11th spot with its first of two first-round picks. At that point, he said the team would be looking for the best available player regardless of position.

As for evaluating the lottery picks, Hill tabbed Michigan forward Chris Webber as his top choice if he elected to enter the draft. Otherwise, he would pick Kentucky forward Jamaal Mashburn and then Indiana forward Calbert Cheaney, the national Player of the Year. Hill didn't know at the time that 7-6 center Shawn Bradley was about to enter the draft, too.

Hill then turned the show back over to O'Neal, who fielded several more questions to complete the clinic.

"Who is the greatest player in the game?" a boy inquired.

Some fans began to shout, "Shaq! Shaq! Shaq!"

O'Neal smiled and responded, "I think the greatest player in the NBA may be Michael Jordan."

Another favorite-type question came from a young girl. She wanted to know what was Shaq's favorite food.

"My favorite food is a cheeseburger," he replied and drew both laughter and cheers from the kids.

Actually, O'Neal had already developed a reputation on the team as a junk-food junkie. His closest teammates, such as Dennis Scott and Litterial Green, always tried to get him to try something different at restaurants. But almost without fail, Shaq would place his usual order for two cheeseburgers and french fries. The coaches and team trainer encouraged him to eat a balanced diet, but he just smiled at them.

Even the reporters who covered the team joked with O'Neal about his eating habits. "If you keep eating like that, you'll look like me by the time you're 30," an overweight writer told him.

The final question of the day came from a cute little girl wearing a Magic shirt. She wanted to know if O'Neal was nervous speaking in front of so many people.

"I like kids. You're so cute," he grinned. "No, I'm not nervous. This is fun. I'm having lots of fun."

O'Neal waved to the crowd and headed toward the portal leading to the team locker room. The boys, girls and parents cheered their appreciation for a fun afternoon with Shaq.

Speaking of Shaq

Greg Kite
Orlando Magic veteran center

"The best thing that Shaq can do for himself is to spend some time working on basketball during the season and in the off-season. Every player needs to put in time working on his game. It will be important to him if he wants it to be. Where he is now, he doesn't have to do anything and he will be recognized as one of the best in the league. But he can get so much better if he really wants to. Guys like Magic, Bird and Jordan put a lot of emphasis on preparing themselves for the season and bettering themselves in small ways. That's the difference between the great athletes and the all-time great players.

"I've never played against anyone who is as physically imposing as Shaq with his 300 pounds and his ability to move the way he does. He is the most imposing player in the league now and the most imposing player in the last 10 years. He's got more power than anyone else: the combination of strength and quickness. That makes him unique right there. He's still a young player. There's no way to compare him to some of the better centers who have played in the league. Jabbar had all the moves and was very polished. He used his moves and his experience to do it all. He was an excellent passer and, of course, he had the sky hook, so he could shoot the ball over people and score. Shaq doesn't have those things yet. That's what is so impressive about him, that he can do so well without being refined. I think if he does get there, he will be able to get his team to the championship level. He went out there and shot 56 or 57 percent as a rookie and about half of his shots were on dunks. That means he was only shooting about 35 or 40 percent on his jump shots. If he gets more proficient at that, he could be shooting better than 60 percent overall.

"It's easy for people to get excited about what Shaq does because he can go up and dunk over people. But the average person doesn't understand everything about Shaq. He likes to play and he plays hard, but he's got some rough edges, where if he keeps working on some things, he could become not just an All-Star, but the best player in the league, and lead his team to a championship. You look at another rookie, like Alonzo Mourning, and you see a better all-around basketball player. He does some things better than Shaq at this point in his career. He has better fundamentals, more moves and better shots. But Shaq has a better upside, more potential. I hope for his sake he realizes that. He's achieved so much so early that it might be hard for anybody to realize that I went out and averaged 25 points and 15 rebounds and shot 57 percent, but I can still get a whole lot better. He can become a better screener, which will not only open up his teammates but create more scoring opportunities for him. He has to get better at putting his body on people, so they don't get good position on him. He needs to become a better passer. He's improved on these things, but he needs to make some progress.

"The reason the Lakers won so many titles was Kareem was such a great passer out of the low post. Shaq has gotten better at it, but there are still too many turnovers. He also needs to work on his shooting form and trajectory. He puts in some turnaround jump shots and hook shots sometimes, but he really needs to get better at that. You don't have to have it all. Good post scorers in this league only need to have one or two good moves. He just needs a bread-and-butter move and something else he can turn to.

"There have been other guys that big, but they can't go and finish with a guy hanging on him like Shaq does. He has incredible size and power. That's an athletic ability, and Shaq has plenty of it. He has so many demands on him. I hope he realizes he needs to take time to make the most of his ability."

five

The Private Life of Shaquille O'Neal

If you think Shaquille O'Neal is a tough guy when guarding his team's basket, you haven't seen anything until you find out how forcefully he protects what little privacy his celebrity life affords. He clings to his private time like a drowning man holding on to a life jacket in a crashing sea. Nobody outside his personal entourage of close friends, family and associates is allowed to peek into Shaq's life away from basketball. If they try very hard, they'll quickly be put in their place.

An Orlando television station did a light-hearted feature story on a local craftsman making a custom bed for O'Neal. To demonstrate the massive size of the bed, the reporter lay down in it.

Dennis Tracey, the $84,000-a-year publicist and privacy protector for O'Neal, was told by the superstar to find out who the reporter was and make sure he didn't reveal any more secrets about Shaq's personal life. Tracey didn't know the news reporter, so he confronted WESH sportscaster Stuart Scott.

"Who was the guy that did the story on Shaq's bed?" Tracey demanded. "We're pissed off. That's none of his business. That's Shaq's private life."

The Florida media made many other attempts to give viewers and readers a closer look at what the most prominent figure in the state was really like. But most of those efforts were in vain.

Soon after his arrival in Orlando, local reporters nicknamed Shaq's house "The Mansion." No reporter, no matter how close to the Magic center, was granted access to his million-dollar, 7,000-square-foot Colonial style home in the Isleworth estates, the most exclusive community in central Florida. His neighbors are corporate executives and other celebrities, such as Lou Holtz, who uses his Isleworth home only in the summer. O'Neal's home is located right on the highly rated golf course, even though he despises the game because "it's too slow and boring."

No reporters can even get a look at the outside of his home, because Isleworth has security gates and only invited guests are allowed to enter the area, much less get close enough to see Shaq's place.

Michael Jordan, on his first trip to Orlando following O'Neal's arrival, was invited to play golf at Isleworth. When someone pointed out Shaq's house, Jordan interrupted his golf game and walked over to the huge estate. But even Jordan didn't get in. He knocked on the door and repeatedly rang the doorbell, but O'Neal had his music blasting so loudly that he never heard him. Many Isleworth residents complained that their rich young neighbor was ruining the peacefulness of the community, and for a short while, he turned down his rap music that usually rattled the walls. After all, he has as much equipment as many radio stations, and he was a part-time disk jockey during his college days at LSU.

Local reporters took it as a challenge to become the first media representative to find a way into "The Mansion." The sportscasters pleaded for just a quick tour of the house, or even a couple of shots from outside. Shaq said no chance.

Orlando Sentinel columnist Larry Guest came up with an interesting idea for a sneak peek into the palace. He merely asked permission to drive out to Isleworth and ride to a home game with Shaq in his customized burgundy Chevy Suburban with license plates that read, "Dunk-on-U."

"I can't do that," Shaq said abruptly.

"Why not? It's just a ride to the game," Guest said.

"I can't do that," Shaq repeated and closed the subject.

After O'Neal was suspended for punching out Alvin Robertson, *Sentinel* reporter Tim Povtak requested permission to come watch the Magic-Charlotte game at Shaq's house, so he could write a story about his reaction to watching his team play without him.

"No, man, I can't do that," responded O'Neal. "I've got a date."

Povtak thought for a moment and then asked if he could just stay for the first half of the game and then leave.

"No way, you'd be the third wheel," Shaq answered. "I can't do that."

Those outside the media who have been granted permission to enter "The Mansion" say there's really not much to see. The expansive two-story house has just one couch in the downstairs living room, a bedroom set, and one small table with some chairs in the kitchen. "You wouldn't have to move much to turn it into a dance hall," said one visitor.

However, his home is well stocked with video games of every kind imaginable. He splurged a little by purchasing Virtual Reality, a high-tech, 3-D, 360-degree interactive video game, which makes you feel like you're actually on the battlefield. The price tag—$100,000—makes you know you're rich if you can afford it.

When he's not playing arcade games or mixing music, he generally sits back and watches old movies with lots of action. His favorites are the gangster and martial arts flicks.

"I love all those Ninja movies, karate movies and anything with a lot of action and violence," he said. "I don't know why, but that's what I like. I'll sit in my big house, on my big old couch, and just have a regular movie festival."

So that he's not lonely in "The Mansion," Shaq allows his former teammate Tracey to live upstairs. Their friendship extends beyond a business relationship, although Tracey is beseiged by 75 to 100 phone calls every day concerning some group, company or individual wanting to get involved with O'Neal one way or another.

O'Neal and Tracey represent their own version of "The Odd Couple." Shaq is the multi-millionaire athlete who spent his whole childhood traveling all over the world as part of a military family. He is also a 7-foot-1, 305-pound black man. Tracey, on the other hand, is a 6-foot, 175-pound white man who spent all of his childhood in New Orleans. He also played basketball, but had to fight and scrap for every opportunity. No major college even called him or sent a letter.

But that didn't stop Dennis Tracey. He wrote a letter to LSU coach Dale Brown, stressing how much his hard-work mentality and leadership ability would add to the team. At the time, Brown had a policy of not allowing anyone to try out for the team unless he had already received an athletic scholarship. He amended that policy because he admired Tracey's guts and determination, and he was rewarded with a player who became the defensive stopper of the team and one of the best leaders LSU ever had.

Tracey and O'Neal became best friends in college and shared an off-campus apartment during Shaq's final year at LSU. Tracey, having completed a bachelor's degree in marketing and business, was offered a job by his old pal.

"I told him I'd only take the job as long as it didn't interfere with our friendship," Tracey explained.

So far, it hasn't. O'Neal, after returning home from a late flight, loves to sneak up on his housemate and scare him out of his wits. They enjoy working together and are still a couple of college kids having a ball now that they have enough money to buy the things they couldn't afford in college.

Last spring, Kenner Toys delivered four boxes of its products for Shaq to test out (Kenner signed a multi-million dollar endorsement deal with O'Neal). He took a Nerf bow and arrow and promptly chased Tracey all over the house shooting arrows at him. For weeks, any guest at the house had to learn to duck the Shaq arrow attack.

Another of Shaq's favorite pastimes is wrestling. He enjoys watching professional wrestling on TV, but really prefers the actual thing. Typically, that means Tracey has to go to the floor with him and find a way to overcome the 100-pound differential. Thus far, he hasn't been injured.

Many of their former college teammates have an open invitation to visit Shaq's house whenever they want. Former teammate Maurice Williamson has made several trips to Orlando to spend time with O'Neal and Tracey. Even some of the team managers have been invited.

"When I start to see him not wanting to play around and wrestle, that's when I'll know something in his life has changed," Tracey said. "But he's still the same. He just happens to have a couple of extra dollars in his pockets."

Of his current teammates, the most regular guests at Shaq's house are Dennis Scott, Litterial Green, Anthony Bowie, Donald Royal and Nick Anderson. They basically just hang out together, playing video games, watching movies, listening to music and kidding around with each other.

But obviously, O'Neal doesn't want the rest of Orlando and the country to get a close look at his private haven.

When asked about his celebrity lifestyle, he said, "It's fun, but sometimes it's difficult. Can't go to the mall. Can't go to restaurants, stuff like that. It's all right. I can handle it."

"He enjoys his private time to himself," Tracey said, "especially on game days and when maybe he's not feeling so great. Maybe he's down about the way he's playing or the way the team is playing. He jumps in his car and goes for a ride for a couple of hours. He'll come back and be all right."

Occasionally, O'Neal disguises himself with a Jheri-curl wig, dark glasses and a big coat so that he can sneak into a movie theater or not-so-crowded restaurant. After some home games, he will ride in Scott's chartered limousine to go eat dinner or take in the music at one of the hot clubs in town. Their favorite spot is Heroes, a nightclub owned and operated by Magic teammate Jerry Reynolds, who happens to be another LSU product.

But many times, his attempts to socialize in public are cut short by the hounding of autograph seekers. There are also groupies who are attracted to professional athletes, particularly stars like O'Neal.

"That's no problem for me," he said. "I don't like girls who throw themselves at me. My parents taught me right from wrong, and I'm not going to get in trouble."

O'Neal told *USA Today* columnist Peter Vecsey, "This may be hard to believe, but I'm not going to [have sex with] every girl I meet in clubs. I like to look crazy. But I go mainly because I love music. Girls who throw themselves at me turn me off. I know their real focus. I keep telling myself, 'They're after you, bro, be careful.' Sometimes, though, it's hard to decipher the good from the setups."

Shaq says he has a girlfriend, although her identity, as could be expected, is kept secret. "If I do anything, I do it safely," he said. "I wouldn't put myself in that risk. My father always told me, 'Don't sign nothing. Don't say yes to nothing. Use common sense, and you'll be all right.'"

O'Neal jokes that the only reason he will get married is to have someone there to prepare home-cooked meals. Most of his meals now are of the fast-food variety. His favorite meal features two cheeseburgers accompanied by a pile of french fries. His freezer is well stocked with ready-to-serve spaghetti and lasagna.

"We'll go go out to eat at a nice restaurant and Shaq will always order a cheeseburger," laughed Green. "I'll tell him, 'Shaq, why don't you try something else for a change?' But he just keeps eating cheeseburgers, and then argues that he shouldn't have to pay the bill."

Actually, the Magic star is extremely generous with

his money, particularly when it comes to those who don't have much. He insisted that his agent, Leonard Armato, give him $20,000 a month in spending money. When Armato inquired as to what he could possibly do with that much money each month, Shaq just smiled. But it's obvious some of the funds are being spent on others.

Shaq has been known to stop by the roadside to pick up one of those unfortunate souls holding a "Work for food" sign and take the guy to lunch himself.

He makes regular visits to local hospitals, usually going straight to the children's ward. In his first month with the Magic, he came up with his own version of "Shaqsgiving"—he bought and helped serve Thanksgiving dinner to 300 homeless people, most of whom had no idea who he was. At Christmas, he bought 1,000 Toys-R-Us gift certificates to hand out to needy children. Then he followed that up in the spring by handing out Easter baskets full of candy.

On each occasion, Shaq asked that no reporters be told of his kind acts. Yet they inevitably found out and reported the story. It seems that he can do nothing that doesn't get broadcast on the 6 o'clock news and spread across the front page of the sports section. He does indeed live his life under a microscope.

Many veterans in the league say there has never been as much attention and pressure placed upon a rookie as O'Neal has faced.

"When I came in, it wasn't quite as hyped," Jordan said. "So, I still kind of took people by surprise. He doesn't really have this. He came in with a lot of eyes on him. I can understand his going through drive-thrus."

Jordan, who entered the NBA in 1984, took about three years to develop into a media megastar whose only private moments came in his own home or on some exclusive golf course.

In 1980, Magic Johnson attracted great acclaim as the rookie star of the world champion Los Angeles Lakers. But living in Tinseltown USA, he was just another celebrity and could venture out into public without being swamped by fans.

O'Neal is not as fortunate.

"In Orlando, the Magic is everything," Johnson said. "He can't escape. It's too bad because a young man that age wants to have some time for himself. But what he has to do is not let it stop him from going places, because once that happens it's over. Then you become a hermit. Then you become irritable with people. You change quickly."

Every once in a while, Shaq will sneak into a mall at an off hour to do some shopping with one of his pals. "He only goes when he has to buy something," Green said.

A necessity for O'Neal might be a glittery shirt, a shiny vest or some bright, baggy pants. The more gaudy an outfit, the more he likes it. He also enjoys the reaction he gets from friends and associates.

When Shaq was scheduled to appear on The Arsenio Hall Show, he dressed up in a radiating red outfit, complemented by gold chains around his neck and wrists. He topped it off with one of his many eye-catching hats.

"No way," said Armato, who insisted that he present the correct image by wearing a suit and tie.

"But I can't rap in a suit and tie," argued O'Neal.

A compromise was eventually reached with Shaq wearing the suit and tie to the show. But he got to change into his casual clothes to sing with the rap group Fu Schnickens.

His collection of unusual hats always creates a stir among the media covering the Magic. They make casual wagers as to which hat he will be wearing for a particular ballgame. Shaq has some hats that are over a foot tall and make him look like more of a Goliath than he already is. He has several Civil War hats and sometimes dresses like Robert E. Lee. Perhaps the crowd's favorite is his "Cat in the Hat" top hat.

"You know he's just doing it to get a reaction," *Orlando Sentinel* reporter Tim Povtak laughed. "And he doesn't like it when you don't pay attention to him. He's just a big kid."

On his more playful days, Shaq may parade around the locker room saying, "I'm Mandingo. I'm well built and I'm well hung." Povtak said the rookie called himself

Mandingo for about a week before he got tired of it and started another act.

"He tells us all the time he's Mandingo," Green said. "He says he's the great man who came over from Africa. He'll say anything."

O'Neal is game for just about anything as well. LSU assistant coach Craig Carse occasionally took him hunting and fishing in Louisiana, known as the Sportsman's Paradise.

When Magic teammate Anthony Bowie invited him to go hunting in Florida, he gladly accepted the invitation. However, the kid in Shaq came out, and instead of shooting wild pigs as he was supposed to, he wound up chasing the baby wild pigs.

"You should have seen it!" roared Bowie in a fit of laugher. "That big guy was running all over the field, diving after those little pigs. They were scared to death."

Yes, he eventually caught one.

It's obvious O'Neal knows how to have a good time. Even though he has yet to make a single friend in Orlando, outside his teammates, he seems content to stay there for years to come.

"As long as I've got my family and my boys," he said, "I don't need anybody else."

Speaking of Shaq

Donald Royal
Orlando Magic forward

"I never expected Shaq to come in and play like he did as a rookie. I'm from New Orleans, so I got to see him play in college. Basically, what I saw was a very raw player. Chris Jackson and Stanley Roberts were the scorers on the team, and Shaq was just filling in the void and blocking shots. But after Chris and Stanley left, the team took Shaq's

identity and he took over. From that point, he started to improve.

"But I watched Shaq come here and he just blossomed into this media megastar. It's amazing. I played with David Robinson in San Antonio and saw how they treated him, and it didn't compare to what Shaq gets. I've never seen a player get the fanfare and attention that he gets. But he has this childlike humor and he doesn't offend anyone. He's still down to earth.

"Shaq is just a fun guy to be around. We go over to his house and just play games and relax. We play Terminator II and stuff like that. He has lots of toys. Then he's got that customized Suburban that I call the 'Truck from Hell' because he plays that music so loud. But he's fun to be around and it's great to see him progress as an NBA player.

"This game is all about confidence, and Shaq has no lack of confidence. He's always been very confident about his shooting ability. He just got by with the dunk in college because he was so much bigger and stronger than everybody else. Now he's got to shoot some jumpers. He thinks he has the best turnaround jumper in the league.

"We get on his ass about his free-throw shooting. We know he plays a lot of minutes and gets tired, but sometimes he just goes up to the line and throws it up there without concentrating. If he concentrated, he could definitely be an upper 60-percent foul shooter. But when he's tired or pissed off, he just throws it up there. We have to remind him that those points count, too. But we have no problem with him. Everything else he does far outweighs his free-throw shooting trouble.

"I think Shaq is hungry. I played with David Robinson and Stanley Roberts, and they didn't have the hunger that Shaq has. You'd never see David or Stanley dive for loose balls, but Shaq does it. Shaq has the great physical skills and has a great attitude. David Robinson relies on his great skills and athletic ability. He's very quick and a great shooter, but he doesn't have the day-to-day intensity that Shaq has. David has other things in his life, being a born-again Christian, that are more important to him than basketball. Not that he's not great, but it's not

vital to him. He doesn't go out there every night to kill people. He's going to have nights when he'll only score five or six points and won't be bothered by it. But if Shaq has a game like that, you won't be able to live with him for the next week.

"David Robinson is just a nice guy. Shaq isn't really that way. He knows how to demand things from his teammates and point fingers. There's nothing wrong with that. Sometimes you need somebody to do that. When he gets mad, he yells at everyone in general. No particular person.

"Shaq loves to trash talk. He'll score on somebody and tell them, 'You can't guard me. Get out of my face.' Then when he blocks a shot, he'll say, 'Don't bring that shit in here.'

"Shaq loves to compete against the great centers. He thinks he's the best player in the league already. He pushed Patrick Ewing around for three games and then Patrick decided he had to take it outside. Nobody can go inside against Shaq. He's the strongest center in the league already and he knows it.

"Sometimes we forget to establish our inside game. We forget to get the ball inside to the big fella. But believe me, we don't forget it for long. He makes sure of that. Everyone understands that the team is expected to revolve around him. We knew that from the day he signed that contract.

"I don't think there's too much jealousy. Just little subtle stuff. Shaq gets a lot of things that the rest of us don't. I get upset when he walks into a club and they won't let me in, or they make me take off my hat and they let him walk in with his hat on. But the rest of us get treated pretty well. We ride on his coattails."

six

How Does Shaq Stack Up?

When Shaquille O'Neal stepped onto the floor of the O-Rena for his first NBA game, it had been more than a decade since a center truly had been the center of attention in the league. Shaq wasted no time filling the void and creating a national stir with spectacular play that instantly brought back memories of the game's all-time great centers and an era when centers were indeed the "big men" in the NBA.

Kareem Abdul-Jabbar won his last of five Most Valuable Player awards at the end of the 1979–80 season, the same year that Magic Johnson and Larry Bird burst onto the scene. In the following years, the NBA style of play evolved into an up-tempo, finesse game, featuring big guards who traditionally would have played forward and lightning-quick forwards who could handle the ball and score from anywhere on the court.

Instead of the classic big-man duels between Jabbar and Wilt Chamberlain, Wilt and Bill Russell, and Jabbar against Willis Reed, the spotlight switched to the smaller players. The superstar role was handed to fabulous forwards like Bird and Julius Erving and later Charles Barkley and Dominique Wilkins, and the top billing went to outstanding guards like Johnson and later Michael Jordan and Clyde Drexler.

From 1965 to 1980, the league's MVP had been exclusively reserved for the likes of Chamberlain, Russell, Jabbar or another center. Bird broke that streak in 1984, winning his first of three MVP titles, and for the next nine years, the highest individual honor in the league went to Bird, Jordan or Johnson.

While O'Neal really had no chance to win the MVP award as a rookie, he did steal the spotlight from Jordan and immediately conjured up memories of the great centers of yesteryear. Shaq, in fact, soared past the likes of Wilt, Kareem and Russell in terms of being endeared to basketball fans throughout the world. Never had a center, particularly such an awesome, overpowering giant, been so adored by the multitudes. He quickly earned the label of "a Goliath that everyone loves."

"It's his physical stature, his power. He's got superstar written all over him," said Cleveland Cavaliers General Manager Wayne Embry, who played behind Russell with the Boston Celtics and was the G.M. in Milwaukee when Jabbar played there. "I'm always glad to see big men come along."

No doubt Shaq is the most marketable and beloved center to ever hit the NBA, but where does he fit in as far as pure talent and ability? The numbers he posted as a rookie clearly put O'Neal in the elite class of centers along with all-time greats Chamberlain, Jabbar and Russell, particularly considering the prevalence of big men in the league now. When Wilt entered the league in 1959, Detroit's Walter Dukes was the only other seven-footer in the NBA. Shaq, on the other hand, made his debut in 1992 having to face 37 other seven-footers and another 22 players at 6-11.

Remarkably, Shaq was the only player in the NBA to finish in the top 10 in four different individual statistics. He was second in the league in rebounding (13.9) and shot blocking (3.53), fourth in shooting percentage (.562) and eighth in scoring (23.4). Among the league's 27 starting centers, he ranked first in both rebounding and field-goal percentage, second in scoring and third in blocked shots.

The only rookie centers in NBA history to outperform O'Neal in terms of combined scoring and rebounding average were Chamberlain (37.6 points, 26.9 rebounds) and Jabbar (28.8 points, 14.5 rebounds). David Robinson, who was 24 years old as a rookie, had a slightly higher scoring average than Shaq at 24.3, but was well behind in rebounding at 11.9. In terms of pure power, Robinson was not even close to young Shaq.

Even comparing Shaq to Robinson and other veteran centers like Patrick Ewing and Hakeem Olajuwon, the strength edge went to the Magic rookie. Some players and coaches say O'Neal was the most dominating center in the league during the 1992–93 season.

"There's not a guy in the league who can handle him," said Cleveland All-Star center Brad Daugherty.

Robinson remarked, "To see a seven-foot guy run like he does, jump like he does and have the strength he has, it's just unfathomable to most people."

"You know what he looks like?" Olajuwon asked. "A bigger me."

O'Neal is most often compared to Chamberlain, because it was Wilt who had the imposing height and weight to go with his great stats. But even Wilt the Stilt would not have matched up physically with Shaq as a rookie. As a 23-year-old rookie in 1959–1960, Wilt stood 7-1 and weighed 255 pounds. O'Neal, on the other hand, carried 50 more pounds as a 7-1 rookie.

"People keep wanting to compare Shaq to other players, especially Wilt," Orlando General Manager Pat Williams said. "I grew up in Philadelphia and I saw Wilt break into the league. He was much skinnier than Shaq. We think of Wilt as an amazingly strong physical specimen, but that didn't happen until later in his career."

Not even Chamberlain and Jabbar, who played in

an era with relatively few seven-footers in the league, managed to shoot as well from the field as O'Neal. Wilt hit 46.1 percent and Jabbar made 53.9 percent.

However, many observers who played with or against Chamberlain and Jabbar say their offensive game was much more advanced than O'Neal's. Although the Orlando Magic don't make their shot chart available to the public, it's well accepted that Shaq scored more than 80 percent of his field goals on dunks, layups or finger rolls from a couple of feet away or closer.

When asked about his team's defensive effort in limiting O'Neal to dunks, Washington Bullets coach and former MVP center Wes Unseld remarked, "Does he ever do anything but dunk?" After waiting for a response, Unseld answered the question himself. "I've never seen him make a jump shot."

Chamberlain made similar remarks about Shaq's offensive game.

"I only point this out to show there's no comparison between Shaquille and me, offensively," Chamberlain told a reporter from the San Francisco Chronicle. "Our games are very, very different, especially when I came into the league. Worlds apart. People have always been confused about what Wilt was about. They only remember the power Wilt of later years. They don't remember my ability to run and leap. I came into the league at 265 pounds. I shot the jump shot off the boards better than anyone except Cazzie Russell, Sam Jones and Dick Barnett. When I averaged 50 and 44, my points came off jump shots, and hooks from time to time. I've seen Shaquille make one jump shot."

Shaq refused to enter into what easily could have turned into a major controversy between himself and Chamberlain. Still, he made it absolutely clear that he expects to become the most dominant player in the game.

"That's his opinion," Shaq said of Wilt's remarks. "I never knock a man for his opinion. That's OK. I'm going to be The Man one day. You underline that three times."

Although O'Neal showed some definite weaknesses in his game as a rookie, most coaches and executives in the NBA say it's only a matter of time before he develops the offensive arsenal to rule the league.

"He'll be the best. That's obvious," said former Los Angeles Clippers coach Larry Brown. "We wanted to change up on him, give him different looks. By the time he has a book on everybody, I hope I'm back in college [coaching]." Brown walked away from the Clippers at end of Shaq's rookie season to become coach of the Indiana Pacers.

At this stage of his career, O'Neal has an offensive game to match his age. He is, of course, the youngest player in the league, having started his rookie season at the age of 20. Before becoming a legal adult on March 6, 1993, he had already taken the NBA by storm, becoming the first rookie to be voted to the starting lineup in the All-Star Game since Jordan in 1985 and leading the Magic into playoff contention for the first time in franchise history. He was also the youngest player to ever appear in an NBA All-Star Game.

"Shaquille is so big and powerful that you tend to forget how young he is," said Magic coach Matt Guokas, who played with Chamberlain on the Philadelphia 76ers' 1967 world championship team. "This is a learning process for him. When he came to training camp, he didn't know how to set a pick and didn't know how to execute a pick and roll. He's come a long way. But he has so much to learn. There are a lot of things he needs to work on. Shooting free throws is just one of them."

It was no coincidence that the Magic never had a shooting coach until O'Neal joined the club. Then the team went right out and hired Buzz Braman from the 76ers. Braman, the son of Philadelphia Eagles owner Norman Braman, works with all the players on the Orlando team, but spends more time with Shaq than with anyone else. Braman said he hoped to spend much of the summer of 1993 working individually with O'Neal, but again that depended on Shaq's busy schedule of commercials, sponsor appearances, singing and filmmaking.

O'Neal's major flaw as a rookie was free-throw shooting. He converted 402 of 684 attempts for 58.8 percent. Often when the game was close, opponents would foul O'Neal to get him to the free-throw line. Usually they were rewarded with misses.

However, with Braman's help, Shaq improved his free-throw percent from the low 50s early in the season to the low 60s during the second half. His was not an uncommon problem for young centers. Russell made just 49.2 percent of his free throws as a rookie, Chamberlain hit 58.2 percent, and Nate Thurmond converted at a 59.4 rate.

"I'm constantly asked if Shaquille will be like Wilt and will never be able to shoot free throws," Braman smiled, "and the answer is no. Shaquille just has to learn to do the fundamental things right. Even if you're Mark Price, you've got to do the fundamental aspects of free-throw shooting correctly or you won't be very good at it."

Braman predicts his star pupil will make the same transition that Karl Malone and Rony Seikaly made. Malone hit 49.6 percent from the line as a rookie with the Utah Jazz in the 1985–86 season, but soon was approaching 80 percent. Seikaly converted 59.2 percent of his free-throw attempts as a Miami rookie in the 1989–90 season and also progressed to near the 80-percent mark.

"Shaquille has made rapid progress with his jump shot and now he just needs to convert that to his free throws," Braman said. "He definitely will be shooting in the mid-70s to the 80s in his career. There's no way it's not going to happen. In our practice sessions, Shaquille has shown he has the ability and the desire to be a very good shooter."

But some question O'Neal's desire to improve his game enough to fulfill the grand expectations cast upon him.

"Right now, he's just basically dunking the ball, so he's got to work on his offensive game," said Hall of Famer John Havlicek, who played with Russell in Boston and opposed the likes of Chamberlain and Jabbar during his career. "I don't like to say negative things about people, but it's obvious he needs some work. His strengths right now are rebounding and defense. I'm sure he will get better with his offense as time goes on. He can't just rely on dunking the ball. He will find some people will start to play him differently. They'll make him do different things. He must become a better passer and a better shooter. But I think he will become a great player.

"As a rookie, he has done a tremendous job bringing his team to the brink of the playoffs," Havlicek continued. "Within his first year already, he has proven to be a force in this league. But what is really going to help the Magic is when he begins to develop his offense."

Tom Heinsohn, a former teammate of Havlicek's, said he wonders if O'Neal will be able to escape the huge demands of the media and marketing world and still have time to work on his game.

"The media is making Shaquille out to be a superstar in this league already, but he's not there yet," said Heinsohn, now the TV play-by-play man for the Celtics. "He doesn't have the skills of the great centers in this league. If the Magic and those people he surrounds himself with don't give him time to work on developing those skills, he'll never get there."

Veteran Orlando center Greg Kite tried to offer some friendly advice to O'Neal, speaking from the perspective of a veteran lending a helping hand to a young teammate. But Shaq was not interested.

"Good scorers in this league have one, maybe two shots that they go to every time. It could be a little jump hook or a turnaround jump shot, whatever," Kite said. "Shaquille doesn't have that yet. I think he will get it, but he's got to work at it. All he needs right now is a bread-and-butter move, and he will become one of the great scorers in the league. Later on, he can add to his repertoire.

"Even though he gets a lot of traveling calls, Shaquille has really good foot work. He does a good job of getting into position to use his body. He just needs a refinement in the mechanics of his shot, where he holds it and how high he gets it off and how he gets his hand under the ball. That's what he needs to work on the most. Of course, he's always going to get a lot of dunks. He's incredible at that. He gets more dunks than anybody I've ever seen because of his power, agility and quickness. Last year, Otis Thorpe led the league with 160 dunks, that's about two a game. Shaq has been averaging four or four and a half per game. That's an incredible difference."

Kite laughed when he reflected on O'Neal's dunk-a-thon against the 76ers. He had 13 dunks in that game.

"Just to be able to get the basketball like that and then dunk over somebody who's just as tall is really remarkable," Kite said, continuing to smile. "There hasn't been anybody that I've played against that could come close. Maybe Wilt or Russell was like that and could get to the goal like he can."

While somewhat critical of O'Neal's offensive style, Chamberlain said upon meeting the new superstar at the shooting of a Reebok commercial that he was very impressed with him. Wilt also said he would be happy to give Shaq a few pointers.

"I had the pleasure recently to film a commercial with Shaquille, Bill Russell, Bill Walton and Kareem, and I was thoroughly impressed with Shaquille as a young man," Chamberlain recalled. "I thought he had a lot of class, style and a lot of enthusiasm. I watched him play in person in New York and on TV against the Clippers and the Warriors, and I've seen a great deal of him on the ESPN highlights. I notice 89 percent of his baskets come on dunks.

"People like to think of me as doing that throughout my career, but that was not how I played basketball," Wilt continued. "The last four or five years of my career, when centers starting getting more lax on defense, I was able to get inside more often and dunk. But during my heyday of scoring, 90 percent of my shots were on jump shots."

Despite his offensive limitations, O'Neal revitalized the NBA with his overpowering shot blocking, defensive play and rebounding, according to Chamberlain.

"He brings a new dimension to the game, he is electrifying, he's a tremendous shot blocker and he's extremely graceful and fluid," Wilt remarked. "It was partly my agility and grace that helped me never to foul out [in 1,205 games] and to move around and get all those rebounds. Shaquille [who fouled out of his first NBA game and had eight disqualifications for the year] is very graceful for his size. I think this man is only going to get better and better, but he's going to have to be taught some offensive skills. He has already established that he's going to the basket, so the defense is back on its heels. If he develops a little five-foot jumper, he's going to be tremendous.

"I'd like to work with him," Chamberlain offered. "I'm not saying he needs a lot of help. Everyone can use help. Someone could've worked with me when I was young. All I'm saying is that I have some offensive moves a guy of his agility and size could use that would only enhance his game. I don't know who would be better qualified to help him.

"He has the power. It's already terrifying, and everyone is going to play him for his power. The league is full of 300-pound guys who will be glad to butt heads with him like two bull elephants, and it's going to wear him down. He's got to learn to score without going inside all the time."

Following his Rookie of the Year season, O'Neal planned to make his second visit to Pete Newell's summer camp for centers. As promised, Shaq first showed up at Newell's Los Angeles training camp shortly after being drafted by the Magic.

Many NBA teams send their centers to work with Newell for a fee of thousands of dollars. The former Cal coach puts the big men through a rigorous series of daily drills and scrimmaging that is considered tougher than what they endure during NBA training camp. Most of the players are not overly enthusiastic about working so hard in the summer.

O'Neal surprised Newell by voluntarily attending the camp. When he got there, Shaq displayed a strong desire to improve, which caught the immediate attention of a coach who is not easily impressed. In fact, Newell is renowned for being critical of such former superstars as Jabbar (needed to become a stronger rebounder), Russell (should have had a better attitude about scoring) and Chamberlain (didn't use his left hand enough).

"What a nice guy," Newell told the Oakland Tribune when asked about Shaq. "The league needs somebody like Shaquille and he's a very modest, engaging young guy. He's not a guy who goes around pumping his hands or anything. He's got a lot of charm to him, and he doesn't try to charm people.

"I'm very impressed," continued Newell. "He's amazingly agile for his size. Very explosive. So many physical attributes. He has to rank at this stage of his career with any of the great centers."

Nonetheless, Newell agreed that Shaq needs plenty of work on his offense. Instead of relying solely on his spin moves to get free for dunks, Newell encouraged O'Neal to come up with a well-rounded offensive game. It was obvious he didn't want Shaq to settle for being like Russell, who was primarily a defensive stalwart, but lacked the offensive skills to dominate the game.

"One thing I tried to impress upon him is he's got to acquire technique," stressed Newell. "He's got quite an explosiveness for his size, but when you have a power game only, you tend to get too physical and you get a lot of fouls. You have to temper your power game with technique."

Without question, foul trouble limited what O'Neal was able to accomplish as a rookie. He finished the season with 321 fouls in 81 games, an average of almost four per game. In addition to fouling out eight times, O'Neal often saw his playing time cut short by foul problems.

Newell believes Shaq will develop an offensive package to go with his overpowering shot-blocking and rebounding ability, but it will take time and a commitment on his part.

"A lot of guys have ability—I'm not saying they have as much as he has—but they squander it," Newell cautioned. "They have money and cars, and the basketball part becomes almost secondary.

"There's a lot of very good players who are satisfied to be good. I've had a lot of them here," Newell added. "But to be a truly great one, you can't be satisfied. Look at Michael Jordan. At one time, he wasn't a very good shooter. Now you can't walk away from him. Shaquille wants to be good and he's very receptive to teaching."

Magic coach Brian Hill called O'Neal a very hard worker during practice. But Hill said Shaq must put in the extra hours of shooting and technique work on his own. Much of the responsibility for Shaq's offensive improvement was thrust upon Buzz Braman.

The Orlando management dictated that Braman keep a low profile during his first season. Amazingly, there was not a single article written about the work he was doing with O'Neal, yet Hill and coach Matt Guokas said Braman was instrumental in Shaq's gradual improvement with free-throw shooting.

Basically, Shaq had a simple technique problem with his shooting. It angered Braman to hear people criticize O'Neal's concentration because that was not the trouble at all, he said.

"It takes two things to become a better shooter: the right diagnosis and the willingness of the player," Braman said. "Those two things are married together."

What held O'Neal back was an improper shooting motion and poor handling of the ball. Whenever he took a shot, his right elbow would fling out, causing the ball to veer off course. His other error involved the way he gripped the ball: too tightly. Braman brought out a number of other minor adjustments, but his work with Shaq focused primarily on shooting form and on gripping the ball correctly.

"It takes time to work these things out, but Shaquille has already made excellent progress," Braman said late in the season. "He just needs to have a good summer now."

Braman, a shooting guru who once made more than 700 consecutive free throws, helped Hersey Hawkins of the 76ers develop into one of the leading free-throw shooters in the NBA. He was shooting around 80 percent before Braman began diagnosing his technique. After some adjustments and lots of practice, Hawkins raised his foul shooting accuracy to almost 90 percent.

However, Braman's most remarkable turnaround

involved Mara Cunningham, a standout for the Vanderbilt women's team. She was hitting only 55 percent of her free throws before working with Braman. By the time he finished with her, Cunningham was one of the top free-throw shooters in women's college basketball, hitting 87 percent of her attempts.

"Most of it is technical," Braman explained. "People think free-throw shooting is all in the head. They say the guy just can't concentrate. They said that about Wilt. But it's really not concentration. You have to use the right technique to make the ball go straight every time.

"My philosophy of shooting is based on two things: Make the ball go straight and judge the distance correctly," Braman continued. "If you can do those two things, you can become a good shooter."

Another question surrounding O'Neal as a rookie was his ability to make his teammates better and ultimately turn what had been the league's second-weakest expansion team into a contender. Interestingly, it had been more than 20 years since the leading scorer on a world championship team was a center. Jabbar averaged 34.8 points in leading the 1971–72 Lakers to the title, but even though he played on subsequent championship teams, it was point guard Magic Johnson who played the leading role.

In recent years, Olajuwon was the only outstanding center in the NBA ever to come close to a title. In his second pro season, Olajuwon and Ralph Sampson led the Houston Rockets to the NBA Finals, but they lost to the Celtics in six games. Prior to the 1992–93 playoffs, the Rockets had failed to advance past the first round six straight years.

The same playoff misfortune plagued Patrick Ewing with the New York Knicks and David Robinson with the San Antonio Spurs. Until this past season, neither player had been able to lead his team past the second round.

"Even before we acquired Shaquille, I always found that interesting," said Matt Guokas. "Yet, every team in the league would want to start their franchise with a

Shaquille O'Neal or an Olajuwon or a Ewing or Robinson. What it really comes down to is championship-caliber teams play good defense. Centers are important. They can dominate defensively at times. They can be rebounders. They can be the hub of your offense. But you also need people who can break down defenses and get out and get after people on the defensive end."

Even Guokas acknowledged the Magic are a long way from being a championship-type team. Small forward Dennis Scott, the fourth player picked in the 1990 draft, failed to fulfill his promise as a consistent scorer in his first three years with the club. In fairness to him, he was slowed by various injuries, including a knee problem that limited him to 18 games during the season before Shaq arrived. Power forward Brian Williams, the 10th player taken in the 1991 draft, also flopped in his first two seasons.

"Brian Williams hasn't shown anything yet as to what we would have expected from him," said Guokas. "Dennis Scott, when healthy, has been a good player for us and helped us win basketball games. But so far, those two draft choices, as we sit here today, have not been productive for us."

Actually, rumors circulated in Orlando and other NBA cities that Scott was on the trading block throughout the 1992–93 season, but a deal could not be arranged.

Prior to the 1993 draft, O'Neal and shooting guard Nick Anderson were the only draft choices that had paid off for the Magic, who essentially needed three more players to become a contender.

"Different strokes for different folks," O'Neal said when asked about the lack of success for the game's top centers. "What happened to them might not happen to me. I think if I'm lucky, the team is playing well and we're doing all right, anything can happen. If I don't win it in a couple of years, I'm going to keep trying, and if I never get it—well, I will have tried."

His team's future success and his own offensive development seem to be the only things blocking O'Neal from achieving the status of one of the greatest centers to play in the NBA. That ultimately may be the only fair way to compare him to Chamberlain, Jabbar and Russell.

Chamberlain, however, said any type of comparison is an injustice to O'Neal.

"I think it's totally unfair to compare Shaquille with me," Wilt said. "In this society of ours, with all the racial unrest, I'm not looking to create any more division or turmoil. I'm just trying to be truthful and honest. And I think it's strange that every time someone tall and black comes out of college, he's compared to Wilt. Ralph Sampson, Patrick Ewing, even Kareem to an extent, and now Shaquille.

"It's a divide and conquer thing, rather than giving praise," Wilt said. "Someone has to come out a loser. They never compared Bill Walton to me. He was compared to nobody. I know it may make nice copy to compare Shaquille and me, but I wonder why he has to be like somebody else, and Christian Laettner doesn't have to. Why doesn't Laettner come in with the burden of having to prove he's as good as Larry Bird? Or as good as me?

"Laettner was a two-time NCAA champ," Wilt continued. "He's 6-11. He was on the Olympic team, not Shaquille. He's more graceful and has more basketball experience than Shaquille. Maybe he should be compared to me. Who's he compared to? Nobody. Right? He's allowed to do his own thing, and Shaquille has to prove he's another Wilt Chamberlain.

"When people make these comparisons, they say I should be honored to be held up as the definition of the apex of a big man," Chamberlain added. "But if that's the highest accolade, how come when they talk about who the best big man of all time is, they throw out four or five other names in there? I see Shaquille as a man totally playing his own game of basketball. The bottom line for me is I'd like to see him given the chance to play basketball with his own athletic ability and style, let him be Shaquille O'Neal and not the next Wilt Chamberlain, or the new anyone else."

Walton, who tutored O'Neal during his college career at LSU, offered a similar opinion about comparing

O'Neal to the all-time greats.

"You don't want to fall into the habit of calling him the next Hakeem Olajuwon," Walton said. "He's the first Shaquille O'Neal. He's going to establish his own identity, and he already has."

Interestingly, when asked how he feels to be compared to Chamberlain and the other greats, O'Neal said, "The only thing I can say is thanks."

Speaking of Shaq

Tom Heinsohn
Boston Celtics TV play-by-play announcer,
   NBA Hall of Famer and former Celtics head coach

"I really like Shaquille O'Neal and think he's great for the league. But right now I have a major concern that they are marketing somebody way past what his abilities are at this point. His potential is certainly what everyone says it is. But his abilities right now on this floor are limited. There are obviously things that this young man has to learn to be able to dominate the game as everyone expects him to do. He's a friendly guy and a competitive guy, but if he succumbs to everything that's being said about him, he will not become a great player. The only way he's going to become a great player is if his peers recognize him as a great player. He needs to be listening to his peers and not the press and all the marketing people. He still has a long ways to go.

"I've never seen a player with his physical talent. There's never been a player with his size and mobility, and he seems to have a competitive spark. But there are a lot of things that he has to learn about basketball, and he must improve his shooting. By the end of the year, he was starting to understand where the double-teams were coming

from and how to pass out of the low post. But he's got to put it all together and do it on a consistent basis. He could be one of the all-time greats, no question about it.

"First of all, he's got to expect that he's going to get double-teamed. If he's going to score, he's got to be able to score over those double-teams and develop the touch to do it. I wouldn't say he needs a medium-range shot, but that certainly would be helpful. He turns to the basket very effectively, which is fine, but he's not going to be able to power everything. He needs a little better touch on the five-, six- or seven-foot shots. If he gets that, he will be un-stoppable.

"You've got to work on it. That's where the competitiveness comes in. If he really wants it, he's got to work on it. The real challenge to Shaquille O'Neal is that he's been given so many kudos before he even stepped on the floor that he's got to be realistic and realize where he truly is and not be swayed by all these great things that people are saying about him. He still has to deliver the goods, and he hasn't done that yet.

"Wilt Chamberlain had a much better game than Shaq coming into the league. But he still had to learn some things. I tell you a guy who was a lot like Shaquille was Darryl Dawkins. He had all the physical tools and the great body, but never became the outstanding player that he could have become. There you have the possibilities of what can and cannot happen. He could be another great player like Chamberlain or he could fail like Dawkins.

"Shaquille is definitely more physical than Bill Russell ever was. Bill Russell used his intelligence. Bill knew how to use his head and his quickness. He really out-thought everyone else on the court, not only the man playing against him, but the whole other team. I don't think Shaquille will ever be compared to Bill Russell. I don't think people will ever look at him that way. Russell was not quite 6-10, but he dominated the boards and was a great shot blocker. And he knew when to go for a block. But he wasn't nearly as physical as Shaquille O'Neal.

"Chamberlain was as big and powerful as Shaquille late in his career. Wilt was a fantastic rebounder,

a great shot blocker, and everyone knows what a great scorer he was. Just look at the record books.

"Shaquille has to learn to use his head. After a while, if he keeps going after everyone who penetrates, they're going to use the movement that he gets. The good players in the NBA, if you just lean toward them, know how to slip the ball past you. So he's got to develop some intelligence and know when to go for the block and when not to go for the block. He's still got a lot to learn."

seven

The Marketing of a Megastar

Pepsi may have produced a commercial for the ages: The sweaty 7-1 giant breaks up a kids' playground basketball game, bends one of the baskets over, dunks the ball, and then goes looking for a cold drink. Finding the cooler empty, he peers across the court to find a little boy holding the last Pepsi. He stomps up to the lad and then flashes that golden smile that belies his intimidating size and makes you think the Pepsi is his. Instead, the little kid says, "Don't even think about it." The commercial ends with the two of them sitting on the bench, and Shaquille O'Neal smiles broadly again and says, "Pleeeease."

Sure, Shaquille has a (multi) million-dollar smile, a handsome face, a sculptured body and worlds of athletic talent and charm to go with them. But guess who's really smiling these days?

Leonard Armato, for one. All Shaq's agent had to do was line up the prospective sponsors, all hoping to get O'Neal to endorse their products in exchange for another

$10 to 20 million. At last count, Armato had worked out deals with nine major industries, pushing Shaq's endorsement take well beyond the $42-million contract that he signed with Orlando. The latest figures had his endorsement package at $70 million and climbing, so his total of future basketball and marketing contracts was worth more than $110 million.

"There's never been a player that's been this hot this quick," Armato said. "The demand has been incredible. It's like Disney managing Mickey Mouse—everybody wants to [link] Mickey with their products."

Shaq's father, for another. Sgt. Phillip Harrison was named the vice-president of the One-al corporate empire, and his former teammate at LSU, Dennis Tracey, was hand-picked by O'Neal to be the publicist. They quickly became one big, rich family.

However, lost in the shuffle of all the millions of bucks being passed Shaq's way was the ripple effect of his mammoth impact on Orlando and the NBA.

Take Ralph Gray, for example. Ralph had been struggling to pick up a few extra corporate sponsors for the Magic. All of a sudden his job changed overnight.

"When I used to go out of town to visit the headquarters of a corporation, I'd tell them I'm with the Orlando Magic and they'd say something like, 'Well, what radio station is that?'" Gray laughed, remembering the bad ol' days.

"Now when I go see somebody out of town and say I'm with the Magic, they always say, 'Oh, you're with Shaq's team,'" Gray said, smiling even more.

Orlando, despite being the home of Disney World, welcomed another super hero with open arms.

"A guy like Shaquille raises the profile of the city," said Joe Mittiga, a spokesman for Mayor Bill Frederick. "People know Orlando as the site of Disney World and other theme parks, but now we're also known as the place where Shaq plays. It's what we call 'top-of-the-head' recognition, something that makes you instantly identifiable in a positive way."

The NBA itself came away a big winner with the arrival of O'Neal. During the '80s, no professional sports league had the marketing success of the NBA. The enormous impact of Shaquille's appeal almost cinched another decade of economic boom times for David Stern's organization. The departure of Magic Johnson and Larry Bird, the cornerstone of the league's emergence, was virtually forgotten in the wake of the O'Neal sensation. For four straight weekends in February, he was shown on the NBA Game of the Week as NBC and league officials acted swiftly to capitalize on the public's love affair with the big man.

"It's no coincidence that we got our highest rating ever (14.3) for an All-Star Game with O'Neal involved for the first time," said NBC sports publicist Ed Markey, who did his part by hyping the controversy between Shaq and his East All-Star backup, Patrick Ewing, and their matchup against David Robinson and Hakeem Olajuwon. "That's his star quality at work. The NBA is star-driven and O'Neal is still a curiosity around the country. People are realizing he's legitimate.

"But I knew he was something special when before the season even started, *The New York Times Magazine* chose him for a cover story," Markey continued. "And then, of course, when he shattered the backboard support in Phoenix, that certainly didn't hurt his image as a Superman."

Of course, Shaq benefited more than anyone else. A lifetime of financial security was assured the moment he signed the record-breaking, seven-year, $42-million deal with Orlando. Once the endorsement opportunities began piling up, it became clear that O'Neal was on pace to become the richest athlete in the world.

Almost overnight, he became the most sought-after athlete for endorsements, stepping over the NBA megastar who seemed untouchable, Michael Jordan. While it will probably take some more time before Shaq starts earning $40 to $50 million a year like Jordan, he is already in more demand.

"In Shaquille, we have the charisma of Magic Johnson, the talent of the NBA's legendary centers and a personality that supersedes Michael Jordan," said Reebok sports division president Roberto Miller. "It took Jordan three years to have the same impact Shaq has made in three months."

Interestingly, Shaq chose to go head to head against Jordan in many sponsorship arenas. Most notably, the battle between Reebok's ShaqAttaq shoes and Nike's Air Jordan is expected to be a fierce one. O'Neal joined forces with Pepsi while Jordan continued to promote Coke. The league's newest superstar also agreed to stay in the NBA products pool, which Jordan pulled out of years ago.

In the case of Reebok, Shaq will share in the profits of his signature shoes, so he could possibly earn more than $20 million over five years. Pepsi will pay him another $10 million over five years. The other major players in the Shaq promotions are Spalding (basketballs), Classic Trading Cards (sports cards), Scoreboard (memorabilia), Kenner (toys), Tiger Electronics (games), Shaq Track (videos) and the NBA (NBA products).

One can only wonder how long it will take for the McShaq burger to hit the fastfood market. There was a deal in the works with McDonald's, but the hamburger king apparently had too much of its endorsement money tied up with Jordan and Bird.

"Basically, Shaquille and Reebok as partners will both profit," said Reebok vice president Tom Carmody. "The more that we sell, the more that we both make."

Evidence of the power of O'Neal's magnetic personality and boyish appeal came at the All-Star Game. At an auction held to benefit the NBA's Stay in School program, Shaq's All-Star jersey sold for a record $55,000. Right afterward, Jordan's jersey went up for bid and brought $20,000. Even at a charity auction in Chicago, a Shaq-signed basketball sold for nearly 50 percent more than a Jordan-autographed ball.

"I wish him well," said Jordan, showing no animosity toward his new rival. "I want him to utilize his position from a business and basketball standpoint. There's a lot he can accomplish."

What Reebok would like to accomplish is to ride the zeal of Shaquille to the top of the athletic shoe empire.

For the last decade, it has been a three-way race among Nike, Reebok and Adidas. L.A. Gear, which is represented by Armato, tried to jump into the middle of the shoe war, but experienced financial woes. Converse, once a big player in the shoe game with Larry Bird and Magic Johnson, slipped well behind the industry leaders.

Amazingly, a superstar the likes of all-time scoring leader Kareem Abdul-Jabbar was paid just $100,000 a year to wear Adidas shoes. Today, even small-time college basketball coaches are paid that much. Some of the bigger names in college coaching receive $200,000 to $300,000 per year from shoe companies hoping that their top players will wear their shoes not only in college but also in the pros. It's a major investment, but often pays off.

In 1983, Nike passed Adidas as the world leader in athletic shoe sales. But the very next year, Reebok captured the aerobics market and quickly soared past Nike to the top of the heap. It didn't last long.

Nike made the shoe deal of the century late in 1984 by signing Michael Jordan to a complex promotional package. It took Nike and Air Jordan less than a year to take over the market again. By September of 1985, Nike had sold 2.3 million pairs of Air Jordans and continued to zoom away from the pack on the heels of the game's greatest and most charismatic player.

Now Reebok hopes to make a run at Nike with the help of the ShaqAttaq shoes and the mass appeal of its own superstar. O'Neal was well compensated with the $20-million contract that might produce even more if his shoes take off as Jordan's did.

Last March, the Shaq shoes officially hit the market with a sizeable price tag of $135. These special sneakers are made of lightweight GraphLite with the air-inflation Pump technology. Reebok had already started selling thousands of Shaq T-shirts, and the entire line of O'Neal athletic apparel was due out early in the summer.

Undoubtedly, Reebok took a major gamble on investing so much of its promotional dollars on one player, but so far it has paid off royally. While Nike cashed in on international promotions with Jordan, Bo Jackson and

Deion Sanders, Reebok stood back in its shadow. The Boston-based shoe company managed to sign up stars like Roger Clemens, Dominique Wilkins and Dennis Rodman, but missed out on landing a kingpin. The problem with Clemens and Wilkins was playing on mediocre teams, while Rodman has had more image problems than almost any other big-name athlete around. Reebok also signed up Rocket Ismail, but turned up a loser when the Rocket snubbed the National Football League and headed north to play in Canada.

"They finally have a big one," said Brian Murphy, publisher of The Sports Marketing Letter. "Prestige and sales go hand in hand. Shaquille is the hottest property to come along since Michael Jordan in 1984. In the athletic shoe business, it is the signature endorser who is the driving force in the industry. It is really guys like Jordan and Bo Jackson who have put Nike on the map in the last few years."

Reebok has the clear-cut goal of reclaiming the throne of the athletic shoe industry. Yet company officials realize that their fortunes are resting on the broad shoulders of Shaquille. If he progresses and becomes a superstar akin to Jordan, Kareem Abdul-Jabbar or Wilt Chamberlain, then Reebok can overcome recent disappointments and make a strong run at Nike.

The biggest bust for Reebok was its pre-Olympic ad campaign centered around decathletes Dan O'Brien and Dave Johnson. The Dan and Dave commercials ran for months and months, leading up to what Reebok billed as the ultimate showdown in Barcelona. The only trouble was Dan never made it. A leg injury caused him to miss three times in the pole vault and drop out of contention for one of the three decathlon spots on the U.S. Olympic team. It was one of the most embarrassing moments in sports marketing history, leaving Reebok with egg on its face. In a desperate attempt to recover, the company tried to land Madonna as a spokeswoman. But that deal fell through as well.

Despite its pitfalls, Reebok remained within striking distance of Nike. With $2.7 billion in sales last year,

Reebok held second place in the shoe race with 25 percent of the market. Nike led the way with 30 percent.

"We'd like to be there again," said Reebok vice president John Morgan. "I seriously believe that the impact that Shaquille O'Neal is going to have for Reebok has yet to be understood by anybody."

Should the ShaqAttaq label even approach the phenomenal success of his Airness, then Reebok could be right back on top. However, the company is putting most of its eggs in one basket.

At last count, Reebok had signed 17 NBA players. In addition to Shaq, Dominique and Rodman, the company had inked Shawn Kemp, Dee Brown, Charles Smith, Reggie Lewis, Rick Fox, Ed Pinkney, John Paxson, Fred Roberts, Mugsy Bogues, Danny Ainge, Sam Perkins, Waymon Tisdale and Danny Manning. It certainly wasn't an All-Star cast. In fact, O'Neal was the only one of the bunch to play in the 1993 All-Star Game.

Nike, on the other hand, has a full cast of All-Stars and members of the U.S. Olympic team. The Dream Teamers with the Nike shoes include Jordan, Scottie Pippen, Charles Barkley, David Robinson, John Stockton and Chris Mullen. Nike's promotional team also features NBA stars Tim Hardaway, Dan Majerle, Sean Elliott, Alonzo Mourning, Kendall Gill, Mark Price, and Kenny Anderson. Nike rounds out its basketball list with B.J. Armstrong, Buck Williams, Kevin Duckworth, Terry Porter, Jerome Kersey, Lloyd Daniels, Alaa Abdelnaby, Kevin Gamble and Sherman Douglas.

Reebok experienced even more misfortune when Lewis, the promising star of the Celtics, collapsed in the playoffs and was found to have a heart problem that could spell the end of his playing days. Likewise, many of Reebok's endorsers play for the Celtics, which now appear to be a dying dinosaur with the possible loss of Lewis and the impending retirement of Kevin McHale and Robert Parish.

If Shaq should happen to be a bust, like big men Darryl Dawkins and Ralph Sampson before him, it would be devastating to Reebok's immediate future. So far that doesn't seem possible. But experts around the league say O'Neal must show the desire to improve his offensive play if he plans on stepping up to the upper level of the NBA with Jordan and the all-time greats. Reebok must also hope there will be no more highly publicized fights like Shaq's attack on Alvin Robertson last season.

Even if Shaq scores big for Reebok, it doesn't necessarily mean the company can catch Nike.

Nike public relations manager Dusty Kidd argues that the endorser must have the right kind of shoe to make the package work. He points to Converse, another Boston-area based company, which had Bird, Magic and Julius Erving as endorsers and still didn't take over the market.

The same opinion was stated by investment expert Gary Jacobsen, who analyzes Reebok and other shoe company for Kidder Peabody Investments.

"I think you need a good company behind it," Jacobsen said. "I don't think a celebrity endorser makes a whole lot of difference. I think people buy Air Jordans because they look neat, not because Jordan wears them. What percentage of sales are Jordan-related? Less than 30 percent."

Other industry analysts attribute the superstar endorser as the driving force behind sales. They point out that all of the top athletic shoe makers are turning out great shoes, but what sets them apart is the player's name on them.

"What you need is someone who can crack that youth market and get the attention of younger people who do buy the shoes," said Murphy of *The Sports Marketing Letter*. "If he [O'Neal] continues to post outstanding statistics, if he can maintain his poise with the press and the public, if he develops a strong public persona that people like and trust, if he isn't injured, if it turns out the camera loves him, he leads his team into the playoffs in the near future, if he becomes an All-Star or championship MVP or season MVP, if he goes by all those ifs, he's a lock as an endorser."

More than 30 percent of Reebok's advertising budget was set aside to promote ShaqAttaq shoes and accessories. The company spent more than $10 million on the initial television and print ads featuring Shaquille. Why was Reebok willing to invest so much so soon on such a young player?

Reebok's Tom Carmody said the decision was well researched and documented. The company commissioned a survey that found O'Neal was the best-known sports personality in the nation among 12-to-18-year-old boys, which is one of the main target groups for athletic shoes.

While Shaq did not fare as well internationally, Reebok made immediate plans to take O'Neal on an international tour.

"That's part of our job to expand his presence beyond the boundaries of the U.S.," Carmody said. "We think his play and personality will both contribute to making that job easy."

Reebok marketing executive John Morgan said, "It's a high-risk business. But it's not just a matter of who you have. It's a matter of what you do with him once you've got him."

The initial ad campaign for Reebok's Shaq line was a huge success. The first commercial featured only a rap song actually written and performed by O'Neal, shown wearing his mammoth size 20EEE shoes and singing, "Don't fake the funk on a nasty dunk."

The commercial spots showed Shaq trying to impress legendary centers Wilt Chamberlain, Jabbar, Bill Russell and Bill Walton and the most celebrated college coach of all time, John Wooden. After Shaq tore down the rim and shattered the glass on one of his power slams, the basketball legends weren't satisfied. They handed him a broom and made him sweep the floor. To this Shaq replied, "This must be some kind of rookie thing or something."

"Reebok needed to get a high-profile personality to compete with the success of Michael Jordan and Nike," said *Sporting Goods Newsletter* publisher John Horan. "Reebok's timing in signing this guy up couldn't be better. It was a 'no-brainer' to go after Shaq."

Studies indicated that sports fans young and old

were beginning to cool on Michael Jordan, who had been the world's top athletic endorser for almost a decade. In fact, Shaq's camp of advisors has been careful to avoid an overexposure problem, hoping not to oversaturate the market place with too much of Shaq.

"The journalists are looking for basketball stories, and they're getting a little tired of writing about Michael Jordan," said Burns Sports Celebrities Service president David Burns.

There was no timetable set up for Shaq in terms of overcoming Jordan in the marketing world. In fact, the O'Neal entourage was as surprised as anyone by the swiftness of his rise. Within a few months of bursting onto the NBA scene, Shaq surpassed Jordan as the hottest commodity in sports marketing. It will obviously take him some time to match the $36 million in total earnings that Jordan picked up in 1992. But that time seems to be fast approaching.

"He doesn't distance people. He rather endears himself to people, which is a wonderful quality to have," said Leonard Armato, who was not nearly as successful in marketing Kareem Abdul-Jabbar and Hakeem Olajuwon, due to their lack of personal flair. "The combination of athleticism, personality and good family upbringing—he's just a great person for kids to look up to."

One of the many public-relations minded moves made by the O'Neal camp was the creation of the Shaq Paq. A paq was distributed to thousands of underprivileged kids in the Orlando area. Each one contained a ShaqAttaq shirt from Reebok, a rookie card from Classic Games (market value of at least $25), a Stuff the Magic Dragon doll (mascot of the Orlando team), and a seat at the otherwise sold-out Magic home games.

Armato is still considering turning the Shaq Paq into a national PR campaign. It could lead to the start of a national Shaq Fan Club.

As president of Management Plus, a Los Angeles-based sports agency, Armato has worked with many of the big names in pro sports. He helped Jabbar get back on his feet financially after he had lost most of his fortune through poor investments. Then he took on the assignment of trying to revamp the image of Olajuwon, who had been labeled a crybaby for constantly complaining about playing for the Houston Rockets. Armato eventually negotiated a new contract with the Rockets, and a happy Hakeem destroyed his NBA competition in the 1992–93 season.

But even Armato had never taken on such a massive task as coordinating the vast marketing campaign aimed at making O'Neal the biggest name and richest man in sports.

The first step was to tie together all of the product endorsements under one symbol. Armato went out and hired a design firm to create a "SHAQ" logo that will appear on virtually every product that O'Neal endorses.

"The object is for people to walk into a store, see his logo and know exactly what it means," Armato said. "He'll only get better as a player and as a vehicle for marketing."

To help promote his ShaqAttaq basketball from Spalding, Armato and his management group came up with the idea of life-size cardboard cutouts that would tower above the counter at every sporting goods stores in the country.

The first phase of the Shaq ball came out in time for the Christmas rush and was, as could be expected, a glowing success. The base model was a rubber high-end orange ball with a wholesale price of about $10. For another fifty cents, Spalding offered a Shaq ball with graffiti graphics and Magic team colors.

Spalding unveiled its second phase of Shaq roundball at the Sporting Goods Super Show. This line featured a black graffiti-covered youth ball as well as mini balls with various graphics and a low wholesale price of $6. There was also a synthetic indoor-outdoor ball for $14 and a micro backboard set.

Naturally, every piece of the line had the Shaq logo shown prominently. Spalding planned to continue to flood the market with new Shaq items over the summer. The company manufactured a Shaq ball made of Spalding's ZK composite material, which is touted as better than leather, and a Shaq slam indoor/outdoor model with a slam-dunk graphic.

Another part of Spalding's deal with Shaq included licenses for Shaq Attaq backboards, rims, sports bags and stationery. All told, Spalding made its biggest investment ever in the young star, surpassing previous deals with Bird and Magic.

In fact, Shaq's impact changed the whole marketing strategy of the company. Spalding product manager Scott Dickey said the company's previous strategy was to sell generic balls at the low end of the pricing scheme, bring in signature balls in the middle pricing level and sell NBA authentics in the high-end pricing. But Spalding chose to sell Shaq balls at all price levels, due to the high demand for anything with his name on it.

Spalding executives projected a 25-percent increase in sales for fiscal 1992. Meanwhile, the total market was expected to climb just eight to 10 percent. Dickey said that was evidence that the competition, headed by Jordan-signature balls, was fading.

The Orlando Magic and the rest of the NBA profited greatly from the emergence of Shaq as a superstar and super seller. Although the Magic had been selling out games before he arrived, Shaq sparked a fire of fan and corporate interest in the team.

The Magic attracted such heavyweight corporate sponsors as Anheuser-Busch, Gatorade, Pepsi, Walt Disney World and McDonald's. The demand to be part of the Magic attraction in Orlando skyrocketed during Shaq's rookie season.

"We don't talk about how many corporate sponsors we have, but let's just say it has increased significantly since Shaq arrived," said Ralph Gray of the Magic sales staff. "Companies that had dropped out began to call us and ask, 'Is there anything we can do for you now?' It's amazing to see the swell of enthusiasm from the business sector."

As the Shaq rookie tour heated up, there was rarely an empty seat to be found, even in some cities with losing teams. Before the All-Star break, O'Neal had played before sellout crowds in every NBA city where he played except Philadelphia and Atlanta. By the end of the season, Shaq had displayed his basketball skills in front of 729,793 fans across the nation in 41 road games. Since the Orlando Arena seats only 15,151 fans, O'Neal actually attracted his largest crowds away from home, drawing an average of almost 18,000 on the road. The only team to outdraw Shaq and the Magic was defending world champion Chicago. Michael Jordan and the Bulls drew 735,994 fans away from Chicago Stadium.

"He [O'Neal] is a happening," said Los Angeles Clippers vice president Mike Williams, who was stunned by the reception O'Neal brought at a Clippers-Orlando game in L.A. "This is the kind of crowd we'd expect when the Chicago Bulls or New York Knicks are in town."

Making the starting lineup in the All-Star game was a major boost to the One-al enterprises. It was also helpful that he enabled the Magic to become the most improved team in the NBA, finishing 20 games better than the previous season at 41–41. He capped it off by winning the Rookie of the Year honor in a landslide vote.

"In the history of the NBA, only three players have hit the ground running with the big marketers: Michael Jordan, Magic Johnson and now Shaq," said Lon Rosen, now Johnson's agent.

The question is now how far will O'Neal and company run with their mass marketing campaign? The target remains Jordan in terms of dollars. But the most prolific athletic endorser is golf legend Arnold Palmer, who has signed deals with approximately 100 companies, according to industry officials.

Armato, however, took a somewhat cautious approach to the early deals for Shaq and plans to continue to be selective. "There is such a thing as overexposure," he said. "We don't want the public to be watching Shaq commercials every time they turn on their television."

Speaking of Shaq

Curly Neal
Orlando Magic Director of Special Projects

*The legendary king of the dribble, Curly Neal captured the
fancy of the world while appearing in more than 6,000
games for the Harlem Globetrotters from 1963–85. Called
the original ambassador of basketball, he promoted the
game in more than 75 countries and traveled millions of
miles helping to pave the way for black players to take
their place in the professional basketball.*

*Neal was an original member of the Magic admin-
istrative staff, first serving as honorary chairman of the
team's season ticket drive in 1986. He accepted a full-time
position with the club in December 1988 and has acted as
director of special projects ever since. He plays a major role
in the NBA's "Stay in School" program and has talked
with more than 50,000 middle school students in Central
Florida.*

*One of the Magic players who is most helpful to
Curly is Shaquille O'Neal.*

"Shaq has been just like Disney World. He's made a
huge impact on the Magic and whole city of Orlando. Anytime you can come in and get your picture on a bus, you
know you're something special. I rode a bus for 25 years
with the Globetrotters, and they never put my picture on
the bus. We've had sellouts before, but the Magic has never
had this kind of impact. Everybody wants to see Shaq. He's
very visible in the community and does so much for this organization. He's a fun guy.

"I just love Shaq. He talks to me as a friend. I love
working with Shaq. He's the talk of the town. For that matter, he's the talk of the country. But when we make appearances together, he's just like one of the guys.

"I can remember seeing Shaq play in college, and you
could see he was going to be one of the great ones. He reminds me most of Wilt Chamberlain, Kareem (Abdul-

Jabbar) and Bill Walton. All of the great centers. When I think of Shaq, it brings back memories of Wilt, because we were teammates together on the Globetrotters. I rank Shaquille right up there with Wilt and that's quite a compliment. I played with Wilt in the early '70s when the Lakers won the world championship. Actually, Wilt played with the Globetrotters right out of Kansas. He was with us for one year before he went into the NBA. Then he traveled with us to Europe in the summer even after he was in the NBA. Wilt was a good person, even though he had his different ways. I really enjoyed playing with him. He sure made it easy to shoot, because he set such great picks. Every day was fun with Wilt. I learned a lot of things from him. He treated me like an older brother. I had been with the Globetrotters for about 15 years, but there was no animosity. We were just happy to be together and happy to perform. We were playing every night, sometimes twice on the weekends. Wilt was great to be with. Every person, whether he's seven feet tall or two feet tall, wants some privacy from time to time, but Wilt knew how to handle it. Shaq knows how to handle it, too.

"I met Shaq when he first came in with his family. He knew me right away. We hugged and rubbed each other's heads. I told him, 'You're stealing my haircut.' They're fine people. We've always got along great. What really makes Shaq so special is he loves to give back to the community. He is always doing something. At Thanksgiving, he helped feed the homeless. At Christmas, he brought presents to the kids. He even brought Easter baskets to the Children's Hospital. Those are the kinds of things we used to do with the Globetrotters, and that's why we were so popular. The same thing is true with Shaq. He really cares about people. He has a big heart, and he gives. Even though he has so much pressure on him, he handles it so well.

"Every time I see Shaq, there's a smile on his face. He always comes right up to me and hugs me. That's what I really like about the man himself. He's such a warm person.

"Shaq is really improving. Now Wilt had more shots when he came into the league. He had the hook, he

had the dipper shot, he could shoot the jump shot backing off. In years to come, Shaq will be able to do that. He'll learn that. When he first came in, he had some problems with turnovers. The pro game is a different story than college. He was fouling out of a lot of games. Everything has been an adjustment for him. He had to get used to the physical play. He had to get used to being on the road so much. But he's handled it very well. He's made a great adjustment. Shaq is forceful and he's fearsome, but he's kept that warm spirit about himself.

"I think Shaq will be a superstar in this league as soon as he gets those other shots. Next year, people will be trying to block him out and keep him away from the basket. It's going to be a lot tougher, so he won't be able to rely just on his dunk. He's going to create a little jump shot, so he'll have two or three ways to score. Shaq is also becoming a good passer. Wilt was a great passer. He led the league in assists one year. Wilt was a great athlete. He was a track star. He ran the 440 at Kansas.

"Right now I see five great centers in the NBA. There's Patrick Ewing, David Robinson, Hakeem [Olajuwon], Brad Daugherty and Shaq. Those are the best. You need a big man to win. Even look at Chicago. Bill Cartwright doesn't play a key role, but Horace Grant does. Plus, they've got Michael Jordan and Scottie Pippen. You've got to have a big man. Shaq is unquestionably one of the best. The only difference between him and Patrick Ewing is Patrick has a jump shot. You saw that in the All-Star Game. They went with Patrick down the stretch when they needed someone who could hit the jump shot. I don't know if it was because Pat Riley was the coach or not. But Patrick can shoot. Shaq is going to work on his jump shot, and he's going to get it. I've been seeing him practice it and he's getting it.

"Wilt, Kareem and Bill Russell won a lot of championships. Of course, they didn't do it by themselves. You need some Jordans and Pippens. You need some Scott Skiles and Nick Andersons, who can dish the ball off or hit those three-pointers. You need it all. A center can't do it by himself. Ewing, Olajuwon and Robinson haven't

had enough help. That's why they haven't won a championship.

"I think the Magic is going to have a championship-type club in a couple of years. We need to get a good power forward and another point guard. Shaq and Nick Anderson are going to be here. I think Scott Skiles is going to be here. Those are the people you can depend on. With a power forward and another point guard, I think we'll be on our way."

eight

Army Brat

Although his stops were short, Shaquille O'Neal never had trouble making new friends in the military-base schools that he attended throughout the world. Former classmates and teachers remember him as one of the most popular boys in school, thanks to his joking manner and constant smile. The principal at Robert Cole High School, his final stop in a globe-hopping scholastic adventure, remarked on how easily O'Neal fit in with the other students, most of whom had been there for several years.

Shaq, however, didn't have such fond memories of his adventurous childhood. He told college friends that he grew tired of all the traveling in a hurry and just wanted to be like other kids who stayed in one town for their whole childhood. If he had been given a choice of where to grow up, it would have been Newark, New Jersey, so he could be close to his beloved grandmother.

Born in Newark, young Shaq started his unsettling childhood by moving with his parents to an Army base in

Bayonne, New Jersey, and then another one outside Columbus, Georgia. His father then served two stints in Wildeflecken, in what was then West Germany. Both times, Shaq and the rest of the family went overseas. He spent his final two years of high school at Fort Sam Houston in San Antonio, Texas.

In addition to constantly being the new kid, O'Neal had to deal with his ever-increasing stature. He was always the biggest boy in his class, and, unfortunately, the most awkward. Some say he became a joker to deflect attention away from his size. He certainly didn't show any impressive athletic skills. As a tall, gangly teenager, he really wanted to be a dancer and envied the young boys who appeared on the network TV show "Fame."

Naturally, some of the tough guys at school would routinely challenge him to a fight. Shaq usually obliged them, though with mixed results. Of one thing he could be sure: If he got caught fighting and word got back to his father, the punishment would be severe.

No matter what it took, Sgt. Philip Harrison was determined to keep his son in line. Harrison said his own youthful trouble-making and mistakes caused him to miss out on an opportunity to become the first person in his family to earn a college degree. He would not let the same fate befall his first-born, even if meant daily beatings with whatever instrument he could get his hands on. Sometimes, it would be just his hands. On other occasions, he would grab a belt. Once, he beat his son with a ping pong paddle.

"My Dad used to beat me everyday," Shaq told *USA Today* columnist Peter Vecsey. "It happened so often, I felt I wasn't being loved. I had no alternatives. I could run away or figure out a way to make my parents be nice."

Ultimately, Shaq found a way to avoid the regular beatings. He made sure he didn't do anything to upset his father. The older he got, the more he came to understand his Dad wanted the best for him, even if it was hard to accept the punishment.

His mother, Lucille Harrison, would often take him aside and comfort him after the stern disciplinary action from his father. She kept him from running away from home and convinced him that he could abide by his father's rules.

"He's real angry. He's been through a lot," O'Neal said of his father. "My mom is a real solid person. Without her, I probably wouldn't have made it. She made things easier for my dad. He yells a lot. She taught me, 'Don't listen to how he says it, listen to what he says.' That helped a lot. He's the type that reacts. I don't react. I'm calm. I have poise. People that try to mess with me, I don't pay 'em no mind. Unless they put their hands on me, [they] can do anything they want. Takes a big man to fight; takes a bigger man to walk away."

Occasionally, his mother administered the discipline as well. Shaq once found a lighter and accidentally burned up a teddy bear with it. He hid the bear under his bed, but his mother smelled it.

"She started sniffing like a hound dog," Shaq said. "She looked under the bed and saw it, and I got tore up.

"Thank goodness I had two parents who loved me enough to stay on my case," he added.

It was Lucille Harrison who came up with the name Shaquille Rashaun O'Neal for her first child, who was born shortly after Philip had been shipped off to Germany. They married when he returned, but their son kept the O'Neal surname.

"He's the oldest male grandchild, and if he didn't use it, the name would die out," his mother explained.

Out of a book of Islamic names, his mother picked out Shaquille, which means "little one." At least, he was little for a few years. His middle name, Rashaun, fits the bill nicely. It means "warrior."

Philip Harrison said he regrets not heeding the advice of his own father. Instead, he "was running wild and playing ball. I didn't realize what he was saying until I had my own children."

More than anything else, Harrison wanted to make sure his four children, particularly first-born Shaquille, took advantage of every educational opportunity they had. No one in his family or in his wife's had ever earned a college degree, and he wanted that to change with the next generation.

Another thing that brought O'Neal closer to his father was their participation together in sports. Harrison was his son's first coach in basketball. A former junior college star himself, he taught Shaq the fundamentals of the game and still advises him.

Actually, Shaq spent much of his childhood playing both football and basketball. But as his height continued to soar, he decided his best sport would be basketball.

"My dad was my coach; I had to be mean," he said. "If I played like a wimp, he'd let me have it. I was real good in football, but I got tackled in the knee one day and said to myself, 'Let's stick to basketball.'"

His first experience in organized basketball came as a nine-year-old at Fort Stewart, Georgia. Harrison had his team running the old Boston Celtics' offense.

By the age of 13, he had already shot up to 6-feet-8 and was still growing. He obviously inherited his tall genes from his 6-5 father and 6-2 mother. He has three siblings—sisters LaTeefah (15) and Ayesha (14) and brother Jamal (12)—who are all very tall for their ages.

"I was known as a child superstar at 14, 15," Shaq laughed. "I think I already went through my bad stage, where I thought I was too good for everybody.

"But I never really thought I was special for a long time. When we were living in Germany, I was awkward, falling down all the time. I might not have played basketball, except that one of the little muscular guys tackled me in the knee."

Soon after giving up football, O'Neal became anxious to learn as much about basketball as he possibly could. It didn't help that he was stuck out in a wilderness Army base in Germany. However, fate would have it that LSU coach Dale Brown, who had visited more than 50 countries during his off-season travels, agreed to conduct a basketball clinic on the base.

At the time, Shaq had never heard of Dale Brown, but he was eager to pick up some new drills from a college coach. He approached him after the clinic and got what he wanted, and a whole lot more. When Brown found out the 6-8 player was only 13 years old, he nearly flipped out and asked immediately to see Shaq's father so he could begin the recruiting process of getting Shaq to LSU, which had never had a great center during Brown's two decades as head coach.

"Excuse me," Harrison told the excited coach. "Basketball is nice, but it's time black people started developing intellectualism—being presidents of companies instead of salesmen, being generals instead of sergeants, being head coaches instead of assistants."

Brown worked out the details with Harrison, and over the next three years, they developed a strong friendship. Even though Shaq wasn't much of a talent in his first two years of high school (he was cut from his freshman team), he continued to grow and his coordination kept improving.

By the time Shaq arrived in San Antonio, he was a 6-10 center with a world of potential. The entire base population at Fort Sam Houston soon heard about the new big kid on campus.

Robert Cole High School athletic director Joel Smith said he will never forget the day that Shaq showed up at school in the spring of 1987.

"They said, 'You better get up here real quick. We've got a big one coming in,'" Smith said. "He was 6-10 at the time."

Primarily a school for military children, Cole High was one of the smaller high schools in the city. Most of the students stay in town for only two or three years before their families are transferred to another base, so the coaches never know what they're going to get for players.

"O'Neal was like a pot of gold dropped from the sky," former Cole basketball coach Dave Madura said. "Coaching him was the highlight of my life. There was no doubt he was going to be a big-time player, but he never flaunted it. He probably was the most popular kid in school. Because of the way he was, there probably wasn't any jealousy."

Wherever Shaq and the Cole team traveled, the

host school would draw its largest crowd of the season to see the huge center. In fact, rival Summerset High School asked to waive the rule banning pre-game dunking so O'Neal could put on a show to entertain the packed crowd.

At Southside High, Shaq dunked so hard that he bent one of the rims in three places. It looked like a back-yard goal before he was finished that night. Other schools realized they needed to install collapsible rims and quick-ly made that adjustment to prevent O'Neal from tearing up the baskets.

Actually, he didn't become prolific at dunking until after his junior season when Cole went 32–1 and lost the state championship game by one point. One day, he got into an argument with his father and stormed out of the house. He went right to a playground and in his fury, found out he could now dunk the ball.

"I loved it," he said. "I just kept dunking and dunk-ing all day. That's all I ever wanted to do after that."

As the local legend of Shaquille O'Neal, the teenage dunking machine, grew in the San Antonio area, his ego swelled with it. All the hype surrounding his se-nior season didn't help, either. Coach Madura told Shaq and his teammates before the season, "Anything less than a state championship will be unacceptable."

Although O'Neal had not attended any of the major summer camps, he did play in the Basketball Congress In-ternational tournament, which gave some college coaches a chance to see him for the first time.

Of course, Dale Brown had been hot on his heels for three years. But Shaq, his family and coaches were soon swamped with letters and calls from many of the top programs in the country.

"It's easier to talk about who didn't call," Madura said. "We heard from so many schools and coaches. Dean Smith, Lou Henson, Denny Crum, Jerry Tarkanian and the late Jim Valvano all visited. Dale Brown always seemed to have the edge."

Shaq took official visits to LSU, North Carolina, Louisville, North Carolina State and Illinois. During the early signing period in November of 1988, he signed a national letter of intent with LSU. His father would later say his first choice had been North Carolina, but he let Shaq make up his own mind.

"I think signing early took a lot of pressure off Shaquille," said Madura, who announced that Shaq's senior season would be his final year of coaching. "It was much easier for the team."

To help prepare Shaq for his senior year and future college career, Madura hired one of his former players, Herb More. The 6-6 More was brought in exclusively to practice against O'Neal every day.

"The only thing I taught him was to dunk with people hanging on him," laughed More, who became head coach after Madura's retirement. "My coaching consisted of playing against Shaquille every day in practice, trying to toughen him up."

O'Neal admitted that the attention went to his head.

"I thought I was Billy Bad Boy in high school," he said, and then related the story of how he had blown the state championship game as a junior: "I told all the TV stations before the state championship game that I was going to score 50 points, that nobody on earth could stop me. We played Liberty Hill and their tallest guy was like 6-3. We were undefeated and I was the best player in America. I had like eight points, I had four fouls in the first two minutes and sat out a lot of the second quarter.

"There were five seconds left in the game, and we were down by one. I got fouled. People were screaming and shouting. I missed the first one, and then missed the second one. And that was the game. That was the last time I even said that I was bigger than anyone."

In his senior year, there would be no denying O'Neal and the Cole ballclub. They had an athletic team that would have been a title contender without their big man. But with him, they were invincible, winning all 36 games they played. In one regular-season game, he delivered 27 points, 36 rebounds and 26 blocked shots. His season average was 32.1 points, 22 rebounds and eight blocks. In the Texas Class AAA state playoffs, he had impressive performances with 46 and 44 points.

Even though he was the big man on campus, Shaq didn't play the role of the super stud. He fit in with his classmates and left a lasting impression, albeit a brief one. He led the Cougars to a 68–1 record and then was off to LSU.

"You couldn't help but like Shaquille," Joel Smith said. "He was just that type of kid. Even though he was a great athlete, everyone liked him."

Cole Principal Buddy Compton called him "a super young man. I'm just glad we had the opportunity to have him over here for the time we did. What I remember most was his great leadership quality. He had great leadership and had a great effect on our kids in school and still does. That's what we enjoyed most about him. He was never somebody who wanted to stand out, he just did."

Speaking of Shaq

Herb More
Robert Cole High School Basketball Coach

"I played at Cole myself, but was coaching at a little school called Sheryland High School when he first came to San Antonio. Of course, I remember all the excitement that he created. You never know what kind of players you're going to get on a military base, because they come and go all the time. So when a 6-10 junior comes to the school, there's naturally going to be a great deal of excitement.

"Coach [Dave] Madura had to coach football as well as basketball, so mainly we had Shaquille working on strength and conditioning. He spent a lot of time in the weight room and we had some drills for him to work on. He worked on a hook shot and turnaround jumper and practiced his moves around the basket. He had some pretty good moves. He's showing that now in the NBA.

"They brought me back to guard Shaquille in practice, because none of the players was tall enough to stay with him. I tell everyone that the only thing I taught Shaquille was how to block shots, because he blocked so many of mine.

"Basically, he complained that I fouled him too much. Later on, we were playing a team in the state tournament and they were fouling him so much that we told him, 'Just go up and slam it.' So that's when he started dunking the ball all the time.

"Not only did I coach Shaquille, I also had him in a geometry class. He was one of the most polite kids I've ever been around. He was a hard worker. Now he wasn't an A student, but he did make B's and C's. He could probably have done better if he had applied himself a little more, but that's true of most kids.

"Shaquille was very humble about his ability. He didn't flaunt it at all. We had about 300 kids in the school at that time, and he was one of the most popular students.

"We had a very talented group of basketball players. Coach Madura told them before Shaquille's senior year that they should win the state championship. There were a lot of good players on the team who were capable of scoring 20 points a game, but they sacrificed their offense to get the ball to Shaquille. Doug Sanberg and Dwayne Cyrus were very good players. Cyrus was probably the best all-around athlete in the school. He played football, basketball and baseball. Jeff Petruss, Daron Mather and Joe Cavalaro were also excellent players for us. We had a very balanced team. Of course, Shaquille was our best player.

"During his junior year, we played AA ball, so the competition wasn't very good. We had so many lopsided games that they moved us up to AAA for his senior season. Every game we went to was sold out. Everyone wanted to see Shaquille play.

"Before his senior year, he played in the BCI [Basketball Congress International] Tournament and a lot of college coaches were impressed with him. That's when the recruiting really began to get hot. About the only major school that didn't recruit Shaquille was Georgetown.

Somebody told us John Thompson wouldn't recruit a player that was being recruited by North Carolina, because he and Dean Smith were such good friends. We heard from just about everybody else. It was amazing. We were very glad that Shaquille signed early, because it took away a lot of the pressure.

"Coach Brown was a fun person to be around. He's a great motivator and a great speaker. I still go to his summer basketball camp, and I always pick up something from him. I think he's very sincere. Of course, he's different from most of the other coaches. Some call him an evangelist and stuff like that. I just know I like him.

"Some people say Shaquille made a mistake by going to LSU. Now he didn't win a championship like he hoped. But I think Dale Brown did a good job with him. Look where he's at now."

nine

Dale, Sarge, Shaq and the Shoe Contract

What started out as a match made in heaven developed into a battle of wills between Shaquille O'Neal and Dale Brown. Shaq came to LSU on the premise that he would have a chance to win several national championships with Chris Jackson and Stanley Roberts. Instead, all they did was bicker amongst themselves for a year, and then Chris and Stanley were off to the pros. Meanwhile, Brown was convinced the Tigers could still win national titles if he could get O'Neal to expand his offensive game. He just couldn't convince Shaq and his father that the Tigers, and Shaq as well, could only go so far with a slam-dunk offense. His friends and associates say it was the most frustrating experience in his 35 years of coaching. He had the center of his dreams, but couldn't get him to reach his potential.

The fortunes of LSU basketball, in terms of wins and losses, weren't the only thing that tied Brown to Shaq. At the end of O'Neal's freshman season, Brown's shoe contract with Converse ran out and thus began a bidding war for the opportunity to have Shaq wear a certain basketball shoe. L.A. Gear, Nike and Reebok all delivered multi-year bids in the million-dollar range. Brown eventually signed a three-year contract with L.A. Gear worth a reported $900,000. The contract began on June 1, 1990, and extended through May 30, 1993, which would have marked the end of Shaq's senior season. Interestingly, the contract was negotiated by L.A. Gear attorney Leonard Armato, who later had Brown introduce him to O'Neal and eventually became Shaq's agent in the biggest contract that an NBA player ever received.

In the meantime, Shaq, heeding his father's command to "dominate and dunk," became more and more obsessed with dunking hard enough to bend the rim or break the backboard. He even developed his own term—rimology—for the art of destroying rims, which he did at the Olympic Festival and several times at LSU in pickup games. In fact, LSU maintenance workers had to install heavy-duty bolts to protect the basket standards from constantly coming loose in the Pete Maravich Assembly Center.

Brown grew more and more dismayed with the sergeant and his son. Every time Brown would try to teach Shaq a new move or work on a different kind of shot, O'Neal would get a call from his dad and his game would revert back to dunk and destroy.

It wasn't that Shaq didn't listen to Brown or follow his instructions in practice. Brown worked individually with O'Neal during every practice session right from the beginning of his college career. They practiced a hook shot, crossover hook shot, jump hook, turnaround jump shot, turnaround bank shot and various power moves. Shaq would work hard in the individual drills for a half hour or more. But once the team started scrimmaging, he would go right back to dunk, dunk, dunk.

Teammates would offer to work with O'Neal after practice and on weekends, but he refused to spend his free time working on basketball. In fact, he tried to get as far away from the game as possible, devoting his time to playing music, going out to eat or to a nightclub or simply fooling around with friends.

"Shaq would rather throw a football around than go back to the gym to work on his jump shot or free-throw shooting," teammate Mike Hansen said. "Basketball wasn't his first love."

Even before Shaq's sophomore season began, Brown was reconciled to the fact that he couldn't get his star center to listen to him. He couldn't even get O'Neal to cooperate during the Olympic Festival even though he was alone with Shaq for 10 days in Minneapolis. During practices, Shaq would oblige his coach and shoot some jump hooks and turnaround jump shots. But once the game began, he would power inside every time and look for a dunk, whether or not there was an opening.

Brown made up his mind he would bring in shooting instructors to work with Shaq, so he could hear someone else tell him that he needed to expand his game. Both Bill Walton and Kareem Abdul-Jabbar came to LSU to work with O'Neal. Their instruction, which was virtually the same as Brown's, made an impact on Shaq for a few games, but after that, he was back to his old self. Of course, it didn't help matters that there were no other centers in the Southeastern Conference who could come close to handling O'Neal. Consequently, he saw double- and triple-teaming in every game.

"Seven foot means dominance," Shaq was fond to say. "When you're seven feet, you're supposed to kill, and I go for the kill. My father always taught me to go out there and show everyone that 'this is my court, this is my ball, so you'd better get out of my way.'"

A frustrated Brown struggled to keep the dilemma to himself. He believed Shaq wanted to heed his coach's advice and develop his offense beyond the dunking stage. But he also knew O'Neal had to answer to his father after every game and often after every practice.

"He's a great player, but he has an awful lot to learn," Brown said after the Olympic Festival. "He's got to learn to play preventive defense. That means keeping people from getting the ball. He's aggressive, but he hasn't really learned that. He began to learn it the 10 days we were up in Minneapolis. He understands he needs moves. He was double- and triple-teamed in the championship game."

Privately, Brown expressed even more dismay over O'Neal's progress. He saw a player who was so big and talented that he could have been a great scorer, but he just couldn't get him to work consistently on his offensive game.

Brown and the other LSU coaches debated about what the problem was. At times, it seemed Shaquille was embarrassed to be getting any help. Since he was the biggest and most publicized player on the team, he seemed to take the attitude that he shouldn't have to be tutored. However, Brown and his assistants would later find out that Sgt. Harrison had ordered Shaquille to get dunks and forget about shooting a jump shot or hook. "Just go out there and pull the backboard down," his father would tell him.

It didn't help Brown's position when O'Neal thoroughly dominated the competition at the Olympic Festival and was able to dunk at will, even against such outstanding opposition as Eric Montross. Some college coaches and pro scouts had already tabbed O'Neal as the top talent in the NCAA ranks. But after his impressive outing in Minneapolis, there was little dispute that he was the best center outside the NBA, even if he had no offensive moves.

During O'Neal's final year at LSU, Brown even resorted to calling friends in the NBA. He asked them to talk about the importance of possessing a well-rounded offensive game. They told Shaq that it would be difficult, if not impossible, to make it in the NBA relying primarily on dunks. He listened intently and was polite as usual, but there was little change in his shot selection.

As far as Brown was concerned, Shaq had become the world's greatest center without a jump shot or hook. And there was little he could do about it, except keep trying to persuade the big guy to listen to his coaches and not his father.

Did Dale fail? Or was Shaq a slouch?

Those questions are difficult to answer. Brown had never before coached a legitimate center, so there was no one else to compare Shaquille's progress with. Shaq had little basketball training as a youth, so it was hard to tell if he was just a late bloomer in terms of his offensive skills or if he would never develop.

One thing was for sure: The LSU basketball team fell way short of reaching its potential during the O'Neal-Jackson-Roberts era. Not only did the tremendous trio not win a national championship, they never even came close. From 1989 to 1992, the Tigers failed to advance past the second round in eight postseason tournaments. Their SEC Tournament record was 1–4, and their NCAA mark was 2–4. Those years proved to be some of the leanest ever for Brown, who had made two Final Four trips and two Final Eight appearances in the nine years before the superstars arrived on campus.

Ironically, Brown had been able to lead LSU to the Final Four with a 6-foot-6 center who couldn't even dunk the ball. But he couldn't come close with a 7-1 center who wanted only to dunk.

Dale Duward Brown, whose father abandoned him at birth in the little railroad town of Minot, North Dakota, has been battling for respect all of his life. He served stints as an assistant coach at Utah State and Washington State before getting the LSU job in 1972, only after at least a half-dozen coaches turned down the position because it was deemed to be a losing situation.

Unfazed by his coaching peers' warnings that Baton Rouge was a graveyard for college basketball coaches, he charged into the job with a fury, traveling around the state selling his program and hanging purple-and-gold nets on every backyard and playground goal he could find. He turned his first ballclub into a group of scrapping hustlers who knocked off second-ranked Memphis State in the first game of the season and won more than they lost the rest of the way. Brown was named SEC Coach of the Year and immediately set the higher goal of challenging Kentucky as the dominant team in the league.

In the 63 years before Brown, the Tigers had beaten Kentucky a grand total of two times. Brown picked up his first win over the Wildcats in 1974, and four years later, his team of overachievers knocked off top-ranked Kentucky in overtime even though all five of the LSU starters had fouled out of the game. The next year, the Tigers captured their first SEC title in a quarter of a century and also made their first appearance in the NCAA Tournament under their new coach. Soon they were beating Kentucky on a regular basis, and it was Brown's team that would be known as the SEC's team of the decade in the 1980s.

For three straight years, LSU moved closer and closer to a national championship. Brown guided the Tigers to a Sweet 16 berth in 1979, they made it to the Final Eight in 1980, and they landed in the Final Four in 1981. All three times, they lost to the eventual national champions—Michigan State, Louisville and Indiana. Many speculated that if star forward Rudy Macklin had not broken his finger late in the 1981 Midwest Regional championship game, the Tigers would have been able to beat Indiana in the Final Four.

After two appearances in the National Invitational Tournament, LSU returned to the NCAA playoffs in 1984 and is now working on a streak of 10 consecutive berths in the NCAA field. North Carolina and Duke are the only other teams in the nation to have qualified for at least 10 straight NCAA Tournaments.

Brown's club made NCAA history in 1986 when the Tigers, seeded 10th in the Southeast Regional, knocked off the top three seeds and made it back to the Final Four. No other team seeded that low has ever won a regional championship and played in the Final Four. The Tigers almost repeated the feat in 1987, drawing the 11th seed in the Midwest Regional and coming within a basket of beating Indiana to win the regional title and return to the Final Four.

All of this was accomplished without the benefit of a top-rated center. Brown brought his first heralded big man to campus in the spring of 1988 when he signed

Roberts, who narrowly missed the NCAA qualifying standards and was ineligible for the 1988–89 season. That LSU team belonged to freshman Chris Jackson. In the fall of 1988, O'Neal signed with the Tigers, giving them two great young centers and a fabulous guard.

Brown proclaimed his talented youngsters to be the college team of the '90s. However, he had to eat those words and wished he could have kept his underdogs of the '80s. Brown called the 1989–90 season his worst job of coaching ever. No one argued the point.

After the early departure of Jackson and Roberts, Brown knew all too well that his team's fortunes were tied directly to the 7-1 center whom he couldn't get to follow his advice.

The L.A. Gear contract also linked Brown with Shaq, but didn't become a major issue until after O'Neal had already announced his decision to leave LSU in the spring of 1992 and join forces with Armato. Both Brown and Armato denied that the L.A. Gear contract was used to help the shoe company sign O'Neal. Actually, when the time came to bid on Shaq, L.A. Gear was hurting financially and couldn't get involved.

Armato told Roy Firestone on ESPN that he did not use his position with L.A. Gear to help land O'Neal as a client.

When asked about the Armato-O'Neal connection, Brown just smiled and said, "I'm not getting in any pissing match with anyone."

In an effort to avoid possible sanctions against LSU, Brown insisted that Armato meet with NCAA executive director Dick Schultz to make sure this kind of arrangement was not a rules violation. Brown called Schultz himself and emphasized, "This deal has nothing to do with Shaquille O'Neal. I left Converse for the very same reason I signed with L.A. Gear: Players shouldn't be required to wear a certain shoe just because their coach is under contract to that company."

Another interesting piece of the puzzle was LSU athletic director Joe Dean, formerly the vice president of marketing for Converse. Dean had to sell his substantial interest in Converse before taking over at LSU, but he still had a son working for the company and had other ties to the organization.

Brown ultimately made the decision to drop Converse because corporate executives had complained bitterly when Chris Jackson was shown on the cover of *Sports Illustrated* wearing a pair of Nikes. "That was totally wrong of them," said Brown.

When Brown was swamped by offers from the shoe giants after Shaq's freshman year, he was adamant that his players should not be forced to wear one shoe brand.

"Other companies offered me more money; I had two higher offers," Brown said. "But L.A. Gear was the company that agreed to let the players decide what kind of shoes to wear. That's why I signed with them. The money didn't have anything to do with it."

Brown did offer to give all of his shoe contract money to the NCAA to set up a fund to give stipends to players. The NCAA turned down that offer, so Brown gave 25 percent of the annual shoe payment to LSU. But he still picked up more than half a million dollars for himself.

Speaking of Shaq

Dale Brown
LSU head basketball coach

"Shaquille is not at all what he looks like from the external. He looks tough. He may even look aloof. But he's far from that. Shaquille is a very loving guy. He's someone you always want to hug and he's always embracing others. The best part about Shaquille is the way he treats other people. He loves kids. I'll always remember him leaning over and hugging some little girl, or smiling as he signed an autograph for a hat or a shirt for a young boy.

"Shaquille never once failed to come over and hug my daughter, Robyn, or kiss my wife, Vonnie, and call her Mom. He's just a big, loving kid.

"His parents taught him some very important lessons. That's obvious. He was always very neat and well groomed. He's very conscientious. Shaquille always wanted to improve himself mentally. Philip and Lucille Harrison instilled some excellent qualities in their son. Lucille is such a wonderful woman. She still writes to me and she took the children to see us play even after Shaquille had gone pro.

"Despite our differences, I will always have a warm spot in my heart for Philip Harrison. He hurt me deeply and he hurt our program when he made those statements after Shaquille left. But I have totally forgiven him. You can't be perfect. Philip has some wonderful qualities himself. I'll never forget the way he placed so much emphasis on making sure his son got an education and improved himself. He never asked for a single thing. He had tremendous integrity. That's the way I will always remember Philip Harrison. I had known the family for four years before we actually recruited Shaquille, so there was a great deal of trust built up there. But there was more than that. We established a bond that I hope will transcend these problems we've had and last forever. I plan to go see Philip one day and tell him how much I appreciate what he stands for.

"Shaquille knew how badly his parents wanted him to get an education. He worked very hard in school and never had an academic problem. I can remember one time Shaquille asked me to go to speech class with him. He just wanted me to interpret his speech, so he could get better.

"There was a real innocence about him. When he first came here, he told me that he didn't want to be an offensive threat. He said, 'All I want to do is help the team by being a defensive player. I don't know enough about offense yet.'

"Of course, he didn't get off to a very good start offensively, and I had to bench him. I told him to sit back and watch the flow of the game, and that helped.

"Keep in mind Shaquille was only 17 when he came here and he had just turned 20 when he left, so he was a very young player. He's going to get better and better. He improved while he was here. He improved enough to be the Player of the Year as a sophomore.

"What really hurt Shaquille was all the grabbing and holding on that was allowed to happen. The intentional foul has no place in basketball. It was hard for him to go out there game after game and have to carry smaller guys around as they held on to his shirt. I was afraid he was going to get hurt. I could see him going up for a shot and getting knocked to the floor by a couple guys pulling on him. I really thought he was going to get hurt. That's why I complained to the SEC officials.

"I believe Shaquille had good intentions of returning for his senior year. But he got tired of all the fouls that went uncalled. The Carlus Groves incident was the last straw. When he tried to pull down Shaquille, I wasn't going to sit still and watch Groves start something.

"When Shaquille left here, he told me that he wasn't as afraid of being permanently injured as he was afraid that he would get mad one day and break somebody's face open. He didn't want to be remembered for crushing somebody's face.

"The game just wasn't fun any more for him. Everybody was triple-teaming him and he couldn't do what he was capable of doing. It took all the fun out of the game for him. I could see that, and that's why I advised him to turn pro.

"Isn't it funny that Rick Pitino was hailed for advising Jamal Mashburn to turn pro? How many people have said Dean Smith puts his players' interests ahead of his own when he has advised players to turn pro early? Why is it when I do the same thing I get criticized and it's controversial? Other coaches are hailed as doing a wonderful job.

"I will always advise my players to do what is best for them. I recruit them as a human being first and a basketball player second. No rule will ever change that. You can make all the rules you want to make, and that will never change. Now when it came time to advise Shaquille,

if I was going to be selfish, I would have told him to stay. But I advised him like I would my own child. I advised him as a human being and told him the same thing I would tell my son or your son. It's like Civil Rights laws. You can't just have a rule that says a black man must be served at a restaurant. You've got to feel it. You've got to want it. It's got to come from your heart and from your soul. I'm always going to advise a person as a human being first and a basketball player second, no matter if it's Shaquille O'Neal or a walk-on guard."

ten

Shaq: We Had Too Many Superstars

No wonder Shaquille O'Neal had difficulty accepting his role as a shot blocker and defensive specialist during his freshman season at LSU. Everywhere he turned, basketball experts were calling him the next great center in America. His father, meanwhile, kept urging him to take over the team and establish dominance right from the beginning of his college career.

Shaq tried to do just that on the first summer afternoon when he stepped on the court for a pickup game against Stanley Roberts. The warrior-like O'Neal made it clear from the start that his rivalry with the generally gentle Roberts would not be a friendly one. There was pushing and shoving and the "in-your-face" kind of stuff, which is not conducive to forming the bonds necessary to a close-knit team.

In these early playground-type games, the groundwork for the 1989–90 season was being laid. While Shaq and Roberts struggled against each other under the basket, Chris Jackson would stay outside putting on his usual blur of between-the-legs dribbling and flashy moves leading up to another jump shot that ripped through the net. Passing was virtually taboo in these games, and it didn't change much once the season officially got under way.

Shaq would later complain, "We were all messed up. I think we had too much talent." The real problem was they didn't have enough basketballs to keep everyone happy.

The biggest ego belonged to O'Neal, insiders say. It got so bad early in the season that Brown had to bench the young superstar for several games. Brown used the excuse that he was only trying to take the pressure off O'Neal, but in reality, he had to bring him back down to earth and make him realize he wasn't the star attraction and central focus of the team.

Brown certainly had not helped the situation at all by predicting LSU would dominate college basketball in the '90s. As soon as he had assembled the team, he talked about only one goal: winning the national championship. To make matters worse, he kept telling the media the same thing.

Wilting under such great pressure, the Tigers would eventually blow a golden opportunity to win the Southeastern Conference title, throwing away a 19-point lead against a slightly above average Georgia team. Their problems continued in postseason play with a first-round loss to lowly Auburn in the SEC Tournament and a second-round setback to Georgia Tech in the NCAA tourney. Jackson and Roberts would both depart after the season. Publicly, they said their decision was based on financial considerations. But privately, they told team members that they were fed up with O'Neal.

"The difference in this year's team will be the number of superstars," Shaq would say shortly after Jackson and Roberts turned pro. "I think last year's team had too many superstars. This year we'll have only one...maybe two."

No one was sure who O'Neal thought the other superstar would be on his second team at LSU. Insiders say Shaq thought there was just one superstar on campus right from the first time he put on a purple-and-gold uniform.

Prior to signing with LSU, Shaq had been recruited by such national powers as North Carolina, Louisville, Illinois and North Carolina State. But he really didn't gain acclaim until after his senior season at Cole High School in San Antonio, Texas. He had gone relatively unnoticed as a high school player because Cole High School played against only small schools in the state. It didn't take much effort from a seven-foot wide-bodied giant to swat away shot attempts from 6-2 centers on the opposing team.

His first opportunity to face real competition and his first appearance on national television came in the Dapper Dan Roundball Classic and then in the McDonald's All-American Classic, both of which he thoroughly dominated, causing national commentators and coaching greats to label him as the next Chamberlain or Jabbar.

By the time he got to Pittsburgh for the Dapper Dan, Shaq had already filled out to seven feet tall and weighed 270 pounds, even though he had just turned 17 years old. Playing alongside future LSU teammates Shawn Griggs and Lenear Burns, O'Neal overwhelmed his smaller foes and collected MVP honors with 14 points, 12 rebounds and seven blocked shots.

ESPN analyst Dick Vitale wasted no time singling out O'Neal as "the best [high school] big man in the country. He's got power and quickness. Put him on a front line with seven-footer Stanley Roberts and Dale Brown's team will be awesome."

Soon after, Shaq was off to Kansas City for the McDonald's All-American Classic, considered the cream of the crop for high school all-star games. And the cream rose to the top with O'Neal looking even more impressive in his second outing against comparable talent. Despite being in foul trouble most of the game, he totaled 18 points, 16 rebounds and six blocked shots. Once again, he was selected the top player in the game.

Before O'Neal went to pick up the MVP award

from coaching legend John Wooden, Vitale proclaimed him to be the best young player in the nation at any position. Wooden offered similar praise.

"I'm really impressed with him as a player and as a person," said Wooden, who produced 10 national championship teams at UCLA and coached Lew Alcindor [Kareem Abdul-Jabbar] and Bill Walton to greatness. "I'll have to tell you it looked like a man among boys.

"I can envision him playing with Chris Jackson, and I know Dale has other good players, although I haven't seen them. With O'Neal and Jackson, Dale will have a chance to win the national championship next year. The only problem is they'll be so young. When Jackson is a senior and O'Neal is a junior, they should really have what it takes."

Wooden didn't realize that the main problem on LSU's next team would be not its abundance of youth, but its overabundance of egos. Maybe if he had assembled Walton, Jabbar and Jamal Wilkes all on the same team, he would have found out what Dale Brown had coming. It didn't help when the preseason forecasts began to come out early in the summer and LSU was a consensus top 10 team. In fact, Billy Packer tabbed the Tigers to finish No. 3 in the nation and Vitale picked them in the seventh spot. Several magazines would make it even tougher on Brown and his ballclub by ranking LSU either first or second in the land and naming Jackson the preseason player of the year.

Of course, Brown compounded the problem by focusing the entire season on getting to the Final Four and then winning the national title. In fact, he stressed that the Tigers should set their sights on two Final Fours—the semifinals and final of the Preseason NIT and the last two rounds of the NCAA Tournament.

LSU opened the 1989–90 season with its *big* lineup, featuring not only big men but big names as well. Jackson would be the point guard, although it was evident he had the mentality and scoring ability of a shooting guard. He would be featured in the offense along with the Tiger Twin Towers—O'Neal at center and Roberts at power forward. Some speculated that the Terrific Trio could play three against five and still win the SEC title. As it turned out, each of these stars went in a different direction and the team never gelled.

In an effort to salvage the season, Brown tried benching O'Neal first and later sent Roberts to the pine. Both moves seemed to help for a short period, but then the unity of the team would come crumbling apart. It showed up whenever the Tigers got a big lead. Then their leaders would go in different directions and the door would open wide for the opposition to come back, which it usually did.

Jackson was the lone player on the team to start all 32 games. The Tigers' part-time starters included guards Maurice Williamson and Randy Devall and forwards Vernel Singleton, Wayne Sims and Harold Boudreaux. Brown didn't stop juggling the lineup until the last four games of the season, when he settled on Jackson and Williamson at guard, Roberts and Singleton at forward, and O'Neal at center.

Most of the attention focused on Jackson following his brilliant first year. He had turned what was thought to be a rebuilding season into a thrilling run for an SEC title and NCAA Tournament berth. Despite C.J.'s heroics, the Tigers narrowly lost the SEC crown to Dwayne Schintzius and the Florida Gators. But they managed to win 20 games and make it to the NCAA Tournament before losing to Texas-El Paso and Tim Hardaway.

Jackson, featured on the cover of *Sports Illustrated* after playing his first four college games, fell only 35 points short of becoming the 11th player in NCAA history to score 1,000 points in a single season. Nonetheless, he did set the NCAA record for a freshman with 965 points and a 30.2 average, second in the nation behind the late Hank Gathers of Loyola-Marymount. C.J. was also selected as one of the five finalists for national Player of the Year. He finished third in the voting behind seniors Sean Elliot of Arizona and Danny Ferry of Duke.

As the only underclassman to earn first-team All-American honors, Jackson was the odds-on choice to be Player of the Year as a sophomore. He was featured on the cover of virtually every preseason basketball publication and talked about on every sports show on television and radio.

"I feel good about what we did," Jackson said of his freshman season, always putting the team ahead of himself. "Most people didn't expect us to go very far and we did. Even though we didn't accomplish all of our goals, we got to the NCAA Tournament and we won a lot of big games. I feel good about that. And working with the guys all year long, that was fun. With the guys we've got coming in, it should be a great year for us."

Despite his phenomenal offensive moves and shooting touch, Jackson was not the type to take charge of a team. Listed at 6-1, 165 pounds, he was actually a hair under six feet and had the frame of a 150-pounder. His physical frailty would later lead NBA super scout Marty Blake to say, "Jackson will get eaten alive in the pros." That was exactly what would happen in his first two years in the NBA.

However, few NBA players have ever overcome what Jackson has had to endure. He grew up in a poor section of town in Gulfport, Mississippi, and never met his own father or even knew who he was. About the time he was beginning to show a gift for basketball, he also began to show signs of a nervous disorder, eventually diagnosed as Tourette's Syndrome. The ailment has no known cure and causes many problems, including eye blinking, head jerking and other types of twitching. The only treatment is medication that reduces the severity of the spasms but has a side effect of fluid retention leading to significant weight gain. Jackson sometimes avoided taking medication because he would gain weight, which would hamper his basketball skills.

There was also the occasional public ridicule that Jackson faced. His twitches and tics would cause stares and sometimes remarks from strangers who didn't understand Tourette's Syndrome.

"There were times when I didn't understand it, and I'd think, 'Why me?'" Jackson said. "But you can't question the Lord. I just left it alone and accepted it. I just decided it was something I would have to deal with. It's life. I knew I had to stop worrying about people thinking things about me, because if they don't accept it, I can't do anything about it. That's just me."

Despite extensive medical and family problems, Jackson was a kind-hearted, loving individual. No one on the LSU team was more willing to go speak to schoolchildren or visit hospitals. He was always obliging with the fans, often signing autographs for an hour after a ballgame.

Jackson's gentle nature, though, couldn't stand up to the typical shouting and hollering that goes along with athletics. His high school coach, Bert Jenkins, had cautioned Brown about being careful in dealing with Jackson. Brown heeded the advice and never raised his voice at Jackson. It was also understood among his teammates that no one was to criticize C.J. And nobody did during his freshman season.

But when O'Neal thought Jackson was shooting too much, he didn't hesitate to tell him so. Shaq also made it clear that he wanted the ball more inside.

O'Neal's college debut was less than spectacular as the Tigers opened the Preseason NIT at home against an average Southern Mississippi team. A capacity crowd packed the Pete Maravich Assembly Center to see what they expected to be a blowout, but it turned out to be a close game, thanks in part to Shaq's lackluster performance. Actually, he got more fouls in the first half (three) than he did rebounds and was in foul trouble all night long. He finished with 10 points, five rebounds and four personal fouls in a mere 16 minutes of play and did not manage to block a single shot. The other half of the Towers wasn't much better. Playing twice as many minutes, Roberts collected 16 points and 13 rebounds, but did come through with three blocked shots.

The only thing that prevented an LSU defeat was the sensational perimeter shooting of Jackson, who picked up where he left off in his record-setting freshman year. C.J. played the entire 40 minutes and knocked down 18 of 29 shots from the field to finish with a game-high 37 points. He even handed out seven assists, which would turn out to be just two off his season high.

Two days later, the Trio was back on its home court, this time playing Kansas for the right to advance to the Final Four of the Preseason NIT. This time, foul trouble and the coaching of Roy Williams would haunt the Tigers. Williams, in his rookie season as a head coach, had the unranked Jayhawks executing a motion offense with great precision, while the Tigers were still struggling to find any offensive threat other than Jackson going one on one and often facing double-teaming.

O'Neal hurriedly got in foul trouble again. He was able to log a few more minutes, but still didn't block a shot and didn't have much of an impact. Before fouling out with five minutes left, Shaq scored 10 points and grabbed seven rebounds in 24 minutes of play. Roberts was slightly more helpful, adding 12 points and 12 rebounds to the cause and blocking two more shots. But from an offensive standpoint, it was Jackson or it was nothing for LSU. He just kept firing away and firing away from short and long range. He missed 19 of his 30 shot attempts, but still led all scorers with 32 points. However, it was not quite enough as Williams's Jayhawks earned their tickets to New York City for the Final Four.

Naturally, NIT officials had hoped to be entertaining the Tigers in the Big Apple, giving the tournament a chance to showcase such a high-ranked team and highly publicized players. Already, sportswriters all over the country were comparing the O'Neal-Roberts combo to such former Twin Towers as Kentucky's Sam Bowie and Melvin Turpin, Georgetown's Alonzo Mourning and Dikembe Mutombo and Jacksonville's Artis Gilmore and Pembrook Burrows. Like Shaq and Stanley, these dynamic duos were all made up of seven-footers with glowing credentials. The common thread connecting the other schools' Twin Towers was not only size, but success. They had all led their schools to at least the Final Eight of the NCAA Tournament. Jacksonville, with Gilmore and Burrows, advanced to the 1970 national championship game before losing to UCLA, Bowie and Turpin guided Kentucky to the

1984 Final Four, and Mourning and Mutombo led the Hoyas to the Final Eight in 1989. Actually, Kentucky had enjoyed an earlier pair of 6-11 centers, Mike Phillips and Rick Robey, who led the Wildcats to the 1978 national championship.

With its two heralded seven-footers and one super soph guard, LSU was expected to follow in the footsteps of these great players and teams. There was only one drawback: Brown could not get them to play together as a team.

The rivalry between Shaq and Stan would continue to detract from the team. After one game, O'Neal was asked by a reporter if he was trying to outdo Roberts on a dunk. "Maybe. Maybe not," he replied gruffly. Then he abruptly got up and left the interview area.

Roberts's personality was in stark contrast to his colossal physique. You rarely saw Stanley without a smile on his face and a joke to share. He was without question the most fun-loving, easy-going player Brown had ever had on his team. If it had been up to Stan, LSU's basketball practices would have been held every other day for about an hour. His favorite conditioning work was getting up off the couch to get something else out of the refrigerator.

In fact, Roberts would never have bothered to play basketball if not for Jim Childers, who discovered him as an eighth-grader in Hopkins, South Carolina. Back then, Roberts was just barely getting by in school with absolutely no ambition to do anything with himself. As soon as school ended each day, he would head home and sit in front of the television all afternoon and evening.

Childers, already a highly successful coach at Lower Richland High School, was told that one of his players, Wayne Roberts, had a "little" brother who had already grown to 6-7 as a junior high student. Childers wasted no time in looking him up and taking him under his wing. There was no doubt Roberts had the natural ability to be a good basketball player, and Childers took care of the rest, bringing him to basketball camps all over the region. Stanley spent several weeks studying the game under Alex English at his summer camp.

"Right away, you could tell he had good hands and

a good shooting touch," Childers remembers. "As a coach, you would like him to be more intense."

Academically, Roberts wasn't any more intense. He floundered in school trying to remain eligible and hoping to meet NCAA qualifying standards so he could play as a freshman with Jackson at LSU. He came within a few points of meeting the mandated 700 on the Scholastic Aptitude Test, but never managed to improve enough to make it.

So while Jackson became the most celebrated young player in America, Roberts had to sit back and watch. He languished in his disappointment over missing his freshman season. Already troubled with low confidence problems, his self-esteem declined several more notches.

Brown had difficulty getting mad at Roberts for his lazy ways, because he was just such a nice, likeable guy. Everyone on the team liked him, except O'Neal. Team members say he loathed Roberts for being overweight and out of shape.

After the Kansas loss, Brown realized he had to make a move to shake up the team. There were five easy wins awaiting the Tigers, but the SEC season was looming just a month away and there were little time left to begin to blend things together.

Brown decided his only recourse was to bench one of the Towers and go with a single post player. Since Roberts was clearly outplaying his younger counterpart, it was determined Shaq would be the one to go to the bench. The original plan was to keep O'Neal in a reserve role for a few games and then re-evaluate the center position. If the plan was working, Brown considered staying with it for a prolonged period, perhaps the whole season. The new rotation produced several positive results: Shaq got his first double-double (13 points, 11 rebounds) in the third game of the season against McNeese State and blocked three shots without fouling anyone, and he followed that with two more double-doubles—26 points and 17 rebounds against Lamar and 22 points and 11 rebounds vs. Cal State-Los Angeles.

While the move served to relax O'Neal and get him

out of foul trouble and more involved in the game, Brown eventually elected to scrap the idea because O'Neal was clearly unhappy as a backup. His father was even more displeased with the arrangement. Sgt. Philip Harrison's collect calls became more and more frequent and his disapproval grew more and more pronounced.

"Shaquille handled it magnificently," Brown said publicly about the benching. "He understands what we're trying to do. This is not meant to demean him. We just want to take some of the pressure off him. He's only a freshman, and he needs some time to adjust. By sitting on the bench, he can watch what's happening and get a feel for the game before he goes in."

Actually, O'Neal moped and complained to teammates about the benching. He told them that he should be the starting center and Roberts should be on the bench. He even talked about leaving the LSU team and transferring to a school where he would be the only seven-footer around.

"Shaq was very upset about it," teammate Mike Hansen recalled. "He didn't understand what Coach Brown was trying to do. He thought he should be starting all the time."

After four decisive wins and four improved performances by Shaq, Brown opted to send O'Neal back into the starting lineup, hoping to keep harmony on the team and still keep the team playing well.

On the contrary, the rest of the season was a rollercoaster ride. The highs came in victories over eventual national champion Nevada-Las Vegas and nationally ranked Loyola Marymount and impressive outings against Notre Dame and Texas. But the lows included two straight losses to a mediocre Georgia team, a 15-point loss at Alabama and a horrendous 13-point loss to league cellar dweller Florida.

LSU looked like a national championship-caliber team on some nights, but resembled one of the worst clubs in the conference on others. The SEC title was in the Tigers' grasp, but they gave away a huge lead at Georgia and followed it up with the embarrassing loss at Florida.

O'Neal had his most celebrated moments against Texas and Loyola Marymount. Yet, he remained unsatisfied in his complementary role to Jackson and Roberts.

In a game played in the Summit in Houston, O'Neal put on a mighty show in his first appearance back in Texas. He scored 16 points, took down 19 rebounds and blocked 10 shots to record the first triple double of his college career. However, he played third fiddle in the game. Jackson blazed away for a season-high 51 points, and Roberts shone with 25 points and 16 rebounds to lead the Tigers to a 124–113 shootout win over Texas.

The high-flying Tigers entered the SEC season with a solid 7–1 record; their only loss was to Kansas. They continued to rise to the occasion against highly touted, non-conference opponents, but couldn't take care of the teams they were supposed to beat in the SEC, which were basically all of them.

No team in the conference was remotely close to LSU in terms of talent. Georgia, the eventual champion, had Litterial Green and Alec Kessler, who would later play in the NBA, but that was about it. Kentucky was just beginning the rebuilding process under Rick Pitino. And no other team in the conference was expected to challenge the talented Tigers.

However, LSU lost its conference opener on the road at Mississippi State. This time, Jackson and O'Neal had to carry the team by themselves as Roberts got in early foul trouble and eventually fouled out with just four points. Jackson delivered 40 points, and O'Neal added 23 points and 13 rebounds. But the Tigers dropped an 87–80 overtime decision.

The Tigers won their next five games, including a 13-point victory over Kentucky at home. In a non-conference contest, LSU's Terrific Trio attracted a crowd of 44,233 in the Louisiana Superdome and treated them to an easy 87–64 rout of Notre Dame, thanks to balanced scoring from Jackson (21), Roberts (18) and O'Neal (17).

But the next day, LSU had to play at Alabama and was completely embarrassed. Jackson fouled out with only 11 points, while Roberts and O'Neal provided just eight and six points, respectively, allowing the Crimson Tide to roll, 70–55. LSU made it two straight losses by letting a big lead get away at home against Georgia, which pulled out a 94–92 win without the services of an injured Green.

Two games later, the Tigers appeared to be back on track as they thrilled a home crowd and national TV audience with a 107–105 win over UNLV, which would not lose again that season. Jackson led the way with 35 points, and Shaquille came through with solid play inside, scoring 17 points to go with 14 rebounds and four blocks.

LSU staged another national show a week later when it held off Hank Gathers and Loyola Marymount in what has been called the most exciting game ever played in the Pete Maravich Assembly Center. The action and scoring was so fast-paced that it burned up the typewriter used to keep the play-by-play summary. As would be the case all year, LSU was at its best with balanced production from its three young stars: Jackson with 34 points, Roberts with 21 points and 12 rebounds, and O'Neal with 20 points, 24 rebounds and 12 blocks. Shaquille blocked seven shot attempts by Gathers alone, but the sensational forward still scored a game-high 48 points in one of his final performances before dropping dead on the court just weeks later. The game went into overtime with the Tigers prevailing 148–141.

LSU went on to beat Mississippi State, Auburn and Tennessee to extend its winning streak to seven straight and boost its record to 19–4. But that was about it for the season's highlights. The Tigers found a way to lose five of their final nine games and fell flat on their collective face.

Despite 41 points from Jackson and 21 rebounds from O'Neal, Pitino's out-manned Wildcats knocked off the Tigers in Lexington to start the club's late-season skid. They had a chance to save face after beating Vanderbilt and Alabama to improve to 12–4 in the conference. All they needed was a win at Georgia to wrap up the conference title or a win at Florida to earn a possible co-championship. But they got neither.

At Georgia, the Tigers led 47–36 at halftime and stretched the lead to as many as 19 in the second half before Hugh Durham's Bulldogs came roaring back. O'Neal fouled out with only two points, and Roberts, being disciplined for his ongoing weight problem, played only one minute and did not score. Jackson, meanwhile, missed 15 of his 25 shots, but still scored 31 points. Georgia rallied behind Kessler's 30 and Green's 17 to take an 86–85 win to clinch a share of the title.

A disgruntled and embarrassed LSU team stayed on the road to play at Florida, which was having a horrible rebuilding season. But the tumbling Tigers were up to the task of blowing yet another chance for a championship. They squandered an early lead and dropped a 76–63 verdict to finish second in the conference at 12–6. Their 22–7 regular-season record was a far cry from what was expected of this heralded team.

As preparations began for the SEC Tournament, ironically to be played in the Orlando Arena, reports of Jackson's decision to leave the team leaked out. Brown and other school officials denied the reports, but there was clearly dissension on the team.

Somehow, LSU found a way to lose its first-round SEC playoff game to lowly Auburn, a team that it had swept easily during the regular season. The Tigers were one-and-done and returned to Baton Rouge with more reason to want the season to end.

Yet there was still hope left with the NCAA Tournament yet to be played. Brown reinstated Roberts to the starting lineup and asked Jackson to cut down on his shooting sprees and pass the ball inside more often. C.J. took only 12 shots in the Tigers' first-round NCAA game and still scored a team-high 16 points, while O'Neal and Roberts had 12 points each to pace a respectable 70–63 victory over Villanova.

The club seemed to be building back up to the level of play shown against UNLV and Loyola Marymount. In fact, the Tigers played their best 10 minutes of the season to open their second-round game against a strong Georgia Tech team that featured Dennis Scott and Kenny Anderson. Roberts and O'Neal dominated inside as the Tigers raced out to an incredible 18-point lead and were on the verge of blowing out Bobby Cremins's Yellow Jackets.

But it was almost an exact repeat of the Georgia game that cost the Tigers an SEC title. This time, the lapse cost LSU a chance to move on to the regional semifinals in New Orleans. Instead, Georgia Tech rallied for a 94–91 win and went on to win the Southeast Regional crown in the Superdome, good for a trip to the Final Four.

Jackson announced after the game that he was making a trip to the NBA. Just weeks later, Roberts had more academic trouble and opted to turn pro and play in Europe. That left O'Neal as the only star left in Baton Rouge, and that, as he said himself, was just the way he wanted it.

Speaking of Shaq

Chris Jackson
Denver Nuggets star guard and former LSU Tiger

"Shaq got upset if he didn't get the ball when he thought he should. I'd tell him, 'I missed you this time, but you'll get it next time.' I didn't mind him saying he thought he was open, but he didn't say it in a good way. He'd come right at me. He didn't need to be mean about it. There's a better way to do things on a team. There's a better way to work things out.

"Shaq didn't communicate very well. I guess he just didn't understand what we needed to do and what I was being told to do. Coach Brown told me to shoot the ball if I could take my man. Shaq didn't understand that. He was the star in high school and he thought he should get the ball a lot of the time. But he was not our best offensive player. Stanley [Roberts] was further along offensively than Shaq, so I tried to get the ball to Stanley. Shaq didn't accept that.

"It got so bad that Coach Brown had to call us into

his office so we could talk things over. The problem was Shaq didn't understand what we had to do to win. He didn't see that we could work together. If he set a pick for me and I got a shot, then the next time I'd get it to him and he'd get a good shot.

"We wanted that balance, but sometimes we didn't connect. It wasn't Coach Brown's fault. Sometimes we connected and sometimes we didn't connect. You can't fault any one person. Someone may be tired. Someone may be hurt. It was no one's fault.

"I've thought about it, and a lot of times I wished we had better chemistry. We really needed more chemistry and we needed more balance. I wish we had had more time to grow. I wish we didn't have all that pressure on us. I just wish we had had more time to grow and gain more maturity.

"Thinking back, I wish I could have gotten more people involved. Shaq, at the time, was a strong guy, but wasn't as offensively productive as Stanley. Stanley was older and had a very good offensive game. At times, I needed to put up the shots. I felt that was our best chance to win, and that's what I wanted to do more than anything else. Coach Brown told me to keep shooting. I felt if I could beat my man, I'd shoot the ball whenever I could. Coach Brown gave us a lot of freedom in the offense. He made us work hard in practice, but in the games, we had a lot of freedom. That's the way I like it.

"Unfortunately, we weren't on the right track. We had guys who were used to being stars in high school. They had to take a role, and it just didn't work out very well."

eleven

At the Top of his Class

Even before Shaquille O'Neal destroyed all the basketball records at the 1990 U.S. Olympic Festival, he was already being hailed as the best young center in the game. Pro scouts, eager to get him in the league, and college coaches, anxious to see him leave, tabbed him as a certain No. 1 draft choice in the NBA. It was just up to him to decide when he wanted to get rich.

Those close to O'Neal said he was eager to prove he could join the ranks of Kareem Abdul-Jabbar, Bill Walton and Wilt Chamberlain as one of college basketball's all-time greats.

"My father always told me, 'When you go in the game, let them know it's your game, your gym, your everything. No matter who you're playing against,'" O'Neal said. "I take that attitude into every game. Every game is mine. Every rebound is mine. Every time I get it, I'm going to dunk it. And if you try to stop me, I'm going to take you up with me and dunk it over you."

Pro scouts had been smitten with the young center since he arrived at LSU as one of the finest post prospects in years. While he was primarily a complementary player to Chris Jackson and Stanley Roberts on the offensive end, he controlled the boards and defensive play of the team.

During his freshman year at LSU, O'Neal set a Southeastern Conference record with 115 blocked shots and led the league with 385 rebounds. He was named honorable mention All-American by several media services and was chosen first team Freshman All-American by *Basketball Times* and *Basketball Weekly*. But his greatest compliments came from pro scouts, who labeled the 18-year-old phenom as the best talent in amateur basketball.

"Shaquille is an intimidating factor, no doubt about it," Georgia guard Litterial Green said. "He's so big and strong. He changes everything you do. And I think he's just scratched the surface. He's already a great basketball player and he's going to get better. The sky is the limit for Shaq."

Unlike former teammate Chris Jackson, O'Neal turned his back on a multi-million dollar NBA paycheck and returned to LSU for the 1990–91 season. It was a decision the sophomore figured to face the next season and the year after, but he said he'd abide by a promise he made to his mother and remain at LSU until he earned a degree.

"You always keep your promises to your Mom," Shaq said matter-of-factly. "Every kid wants to make his Mom happy."

Pleasing his mother, Lucille Harrison, also helped O'Neal stay on the good side of his father, Sgt. Philip Harrison, whom he called "a great disciplinarian." "When he tells you to do something, you do it or else," Shaq added.

The LSU center's twofold pursuit of athletic superiority and academic excellence was something his father instilled in him at an early age. Shaq never had to worry about the "No Pass, No Play" legislation in Texas. If he didn't bring home good grades, he had to answer to the sergeant, and that fate was worse than not playing basketball.

"I just want to maintain a 3.0 grade-point average and get a degree," he professed. "I was always taught at home that if you didn't pass, you shouldn't even think about playing again."

All that notwithstanding, Shaq was always in the public eye for the way he banged under the backboard. His greatest pleasure came from swatting a blocked shot into the stands or atomizing a rim with a thundering, full-body dunk.

"Most people, when they go up, they dunk it straight-legged," he explained. "I try to bend my knees up in the air and when I come down, I come down with all my weight on the rim. Dunk hard enough that if anyone tries to block it, they won't be able to."

Collapsible rims didn't always survive the Shaq impact. LSU maintenance crews had to replace the steel support bolts that anchored the basket to the floor of the Pete Maravich Assembly Center, because he had bent them in a matter of weeks. In the Metrodome, he sheared off the rim while leading his team to a gold medal in the U.S. Olympic Festival.

"I wasn't really worried about breaking the rim," he laughed. "When I went up and the rim broke, I thought, 'Darn, I am strong.' But I wanted the glass, too. That would be the greatest feeling. If I break the glass, it would make me feel like the strongest man in the world."

All of these search-and-destroy missions stem from another lesson taught to him by his father. "I just like to dominate and let them know that everything is mine," he said.

Most players who went up against Shaq as a young freshman were dealt a quick lesson. He averaged 13.9 points, 12.0 rebounds (ninth in NCAA Division I) and 3.6 blocks (sixth). He was a consensus All-Southeastern Conference first-team selection.

But Shaq saved his best act for the 1990 Olympic Festival, where his dominance on the basketball court was called one of the most impressive performances in the history of the event, regardless of the sport.

O'Neal established Festival records with his scoring average of 24.5 points. He also set records with 13.7 rebounds per game and 6.7 blocks. That put him in a class above the likes of current NBA stars, such as Charles Barkley, Patrick Ewing, Danny Manning and Danny Ferry.

When he wasn't busy busting rims or displaying his awesome physical power, he showed another side of himself, which wasn't all toughness. He got his off-the-court demeanor from his mother, a thoughtful, gentle person.

"Shaquille has always been a very loving boy," said Lucille Harrison. "He's extremely unselfish. He was always a very sharing boy. Everything that he got, from his toys to his food, he wanted to share with someone."

Shortly after the gold medal ceremony in Minneapolis, Shaq had a medal around his neck, flowers in his hand and a throng of kids encircling him. When a small girl edged close enough to ask if he'd pose for a picture, he scooped her up in his big arms, squeezed her with a soft hug and grinned for the photo.

Before his young acquaintance left, he gave her the bouquet of flowers. The child was delighted by the gift, which Dale Brown said was nothing out of the ordinary for the kind-hearted star.

"He may not show it by the way he plays basketball, but Shaquille has a big heart," Brown said. "He'd do anything for kids."

On this occasion, there was more to it than a simple gesture of kindness. The little girl was white, and Shaq wanted to make a lasting impression on her.

"When a little white girl like that sees a big black guy give her something and be nice to her, it may have an impact," he said. "In the future, she might not be a so-called racist or a bigot. If one of her friends should tell her, 'Don't talk to him because he's black; black people are dirty,' she could always remember, 'I know one black guy who was nice to me.'"

His reputation was already vitally important to O'Neal. He worked hard to establish it and didn't want it to be spoiled. He was a dedicated student and a very conscientious employee during the summer months. His supervisor on a construction crew said that Shaq was one of the hardest—and most polite—workers in the entire company of 600.

"Shaq is a very unusual person," said Richard Gill, the owner of the construction company. "He never says anything bad about anybody. He's very polite and courteous. I think he's a fine young man. Shaq is very special."

One of his assignments was a little out of the ordinary. He and two co-workers were dispatched to Gill's home to clean out the gutters. They scaled a ladder to get on the roof and completed the job just as Gill's wife came out of the house. While his fellow workers climbed back down the ladder, Shaq took the quick way down, leaping off the roof and landing feet-first on the ground with a pronounced thud.

"My wife almost had a heart attack," Gill recalled. "One thing we make sure of is not to give Shaq any kind of work that might lead to an injury. I don't want to be known in this town as the guy who ruined Shaquille O'Neal. Then he goes and jumps off my roof."

Many of Shaq's peers marveled at the way he worked out on the basketball court as well. During summer pickup games, he was one of the few players who never sat down. He thrived on his slam dunking exhibitions, but also enjoyed the run-and-gun fun of pickup games.

"I just want to keep running as long as they'll keep playing," he said. "I want to be known as the big man who runs like a guard. Most big men today seem to have bad knees and can only run up the court at half-speed. But me, I want to run with the guards. I want to start the fast break."

Former LSU forward Oliver Brown, a member of the Tigers' Final Four team in 1986, had played against some of the best big men in college basketball from 1983–87, but quickly learned to get out of Shaq's way during those playground-style pickup games.

"I've never seen a big man move like Shaquille," said Brown. "When Tito [Horford], Jose [Vargas] and Zoran [Jovanovich] were here, they'd run up and down the court a couple times and start to slow down. Then they'd want to sit down after every game. Shaq just doesn't get tired. He's the quickest center I've ever seen."

O'Neal credited Stanley Roberts's presence at LSU as the chief reason that he played so hard in summer contests. When Shaq arrived, Roberts had already been on campus for a year and was established as the team's dominant big man. However, the newcomer from San Antonio quickly set out to change that status.

"Stanley and I had to find out who was the best," he explained. "So every time there was a rebound, I tried to outrun Stanley down the court. I was doing it so much it became a habit."

Almost without exception, Shaq outsprinted Roberts and got position for a dunk, rebound or blocked shot. The two seven-footers went nose to nose until Dale Brown eventually settled on O'Neal as his starting center and moved Roberts to power forward.

"Stanley is like the big brother I never had," said Shaq, offering one of his rare compliments to his ex-teammate. "But when we get on the court and play against each other, he wants to be dominant and I want to be dominant. But that's all about competition. There's no conflict between me and Stan."

The Tigers' Twin Towers formed an imposing double low-post presence, with Roberts overcoming a late-season weight problem to average 14.1 points and 9.8 rebounds, virtually on a par with Shaq's numbers. Roberts, however, didn't fare as well in the classroom and was unable to pick up the necessary hours he had to have to remain eligible. Rather than continue to battle O'Neal and his academic troubles, he decided to leave LSU early and head to the Spanish pro league.

Classwork wasn't the only thing that set the two Tiger centers apart. Roberts was an exceptionally gifted athlete with quick moves and a delicate shooting hand. O'Neal, on the other hand, appeared awkward on offense. He had been teased about his clumsy ways as a youth and couldn't even dunk the ball until he was 17 years old and stood 6-foot-11.

"I don't think I have that much talent," said Shaq. "I couldn't always run. I couldn't always shoot. I couldn't always dunk. I had to practice. I don't believe in talent. I believe in working hard. I practice every day. I never miss a day."

Shaq's supposed lack of natural ability didn't stop Dale Brown from pursuing him with the same zeal he put forth to land Jackson, Roberts, Horford and John Williams. When Brown visited the Army base in Germany, he immediately fell in love with the potential presented to him in the person of 13-year-old Shaq, who already towered above him at 6-8.

"I remember when I was first told Coach Brown was coming to the base," Shaq recalled. "I didn't know who he was. I had only heard of Dean Smith, John Thompson and Jim Valvano. But Coach Brown was really funny. He was putting on a clinic and started doing these tricks that everybody laughed at. He stood at one end of the court and said he could shoot the length of the court and make it three out of 10 times if he kept his elbow straight. He made it three times."

Shaq laughed even harder at the story of Brown's mailouts. The engaging LSU coach promised to send his new recruit some information about the school's program as well as some more training tips. Every day, Shaq eagerly checked the mail, but nothing came. However, when he moved back to his grandmother's home in New Jersey, he found a tall stack of letters waiting for him. Over the next three years, he would receive something in the neighborhood of 2,000 letters, brochures and motivational handouts, which are Brown's trademark.

His future college coach also sent along a workout program that helped Shaq improve his leaping ability and overall agility. He blossomed when he moved to San Antonio and led Robert Cole High School to a 68–1 record in his final two years of high school basketball. He earned Parade All-America honors and was heavily recruited by many top programs.

Ultimately, Shaq selected LSU because of his fondness for Brown and the opportunity to join Jackson and

Roberts on a team that could contend for a national championship right away. Of course, that trio of super talents failed to mesh and Shaq endured what he called the most frustrating year of his life. The Tigers routinely blew double-figure leads and could do no better than a runner-up finish in the Southeastern Conference to Green's team at Georgia.

"We didn't play together," Shaq said. "We didn't play as hard as we could. I think we relied too much on talent instead of hard work."

Despite the loss of Roberts, LSU still possessed one of the more powerful front lines in college basketball, due mainly to the presence of Shaq. He would be joined in the frontcourt by 6-7 veterans Vernel Singleton and Wayne Sims. Singleton, a great leaper and defender, had played center before Shaq arrived on campus, while Sims was a tough rebounder and had an outstanding jump shot. They would be joined by backups Harold Boudreaux, Lenear Burns, Shawn Griggs, Geert Hammink and Richard Krajewski.

The Sporting News rated LSU's front line the third best in the nation behind Nevada-Las Vegas with Larry Johnson, Stacey Augmon and George Ackles and Arizona with Sean Rooks, Ed Stokes and Brian Williams. "It may have been a blessing in disguise when Stanley Roberts left early, eliminating any doubt that O'Neal is the big man to turn to in the clutch," read TSN's analysis on the Tigers.

Shaq kept his predictions simple for his final three college seasons, saying he wanted to "win the first game of this season and the last game of my senior season—and every game in between. I just want to win every game I play."

And how many more games would Shaq actually play before turning pro? He remained adamant that LSU would remain on his jersey for three more years, despite the millions of dollars awaiting him in the NBA.

"It [the money] has crossed my mind a few times," he acknowledged. "Every kid's dream is to make a lot of money and be rich. I want to be able to give my kids what I never had and give my parents some things they never had.

"But I don't pay much attention to what the commentators say I could get now. If they say I'm worth $3 million now, why don't I stay three more years and then I'll be worth $9 million."

A business major, O'Neal already had plans for his big payday, even if he didn't expect it to come for a while. He wanted to buy a new house for his mother and father "with a big pool in the back."

Harrison, however, maintained that money would not be a factor in regard to his son's college career. At that point, the family had not even purchased an insurance policy to safeguard itself in the event of a serious injury to Shaq.

"We never had any money, so it's not a big thing to us," Harrison said. "We've always lived from payday to payday. We're happy. We're content. You need money to survive, but it's not important. What his mother and I want for Shaquille is to get a college degree, more than anything else in the world. That would outweigh anything the NBA has to offer."

His mother agreed wholeheartedly.

"I want him to have some education, so he will have a backbone to support himself in life," Lucille Harrison said. "I didn't get to go to college, and my husband didn't get to finish. We want Shaquille to graduate. He would set an example for all of our children."

That was the reason Shaq coined his own acronym to describe his feelings about the NBA: "Nothing Beats Academics."

"I want a degree," he said. "A degree is always going to be there. I want a degree just in case I fall down the stairs or something. Then I'll have something to fall back on. Besides, I'm having a good time. College is supposed to be the best four years of your life. I'm going to keep going until I get my degree."

Speaking of Shaq

Mike Hansen
Former LSU guard and co-captain with O'Neal

"I arrived on campus the same day with Shaq on June 5, 1989. It was a big deal because I had scored 40 points against LSU [while playing for Tennessee-Martin] the previous season, and everyone wanted to see what I could do against Chris Jackson. Of course, Shaq was going up against Stanley Roberts, who had already been there a year and was the team's center. There were all kinds of people in the downstairs gym. We really went at it for two hours. I was really impressed with Shaq because he was so huge. He was all muscle and no fat, and he could run all day.

"That whole summer, Shaq and Stanley really went at it. They were different type players. Stanley was all finesse, and Shaq was all power. I roomed with Stanley at the time, so we talked about it a lot. Stanley and Shaq had a mutual respect most of the time. It was tough to have two superstars at the same position. There was naturally going to be some friction. They got into a lot of arguments and fights.

"It got very intense between Stanley and Shaq. One time, Shaq called a foul on Stanley, and Stan said it wasn't a foul. They argued for 15 minutes. Then they started pushing and shoving each other, and it became a fight. Stanley picked up a garbage can and then started chasing Shaq around with it to try to protect himself. Stanley told him, 'If you come after me, I'm going to hit you with this.' Shaq went to get something to hit Stanley with. But we broke up that fight.

"Vernel Singleton got in a fight with Shaq, too. Shaq was young, while Vernel had seniority and felt he should be given some respect. The same thing happened on a disputed call. We really had some tough pickup games. The guys really wanted to win. This time, Vernel called a foul, and Shaq said, 'No, that's a lame call. I'm not going

to give it to you.' Vernel got mad and said, 'You're just a rookie.' Shaq got mad and said Vernel hadn't done anything yet, either. Then Shaq started swinging at him. Wayne Sims had to pull Vernel off of Shaq, and Stanley got ahold of Shaq.

"Shaq was the most competitive guy I've known. He always wanted to win the pickup games. He argued every call, and he got furious if he ever lost. He could really get mean if he didn't get his way or if he was challenged by somebody.

"He even started a fight with me, and I was his roommate and one of his best friends. It happened during another pickup game. I went up for a shot and he pushed me. So I said something back to him. That was a mistake. He charged me, picked me up and threw me into a steel door. Fortunately, I held on to him. We went at it fighting for a while, before somebody broke it up.

"After all of his fights, Shaq always felt really bad. He'd come up to you and hug you and say he was really sorry. He really is a nice guy. He just has that mean streak.

"Actually, Shaq is a very quiet, private person. He's really very shy. He doesn't make eye contact with many people. He's just very guarded. He doesn't trust very many people. But once you get to know him, he is a very warm person. He really is great to be around. We had some wonderful times together.

"We had the captains' rooms, which are really just one big room divided by a thin partition. That's when he got into being a DJ and started mixing his rap music. He would play the same song—"Tom's Diner" by Suzanne Vega—over and over again from midnight until 3 a.m., because that was the only record he had. I would bang on the wall and ask him to turn it down, and he'd say he just wanted to play it one more time. I didn't get any sleep for the first two weeks, but after a while, it became like a lullaby and it would put me to sleep right away. Finally, he saved up enough money so he could go out and buy some more records.

"Since we were the team captains, we discussed everything together before we would go to Coach Brown with any problem. Of course, Shaq was the dominant force on the team. He controlled everything on the court. That's when he became Player of the Year and got his status.

"As a freshman, he really didn't get the ball enough to develop his offensive skills. Chris was such a great player and Stan was an outstanding offensive player, too, so they took most of the shots. Chris was just a super person to be around. He was an outstanding Christian guy and always wanted to help everyone else. He was one of the kindest people I've ever known. When he was here, he was like a god because he was so good. But you wouldn't have known it to talk to him.

"Shaq would get irritated with Chris when he didn't get the ball enough. Chris was being told to shoot and shoot because he was such a great scorer. Shaq got angry at him for not passing more to him. There were some frustrating moments. Shaq would tell him that he was open and should be getting the ball more. Chris got very upset. He was shocked that anybody would get on him. He was a perfectionist and it really bothered him when Shaq would say something to him. He got very upset.

"In Shaq's second year, he kept telling us he was going to turn pro. We didn't know whether or not to believe him, because he was such a kidder. One day, he told me, 'I've got to hug you, man, because I'm gone. It's time to go to the pros. I'm going to be the first pick. I'm going to grease you guys. I'll be coming around with the money for you next year.' We didn't know if he was serious or not. But during his junior year, we knew he was going to go pro.

"If he didn't have that mean streak, he wouldn't be such a great player. He has such a meanness about him that he's tough to play against. He makes up for his lack of skills by being so mean on the court. Jabbar and Ewing developed great skills, but Shaq wins on his mean streak. Nobody taught him how to play the post.

"It wasn't until Shaq was in the NBA that he realized he had to work on his offensive game. He always thought he could wait and work on that later. He didn't like to practice with us. We'd try to get him to go shoot with us, but he'd say, 'It's not how much you practice, you've just got to have heart.'

"If he wants to really know what kind of player he can be, he has to develop a shot or refine his moves. He needs to put in the time to work on it. Right now he just has the monster dunk and that's it. He's just having fun right now. He's the Rookie of the Year and he's on top of the world. But you can't always rely on your athletic ability, even if you have as much as Shaq has."

twelve

Player of the Year

All those shot-blocking records set as a freshman were nice. The scoring, rebounding, blocked shot and even free-throw records at the Olympic Festival, not bad, either. Of course, the broken rim at the Festival was something to remember.

But the legend of Shaquille O'Neal, college super-star, took off at the start of the 1990–91 season. O'Neal, just a lad of 18 at the outset of his sophomore season, was suddenly the only show left in town. Chris Jackson had exited stage left for the NBA and a $10-million contract with the Denver Nuggets, who took him third in the draft. Stanley Roberts had said adios to LSU and hello to Real Madrid, which paid him over $1 million for one season in the Spanish pro league.

Now LSU was a one-man show, and there was plenty of Shaq to fill the spotlight. The youngster had grown another inch to stand 7-1 and tilted the scales at 295 pounds, which would be almost his identical playing weight as a rookie in the NBA two years later. David Robinson, who spent time with O'Neal in San Antonio after his freshman season was over, pronounced Shaquille ready for the NBA. Kentucky coach Rick Pitino, who had coached Patrick Ewing with the New York Knicks, said O'Neal would be the first player chosen in the draft whenever he came out, and Pitino added he hoped it would be sooner than later. Just a few games into the season, Dale Brown remarked, "If he doesn't get [national] Player of the Year, it will be a travesty."

Now whenever his name came up in a story, it was soon followed by comparisons to Wilt Chamberlain, Lew Alcindor (aka Kareem Abdul-Jabbar), Bill Russell, David Robinson, Patrick Ewing and Hakeem Olajuwon. Shaq's numbers would always be compared to what Wilt and Kareem accomplished in their first season in college basketball. The grand expectations came from everywhere.

Despite just getting started with his college career, O'Neal had already deflected rumors that he might be turning pro. Although he denied there was any possibility of skipping his last three years of college eligibility to jump to the pros, the questions persisted.

"Getting a degree is something my parents and I have talked about for a long time," he told the *San Antonio Express-News* upon returning to his home after his freshman year. "I know what I'm going to do."

"Read my lips: I'm going to LSU for three more years," he insisted. "The longer you wait, the higher the dividends you get. I want to get my degree. I'm going to play at LSU for three more seasons, and then I'll worry about the pros. You can't play basketball all your life."

Privately, O'Neal would joke with teammates and friends that he was waiting for his contract value to go up. Once it got high enough, he said, he would turn pro. "It's got to be $80 million for eight years," he'd say with a wink.

Shaquille, however, never even joked about going to the NBA around his father. Sgt. Philip Harrison remained adamant that no amount of money would lure his son away from college and the ultimate reward of a college degree.

"We've said it from the beginning: Shaquille is

going to college four years," Harrison said. "People always want to ask us if Shaquille is jumping to the pros early, and the answer is always the same: No. He's going to get his degree. We're going for the education. Money is not the big factor. What happens if he goes to the pros and turns a knee? Then what happens? That's why you've got to get your education."

Harrison deeply regretted not finishing college himself. He had had a chance to earn a college degree by playing basketball, but had not taken advantage of it. As a result, he had spent his life taking orders from superiors in the Army, most of whom *had* earned college degrees. Harrison was determined that his son would not be relegated to a lifetime of being an order-taker.

Naturally, Dale Brown was doing everything in his power to convince Shaquille and his family that four years of college basketball was the right move for any great young player. Even though Brown was already fed up with the sergeant's constant complaints, he was willing to put up with them if it meant keeping his only superstar around for three more years.

"The highest-paid big men in the history of the game waited four years," Brown would often say. "Kareem Abdul-Jabbar and Bill Walton did, and they both were great players. Larry Bird waited four years. There are some instances when some players go early. Chris Jackson made a wise decision. That [the 1990 draft] was not a strong lottery class, and he can play in the NBA. I think it all comes down to what is fair for the person."

Of course, Brown was also trying to be fair to his program. If Shaquille left early, the cupboard would be completely bare. Brown would have to start all over again.

While Brown believed Shaquille and his family were serious about their commitment to a degree, he did everything possible to reinforce the advantages of staying in school four years. He had former UCLA coach John Wooden talk to Harrison about Walton and Jabbar and how their four-year college careers benefitted them.

Brown was delighted when David Robinson publicly advised O'Neal to remain at LSU for four years, even though he was capable of entering the NBA at any time.

"He has a tremendous future," Robinson said. "I've got to get ready for him in a few years. He may have a tremendous opportunity his junior year. If he has the ability to come out, and he certainly does, he could be one of the top three picks in the draft. I would say stay in school, but not everybody has to stay in school four years before they can play in the NBA.

"The thing I really noticed about him was the aggressiveness that he had all the time," Robinson continued. "He takes the ball strong to the hole all the time, and he is a tremendous rebounder. Those are the things you look for in a player when he gets to college. I know it took me two or three years to learn those things. He showed all those things as a freshman."

Despite all of his early accomplishments, Robinson said it would be wise for Shaquille to remain in school as long as possible.

O'Neal obviously listened to the words of his new idol. What he admired most in Robinson was his quickness, ballhandling and ability to run the court so well for a big man. Shaquille, though he refused to spend much time working on post moves or hook shots, loved to run up and down the court like a guard. He was particularly excited whenever he got the chance to lead the fast break and toss off a spectacular no-look pass or simply come thundering through the lane for a monster dunk.

In pickup games and even in team scrimmages, Shaquille would seldom try a turnaround jumper or go up for a jump hook. Instead, he'd just run the court, get the ball from a teammate and power in for a dunk. Then he would go back on defense, get a rebound and start running again, looking for another slam opportunity. While that mentality continued to drive Dale Brown crazy, if he wasn't already, it was music to his ears whenever he heard his only star talk about the importance of finishing college.

"The way I see it, the NBA is all business," O'Neal said. "It's all entertainment. It's a job.

"If you're good enough, the NBA will take care of itself," he added. "You'll have more value if you wait four years."

Russell, Jabbar, Walton and Robinson all waited to complete their collegiate eligibility before entering the NBA. Chamberlain played through his junior season at Kansas before turning pro. Among those five players, there were seven national championships, one runner-up finish, one other Final Four appearance and a Final Eight showing.

O'Neal, hoping to win a few national titles himself, had burst onto the national scene as a 17-year-old freshman, while Russell, Chamberlain, Jabbar and Walton were already 19 or 20 by the time they started their college careers. Robinson, as an 18-year-old freshman, had been unimpressive. He averaged just seven points and four rebounds in his first season at the Naval Academy.

Russell was a rebounding machine and defensive standout right from the start of his playing days as a 19-year-old sophomore at San Francisco. In the 1953–54 season, the first in which he was eligible to play, the sophomore center averaged 19.9 points and 19.2 rebounds. Then he improved to 21.4 points and 20.5 rebounds as a junior and led San Francisco to the national championship. Russell capped his college career with a perfect season and another national title.

The year after Russell graduated, Chamberlain turned 20 and got his first chance to play for Kansas as a sophomore. Wilt averaged 29.6 points and 18.9 rebounds in his first college season, and carried the Jawhawks to the NCAA championship game, where they lost in a triple-overtime thriller to North Carolina. Chamberlain boosted his scoring average to 30.1 points as a junior, but Kansas did not return to the title game. Wilt turned pro after his junior year and joined the Harlem Globetrotters before eventually playing for the Philadelphia Warriors.

Nearly a decade passed before a seven-footer dominated college basketball again. John Wooden was the coach who brought the big man back into the limelight as he used the skills and size of Jabbar and Walton to string together seven straight national titles. Jabbar was almost

20 when he began playing as a sophomore at UCLA. He averaged 29.6 points and 15.5 rebounds in his first college season and powered the Bruins to the 1967 national title, their first of seven straight. Jabbar was the main force in the 1967–68 season although his scoring output dipped to 26.2 points on a more balanced team. He closed out his college days with two more national championships.

UCLA won the 1970 and 1971 titles before Walton was eligible to compete as a 19-year-old sophomore. He contributed 21.1 points and 15.6 rebounds to lead the Bruins to the 1972 title. The following year, "Big Red" came through with 20.4 points and 16.5 rebounds a game, once again leading UCLA to the national championship, its seventh straight. Walton helped the Bruins return to the Final Four in his senior season, but they fell to eventual champion North Carolina State in the semifinals.

O'Neal figured there would be a national championship or at least some Final Four appearances in his future before heading to the pro ranks. After all, Dale Brown's team had been to the Final Four twice and the Final Eight four times during the 1980s, and never had a center over 6-9. Despite losing Jackson and Roberts, O'Neal was sure LSU would return to national prominence.

"When I first got here, I looked around at Chris and Stanley and all the other guys, and I figured we'd be going all the way," O'Neal reflected. "I think we found out last year that talent isn't everything. This team has a different attitude. I think we'll have more fun.

"If people want to focus on me, that's fine. I can take it," he added. "I've always been taught that it's your court, you use it. You control it. It's your place."

No one was disputing that the LSU team was Shaq's. The previous year's team had enough talent to beat any opponent outside the NBA, but the season had ended in dejection. The Tigers finished 23–9, but blew a chance to wrap up the Southeastern Conference championship, lost in the first round of the SEC Tournament and threw away a golden opportunity to advance in the Final Four.

"We were all messed up last year," O'Neal said, "I think we had too much talent."

Not only did Jackson and Roberts opt for professional basketball, LSU lost its other talented guard, Maurice Williamson, to academics. Jackson's likely replacement at point guard, Randy Devall, also was academically ineligible. All told, the Tigers lost nearly two-thirds of their offensive punch and almost half of their rebounding production from the 1989–90 ballclub. O'Neal and forward Vernel Singleton were the only returning starters. Critics were complaining that LSU had put too much of its recruiting efforts into getting superstars, and now that Jackson and Roberts were gone, there was not enough of a supporting cast left to work with O'Neal.

Matters didn't get any better for the Tigers when transfer Mike Hansen, a hot-shooting guard, came down with mononucleosis and was never effective, and power forward Wayne Sims, a part-time starter for the previous three seasons, was suspended from the team after passing out drunk at the wheel of his car.

It was clear that Shaquille would have to do more than provide 12 rebounds and four blocked shots a game. His offensive production would have to improve well beyond the 13.9 points that he averaged as a freshman.

Jokingly, O'Neal told the press that he rated himself at 79.2 percent during his first season at LSU. "It's a C-plus," he smiled. "I can do much better."

Without much of a complementary force, Shaquille had to find ways to score inside. He was still resistant to improving his game to include anything other than dunks. But in most cases, that was enough. He could get five, six or seven slams easily against his 6-7 and 6-8 opponents. LSU's most reliable play was the alley-oop from point guard T. J. Pugh to Shaquille.

O'Neal tried not to let the lack of outside shooting bother him. "I still dream about going to the Final Four," he said. "This is a new team with a new attitude. We've lost a lot of talent, but talent is not everything."

Just the week before the season started, O'Neal got some extra help when Brown called in Bill Walton for a two-day tutoring session with O'Neal. He also scheduled Shaquille an appointment with Jabbar for a month later.

The explanation given the press was that Walton and Jabbar were two of the best big men in the history of the game and could help refine O'Neal's game. But actually, Brown was hoping they could convince Shaq to add some shots and moves that would help him become more than a mere dunking machine.

Walton had spent part of the previous summer working with Indiana Pacers center Rik Smits and proceeded with his instructional duties as a trouble-shooter for several other centers. Brown contacted Walton through his long-time friend John Wooden. Walton was also working with L.A. Gear, so his visit was gratis. Jabbar, on the other hand, was compensated by LSU for working with O'Neal.

For several hours each day, Walton tutored O'Neal on footwork, learning a hook shot, playing defense with his hands up and blocking shots to teammates rather than out of bounds.

"Every player, no matter how good, can improve," said Walton. "After all, basketball players are not born, they develop, and they develop under others."

Long a student of Wooden's system, Brown had already taught O'Neal most of what Walton was showing him. The difference was that this time it was coming from one of the legends of the game, and Shaquille listened carefully and followed his advice.

Brown had long been frustrated that O'Neal would always try to block a shot "somewhere near Pluto or Mercury.

"He [Walton] said, 'Block a shot and save it, block it to yourself,'" Brown said. "I've told him that 4,632 times, but now when one of the greatest players in the game tells him, it makes an impact."

That impact, Brown hoped, would last more than just the week that Walton was in town.

O'Neal smiled when recounting one of the lessons Walton shared with him. He told Shaquille "to keep your hands up. If the ref makes a bad call, don't embarrass him, just play hard and don't worry about the zebras."

Before leaving, Walton also encouraged his new pupil to stay in school and enjoy college life for as long as possible. Brown, naturally, appreciated those instructions as well.

When asked to compare O'Neal with other outstanding centers, Walton gave a long, detailed response: "Shaquille is an outstanding young man who has an unlimited future in front of him. The thing we have to do is remind him that he's only 18. But he's done a great deal already, and he's going to get better.

"Shaquille is more physical and much bigger than Hakeem Olajuwon," Walton said. "They both have great quickness, great leaping ability, great strength and great competitive drive. But you don't want to fall into the habit of calling him the next Hakeem Olajuwon. He's the first Shaquille O'Neal. He's going to establish his own identity, and he already has."

Is he ready for the NBA?

"Physically, there's no question he's ready right now," Walton answered. "But I'm a firm believer that everyone should go to college, and that everyone should stay in college and get a degree. He doesn't need to worry about being chosen high in the draft."

However, O'Neal soon learned that he did have to worry about LSU finishing high in the national rankings or even in the SEC standings. The Tigers opened the season in the Hall of Fame Classic in Springfield, Massachusetts. Their opponent was Villanova, which followed Rollie Massimino's game plan of sagging two or three men inside on Shaquille and making LSU win the game from the perimeter. LSU quickly found out that its outside shooting was suspect, and O'Neal was unable to fight through the sagging defense to make up the difference. Shaquille did create quite a stir when he slammed down a fierce dunk early in the game that relocated the entire basket support. Delighted with his forceful display of power, O'Neal sat back and enjoyed watching the maintenance crew take five minutes to reposition the basket. When play resumed, however, O'Neal could not get free for many more dunks and his teammates didn't fare much better from outside. What ultimately cost the Tigers the game was poor perimeter defense as Villanova downed LSU, 93–91.

O'Neal manhandled the opposition in LSU's next two outings. He came through with a combined 54 points, 29 rebounds and 11 blocked shots in home wins over Southeastern Louisiana and Texas. Following a blowout of tiny Chapman College, LSU faced undefeated, second-ranked Arizona in a home game, and O'Neal put Walton's tips to good work in propelling the Tigers to their biggest upset in his college career.

Featuring Brian Williams, Ed Stokes and Sean Rooks, Arizona's front line was supposed to be the best in the college game. All three were extremely athletic and stood within an inch or two of the 7-1 O'Neal. Despite being outmanned three to one, Shaquille staged what one writer called an aerial ballet followed by a succession of basket-rattling dunks. All of this magnificent display of basketball brilliance and power ignited the Pete Maravich Assembly Center into a frenzy. ABC announcer Dick Vitale, who is always in a frenzy when watching college hoops, appeared on the verge of jumping out of the gym after O'Neal dunked over and around the Wildcat Trio time after time.

"I mean," Vitale screamed into the mike after yet another Shaq slam, "that is frightening."

Saving his best for last, O'Neal rattled off 16 points in the final six minutes as LSU pulled away for a 92–82 victory. Shaquille finished with 29 points, 14 rebounds and all six of LSU's blocked shots, despite being able to play just 28 minutes due to foul trouble.

As a final exclamation mark, Shaquille soared through the air and came down with a crashing dunk with eight seconds left. And when it was all over, he delighted the home fans and national TV audience by celebrating with a rap dance that brought even more cheers. Vitale squealed his approval: "Take a look at this, America!!! Take a look! Oooooooh!!!"

America did take a look at Shaquille and the Tigers. O'Neal, raising his average output to 27.5 points, 5.3 blocked shots and a nation-leading 15.4 rebounds, showed the basketball world that yes, maybe he could carry a team, perhaps further than it had gone with three superstars.

The performance against Arizona launched O'Neal into contention for national Player of the Year and further enhanced his celebrity status. He would soon be on the cover of *Sports Illustrated* and many other national publications. Unfortunately, he would also revert to relying on the dunk-run-block style of play.

"There's no question he's the best big man in the country," said Arizona coach Lute Olson, "and it's not even close, I don't think."

Right after the upset of Arizona, LSU stayed at home to play Arkansas State, which had one of the smallest front lines ever to play against LSU during the Brown era. O'Neal took advantage of the tiny opposition to pour in 53 points and break the Assembly Center record of 50 points set by Chris Jackson. In the second half, Shaquille made 12 of 15 shot attempts, most from within two or three feet of the basket. In addition to his scoring record, he set arena records with 17 free-throws made and 21 free-throws attempted. He also added a game-high 19 rebounds and four blocks.

Ironically, it was about that time that Sgt. Philip Harrison began to complain openly about other teams supposedly getting away with fouls against his son. Harrison's criticism of the officials hit an all-time high after LSU lost at Illinois. Brown even joined the battle, which eventually became a national controversy of sorts.

"Unless we want to continue to lose good big men to the pros, then we have to learn how to officiate big men in college basketball," Brown said after the 102–96 loss to the Illini. "It's ridiculous. It's a joke the beating that Shaquille takes every time out. There are rules against the things that are done. Officiating is a terrible job and we must professionalize it to make it a better job. We have to do away with the conference affiliation thing. It's a joke. Everybody wins at home and loses on the road. It's not just here. It's that way in the Assembly Center. It's that way everywhere. I'd feel that way if we'd won the game."

When Lou Henson learned of Brown's charges of

poor officiating, he merely laughed it off and explained the Illini's game plan of taking the ball right at O'Neal to draw fouls and putting a body on the big man whenever a shot went up. Shaquille was lured into committing three first-half fouls and sat out almost half of the period. He eventually fouled out late in the game, but still had 28 points, 12 rebounds and seven blocks.

Illinois center Andy Kpedi, nearly half a foot shorter than the LSU star, explained the strategy: "We wanted to make him do things he hasn't done before. I think he got frustrated."

Indeed, O'Neal was so perplexed by the situation he threw an elbow at Illinois's Scott Pierce and drew the first technical foul of his career. Had the elbow landed, he would also have been kicked out of the game and suspended for the first time.

Once the SEC season opened in January, O'Neal kept posting big numbers against smaller opponents. *Baton Rouge Advocate* sports editor Sam King dubbed it a season of "Man vs. Munchkin." Even though O'Neal continued to score 25 to 30 points and grab 14 to 18 rebounds every night, Harrison kept complaining to Brown, who ultimately complained to the media about the lack of fouls called against LSU's opponents. Brown and Harrison finally wrote a letter to the SEC Office stating that if the league's officials didn't call more fouls against players holding O'Neal, he would be forced to turn pro.

Reporters covering the LSU team snickered every time Brown brought up the subject. Sure, Shaquille was occasionally being held by some 6-6 runt of a center. But what else were the poor guys going to do? Sam King adeptly pointed out that Brown's past teams, with small centers of their own, had made a living off pushing, grabbing and hanging on bigger players.

"The rules are always against the basketball coach, depending on what he has and what he doesn't," King wrote in a column. "With visions of [former LSU 6-6 center] Ricky Blanton chopping up A-1 centers like a blue chip nose guard at work, one of Brown's remarks about officiating was a bit amusing: 'You can't belly up to a big man the way they did. That's illegal.' If Blanton had shoved big men around no harder than the Munchins did O'Neal Tuesday night, LSU would never have gotten out of Baton Rouge, much less to the Final Four in 1986."

During LSU's historic march to the 1986 Final Four, when it became the only team seeded 10th or lower to ever make the national semifinals, Blanton battered John Salley, William Bedford and Kenny Walker. If Blanton had played against O'Neal, he would have shown Harrison and Brown what a real pounding is all about. What the Munchins were doing to Shaquille in 1991 was mere child's play compared to Blanton and other former LSU centers like Greg Cook, Nikita Wilson and even Vernel Singleton.

The amusing pleas by Harrison and Brown brought so much national attention that even Georgetown coach John Thompson took advantage of the opportunity to lobby for some help for his "abused" centers, Alonzo Mourning and Dikembe Mutombo.

"I personally don't disagree at all with Shaquille O'Neal's father," Thompson said. "I don't think my guards can be as aggressive as my post men are guarded. The NBA's far more conducive for them and if we don't do something about the college game we'll discourage a post player from staying in college.

"People ask me if Alonzo Mourning should stay in college," Thompson continued. "Well, from an educational standpoint and for his psychological and mental development standpoint, yes, he should stay in college. From an athletic standpoint, it's insane. Because it's a technical foul if four people guard you in the NBA. It's not a technical foul in college for four people to guard you. In that regard, Dikembe Mutombo, and remember I told you this, will exhibit a lot of offensive skills you will be surprised at. I know he can't make those moves with four people on him."

Thompson and Brown claimed the officiating was holding back not only their centers, but also the other outstanding post players in the country: seniors Luc Longley of New Mexico and Rich King of Nebraska, both 7-2, sophomore Shawn Bradley of BYU, at 7-6 the largest player in the country but headed for a two-year church mission, and freshman Eric Montross, a seven-footer from North Carolina. Just below that group in size were post players like Christian Laettner of Duke, Anthony Avent of Seton Hall, Mark Randall of Kansas and Doug Smith of Missouri.

Georgetown, though, was the only team in the country with the Twin Towers concept. Thompson was sensitive to the situation because he had been under fire for moving Mourning from center to power forward and using Mutombo at center.

"Next year for certain he [Mourning] will be free," Thompson said, referring to Mutombo leaving for the pros the next season. "He's tried to do everything we've asked him to do this year and he's worked like hell. He's gotten himself to a point where he's got himself so damn tight about things when they go wrong for him now because he was hurt. Physically, he's fine. It's more what happened mentally that got to him, really."

O'Neal was asked to compare playing alongside another big man with being the main focus of the team as the only center. "That depends on the coach, and at this university with the seven-footer it had, that was not a good idea," Shaquille said. "Now one big guy, I think that's a good idea."

LSU's one big guy was too much to stop for SEC foes during the rest of the 1990–91 season. LSU swept through the first half of the conference schedule with a 6–3 record, surprising many coaches in the league who had picked the Tigers to finish in the middle of the pack with only Shaq back.

O'Neal really began to dominate in the second half of the SEC season when the Tigers avenged an earlier loss at Kentucky by blowing out Rick Pitino's ballclub, 107–88, in the Assembly Center. In the first half alone, Shaquille burned the Wildcats for 23 points on nine of 10 shooting (seven dunks) and grabbed 13 rebounds. He finished the rout with 14 of 17 shooting, 33 points and 16 rebounds.

"You play Shaquille by guarding the guys on the perimeter," a bewildered Pitino remarked. "You try to keep them from passing it. Otherwise, forget it. It's not my place to say whether he should turn pro. But if he does, he'll be the No. 1 draft choice. He would have been last year, too."

After watching O'Neal's performance against Kentucky, *Orange County Register* reporter Mark Whicker wrote, "The 7-1, 295-pound, fast-dribbling, quick-jumping, hard-slamming, all-catching O'Neal has been nothing less than the next stage of basketball's evolution."

Whether or not he represented a new age of athletic big men, Shaquille certainly was uncontested in the SEC. He was more than six rebounds per game ahead of his closest challenger in the SEC and was on pace to become the first college player to average more than 15 rebounds a game since Larry Smith in 1980.

Asked why he was so overpowering against UK, O'Neal replied, "We wanted to go for the kill. It was time for me to dominate."

What specifically does dominate mean?

"Dunk on a lot of people," Shaq answered abruptly.

Dunking was enough to power LSU through the conference, which was virtually devoid of centers. In fact, Jamal Mashburn, at only 6-8, was forced to play center for Kentucky.

There was virtually no challenge for O'Neal down the stretch of the SEC race. He averaged 31 points in his final seven league games, all victories. In addition to 33 points against Kentucky, he slammed for an SEC-high 38 points against Georgia, 20 in limited playing time in a rout of Auburn, 36 against Alabama, another 38-point output to crush Ole Miss, 33 against Tennessee, and 19 in a decisive win at Florida that clinched a share of the SEC crown.

"There's no way to stop him," Ole Miss coach Ed Murphy said. "There's nothing more he can do in this league."

O'Neal sustained what was thought to be a deep bruise on his right leg in the Florida game. "He came to my office and told me, 'Coach, I don't think I can play,'" Brown recalled. "So I said, 'That's fine. We've clinched a share of the championship anyway. We don't want to risk your pro career.'"

A bone scan later revealed a hairline fracture of the leg. O'Neal was held out of the season finale against Mississippi State, which beat the Tigers, 76–73, to forge a tie for the conference title. Both LSU and Mississippi State finished league play at 13–5.

Without O'Neal playing a minute, LSU was routed by Auburn in the first round of the SEC Tournament. The 92–77 loss was yet another embarrassing exit for LSU.

O'Neal managed to return to the lineup for the first round of the NCAA Tournament. But limping visibly, he was not his usual self in LSU's 79–62 loss to Connecticut.

Although it was another disappointing finish, LSU still had a remarkable season recovering from the loss of Jackson and Roberts. They finished 20–10 overall and actually won one more SEC game than they had the previous season with all three stars.

Statistically, Shaquille was at the top of the conference in almost every category. He led the league in scoring at 27.7 points a game, rebounding at 14.6. (He would have averaged over 15 if not for the debilitating injury that slowed him in the final two games.) He also led the SEC in field-goal percentage at 63.4 and blocked shots at 5.0.

O'Neal established numerous milestones during his superb sophomore season, including being the first seven-footer to lead the nation in rebounding since Olajuwon did it in 1984. He was also the first SEC performer to lead the conference in both scoring and rebounding since Kenny Walker in 1985, and he became the first player since Charles Barkley in 1984 to lead the league in rebounding for two straight years. Unofficially, he set a new SEC record for dunks with 118. LSU, though, was the only school to keep track of dunks because that was primarily how Shaquille got his points, along with layups and other power moves.

Although Brown said publicly that O'Neal had improved more in one year than any other elite athlete he had coached, he was still baffled by O'Neal's insistence on relying on the dunk exclusively. While it didn't matter against the weak post players in the SEC, O'Neal was no match for Christian Laettner when LSU faced Duke in a late-season game on national TV. Laettner, though two inches shorter and 50 pounds lighter, cut off Shaquille's path to the goal to take away his dunk and leave him offense-less. Laettner finished with 24 points and 11 rebounds, while Shaq managed only 15 points and 10 rebounds. Duke, meanwhile, blew out the Tigers, 88–70, in Cameron Indoor Stadium.

Despite the poor showing against Laettner, O'Neal was still voted Player of the Year, becoming only the fourth sophomore in history to win the Adolph Rupp Trophy. Shaquille received nearly twice as many votes as his closest challenger, Larry Johnson of UNLV. Johnson's teammate, Stacey Augmon, finished third.

"I'm not thrilled about awards," Shaq said in accepting the trophy at the Final Four proceedings in Indianapolis. "But I am glad that I have my name next to the elite players, such as Patrick Ewing, Bill Walton and Kareem."

The only other sophomores ever to win the Rupp Trophy were Walton of UCLA in 1972, Mark Aguirre of DePaul in 1980 and Ralph Sampson of Virginia in 1981. The only question left to be answered was this: Would O'Neal return to LSU and try to win the trophy again?

"I am coming back, but right now I'm going to say might, and that my intentions are to come back," Shaq said. "Rocket [Ismail of Notre Dame] said he was coming back, but something happened that made him change his mind so he left.

"The end of the season was pretty disappointing, but the good thing about America is there's always next year," he said. "We'll be back next year and hopefully make it then [to the Final Four]. If not, then we'll have to come back the year after that."

O'Neal had to travel to Indianapolis from San Antonio, where he had been spending spring break with his family and resting his injured leg. He said he had watched David Robinson and the Spurs take on Ewing and the Knicks.

"Patrick killed 'em," O'Neal said. "I ain't ready for Pat. I need to work on my hook shot. I need to stay one more year."

Speaking of Shaq

Stanley Roberts
Former LSU and Orlando Magic center

"Shaq dunks all the time, because that's the flamboyant thing to do. I'm more prone to take it outside, so I won't get my shot blocked. But Shaq wants to go up and power inside. That's his game, and he's good at it.

"At LSU, Shaq worked on a jump shot sometimes, but mainly he liked to dunk. He's always been a big, strong guy. He loved to run and power to the basket. He still does.

"It was always very physical playing against Shaq. But that's the way to play basketball. If you've got two big guys playing to the best of their ability, it's always going to be a battle. We played hard against each other, and it got very physical. It's always going to be competitive between two seven-footers.

"Playing against Shaq was like being on a field of war. He was rough. There was some pushing and shoving on the court. But when it was over, it would be all hugs and kisses. Off the court, Shaq was a great person to be around. He likes to have fun, and he's always been a good friend of mine.

"Shaquille and I never had what I'd call a real fight. Sometimes one of us would get the better of the other, and then something might happen. The worst time was when he came after me and I grabbed the trash can. That was definitely the worst time.

"But that's part of being a family. You're always going to have fights and squabbles in a family. We got over

them. I accepted the way Shaq was. You've got to remember he was very young at the time, and I'd already been around [at LSU] for a year when he came.

"Shaq is still a young guy. He has a lot to learn about basketball and he has a lot to learn off the court. He has to control the temptation of having a lot of money and wanting more and more. People are going to keep coming after him. He has to surround himself with people he can really trust. He needs a good attorney and a good accountant. He needs people who really care about him and aren't just trying to make money off him. You can trust family members, so maybe it's good that he is working with his family. They're not going to try to cheat you.

"On the court, he's pretty strong around the basket. The only thing he really needs to work on is a jump shot. If he can learn to step back and hit a jump shot, he would be an awesome player. He needs to keep working on his jump shot and some post-up moves. You can't just practice them during the offseason and then not use them anymore. During the season, he has to play around the basket. Last year, they just let him drive in and shoot. That's not going to happen next season. They're going to be looking for that spin move. He's going to need a jump shot. He could be a dominating player in the league, but he's got to put it all together."

thirteen

Basket-brawl

His cherub face and boyish smile covered up the tiger that often roared inside Shaquille O'Neal. His friends and college teammates learned to live by the Shaq rule: Don't challenge me, or be prepared to stand up and fight. Most heeded the warning and didn't mix it up with the powerful seven-footer. Those who did usually regretted making the mistake.

During his three years at LSU, O'Neal was at the scene of or involved in at least two brawls that resulted in other players being arrested. Even the university's top administrators questioned whether the school was giving preferential treatment to star athletes by keeping them away from police prosecution. Neither university officials nor the school's basketball coaches were aware that Shaq got into innumerable fights with teammates during pickup games in the privacy of the basement gym in the Pete Maravich Assembly Center.

In his most serious outburst, LSU police officers

announced they might arrest O'Neal after he was one of the chief instigators in a near-riot between basketball and football players. The November 14, 1991, fight escalated into an ugly scene at the school's athletic dormitory and involved more than 100 athletes.

"It was on the riot stage," LSU police detective Tracy Bobinger said. "Whenever you have to call in another police agency [Baton Rouge City Police] and the Canine Squad, the situation has obviously gotten out of hand. That's the only time I've ever dealt with anything of that magnitude."

Bobinger confirmed the accuracy of the police report that stated O'Neal got into a dispute with LSU football player Anthony Marshall and hit him, thus starting an all-out battle between basketball and football players. Marshall, after much contemplation, decided not to press charges against the school's star basketball player. The only players arrested were four members of the football team.

But an LSU official at the scene of the fight said O'Neal would have been arrested had it not been for basketball coach Dale Brown, who threw up a "smoke screen to deflect attention away from Shaquille."

When the police report was finally released to the local paper in March 1992, it was revealed that Detective Bobinger nearly arrested Brown for public intimidation of a police officer.

LSU Police Officer Lawrence Rabalais filed this report detailing the events of the Broussard Hall fight: "We observed approximately 100 athletes who were yelling, pushing and shoving on each other. As this officer turned around, there was a football player who entered the hallway with a stick in his hand. The subject was later identified as Anthony Marshall.

"While attempting to calm the riot situation down, Officer Shuford was heard calling for assistance. This officer accompanied by other LSU plain clothes officers went to assist Officer Shuford in making an arrest.

"At this point, Coach Dale Brown arrived on the scene causing another confrontation," the report continued. "He stated that this was not going to be covered up by politics as usual. When this officer advised him that Shaquille O'Neal might be arrested, Coach Brown stated, 'You're going to have to arrest me before you arrest Shaquille.' He also stated that LSU Police is a joke.

"Detective Bobinger then attempted to calm Mr. Brown down and try to find out what started the fight. Coach Brown then got very argumentative with Detective Bobinger, calling her 'a fucking bitch' and a 'police groupie.' Brown also told Detective Bobinger that he would have her job by morning, and that if she wasn't a female, he would knock the hell out of her. Detective Bobinger then left of her own accord after realizing that this was causing the situation at hand to escalate."

The police officers managed to calm down Brown and left the basketball area of the athletic dorm to go to the main lobby, where they discussed the events leading up to the riot situation. At that point, football players Harold Bishop and James Jacquet were the only ones placed under arrest by LSU Police.

However, the police officers were alarmed by the unruly behavior of the other athletes on the scene and called for backup from the Baton Rouge City Police, the police report states. LSU football assistant Rick Villareal arrived shortly thereafter and ordered the football players to return to their rooms, which diffused the situation.

LSU police officers booked Marshall, Jacquet and another football player, Shawn King, with misdemeanor summons for disturbing the peace by fistic encounter. Bishop, the fourth football player involved, was involved in a fistic encounter in striking a police officer several times and resisting arrest. He was transported and booked into East Baton Rouge Parish Prison. But the charges were eventually dropped against all four football players.

King later told the *Baton Rouge Advocate* that he received a misdemeanor summons because he attempted to point out to the police that they had unfairly let off O'Neal and another basketball player, Clarence Cesar.

"I was telling them they didn't arrest no basketball players," King said.

LSU Dean of Students Tom Risch said, "There was the possibility—and I don't think we found it was fact—but the possibility that when the authority is the coach and the athletic director, and the troublemaker is the star, is he being treated the same way as the troublemaker who is not the star?"

Sworn statements by witnesses of the Broussard Hall disturbance indicated the incident started over a girlfriend squabble between Clarence Cesar of the basketball team and Shawn King of the football team. Cesar, in his statement to the police, wrote that he was accompanied by O'Neal and teammates Maurice Williamson and Paul Marshall to the football players' wing of the athletic dorm, where they settled their differences with King. However, Cesar claimed football player Anthony Marshall "was cursing everyone and saying he'd kick everyone's ass and got in Shaq's face and called him a pussy." After Marshall pushed Shaq, Shaq slapped him, Cesar reported.

However, other sworn statements reported that O'Neal and Marshall "had a few words for each other, and Shaq hit Anthony." That brief encounter was broken up by the other basketball and football players, but led to more violence.

A statement from Resident Assistant Chris Losack reported that Anthony Marshall led a pack of football players to the basketball wing, where they banged on the door until someone opened it. A large group of football players "went flying in with Anthony leading the pack," Losack wrote in his statement. "Shaq and Anthony were in a full-fledged fight. One time, Anthony was thrown against the crowd, and Leonard Harris [another football player] and I held him. He broke loose, however, and went after Shaq again. Several more blows were thrown until Anthony could be restrained. Almost immediately after this was broken up, the police arrived. I motioned to them to stay back and the crowd was dispersing. About this time, Anthony Marshall came in the back door with a stick. The officers were trying to disarm Anthony when Harold Bishop tried to break up the officers. He pushed on several officers and threw one against the wall. They then

Shaq shows his dominating form against the
Florida Gators, which had no big man to match
up with the likes of the 7'1" L.S.U. center.

(Photo by Brad Messina)

(Right) Shaq throws an outlet pass to start a fast break, which remains his favorite part of the game.
(Photo by Brad Messina)

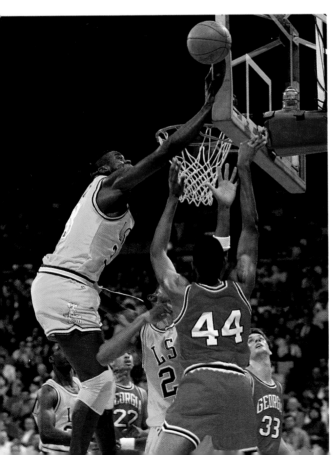

(Left) Shaquille suffered three of his most disappointing college defeats at the hands of the Georgia Bulldogs, including the 1991 loss that cost the Tigers a Southeastern Conference title.
(Photo by Brad Messina)

Envious of NBA point guards, Shaq takes a turn dribbling down court, seeking a chance to dish off a spectacular no-look pass or take it down the middle himself for a thunderous dunk.
(Photo by Barry Gossage)

(Right) The Magic man powers inside against the outmanned Atlanta Hawks, who were forced to try to double-team O'Neal whenever he touched the ball in the low post.

(Photo by Barry Gossage)

(Left) A rare moment of rest is granted Shaq, who showed few effects from the long grind of the six-month NBA season.

(Photo by Barry Gossage)

tried to back him off when he continued to resist and shout obsenities at the police."

Minutes later, there was another disturbance in the lobby of Broussard Hall. This time, a huge group of football players had gathered on the front steps and were hollering at the basketball players, according to sworn statements.

When Dale Brown walked up to the front of the dorm, several football players taunted him with obscenities. Brown attempted to find out the players' names, but they answered, "We're Curley Hallman." Hallman, of course, is the head football coach. He showed up on the scene later, along with Athletic Director Joe Dean.

Brown was incensed by the mere mention of arresting O'Neal and became more infuriated by the misconduct of the football players, even after the police arrived. Brown got in the face of Hallman and accused him of being "a rookie coach" who couldn't control his players.

For several days, LSU police officers received reports that O'Neal battered Marshall, which started the fight. In fact, Detective Carl Boniol reported that he "felt as though the matter should be looked into since verbal allegations were made by practically everyone except the victim, Anthony Marshall. This officer has attempted to contact the alleged victim, Anthony Marshall, on several occasions."

Eight days after the fight, Marshall officially told the LSU police that he did not want to press charges against Shaq.

Marshall issued the following statement to the police: "It was about 10:15 p.m. when four basketball players came up to the football wing looking for Shawn King. King was there so everybody was standing around exchanging words. So I came out of the room and my name was brought up. When I heard my name, I told one of them [basketball players] he was telling a lie and stop putting my name in that mess. I said, 'F--- you.' And O'Neal started walking up to me, and everyone was coming between us. While everyone was between us, he reached around and hit me.

"Shaq ran downstairs while they were holding me," Marshall continued. "When I got down there he had a lamp in his hand, so the other basketball players locked the door. So when the door was opened, we started fighting. I'm glad everything is over, and it could have been avoided. I just want my name cleared. I don't wish to press charges."

O'Neal was questioned by police, but was not charged with any crime. He received no punishment from the police, the university or the basketball team. The four football players were allowed to play in a football game two days after the fight, and all charges were eventually dropped.

Brown apologized to Detective Bobinger later that night and invited her to come to practice the next day. Then he made a public apology to her in front of the basketball team. "I made a terrible mistake," he told her. "No one should treat the police with disrespect. Please accept my apology."

The details of the fight, including the near arrests of O'Neal and Brown, were kept secret until the *Advocate* obtained a copy of the police report and printed a front page story on March 30, 1992, more than four months after the fact.

By then, O'Neal had already left town and was preparing to announce his entry into the NBA draft. He never made a public statement about the riot situation that he reportedly started. Instead, Brown was left taking the heat for cursing and threatening a police officer.

"Coach Brown only did that to protect Shaquille," said LSU assistant coach Craig Carse, who was actually the first coach to arrive at the fight. "There's no way he would have done that if he hadn't been trying to help get Shaq out of trouble."

Brown was later surprised to learn that O'Neal had been in fights with teammates throughout his three years at LSU. Those skirmishes were hushed up by other players and members of the coaching staff, who feared Brown would have suspended Shaq or kicked him off the team if he had known about the fights.

Speaking of Shaq

Craig Carse
LSU assistant basketball coach and recruiting coordinator

"When we were recruiting Shaquille, we already had Chris Jackson and Stanley Roberts, so we were really in a good position. Some people said we were on our way with Chris and Stanley, and then Shaquille complicated things when he came in. Remember, Shaq was not nearly as well known as Chris and Stanley had been. He didn't become a national figure until the all-star games after his senior year in high school.

"Personally, I looked at Shaquille as the finishing touch to what I thought was going to be a dominating team. Chris was the best guard in the country, Stanley was the best offensive center, and Shaquille would be the defensive standout. Now Shaquille didn't have a lot of skills when he first came here. That's why we had to sit him on the bench for part of his first season. But he started to come into his own as a freshman, and just got better and better as a sophomore and junior.

"I think the thing we enjoyed in recruiting Shaquille was they were so up front about everything. Shaq and his father were very genuine. You knew where they were coming from, and they followed up on everything they said they were going to do.

"Sgt. Philip Harrison was a very honorable man. He didn't play any games. He didn't ask for any favors. You had to respect that about him. When Shaquille got the celebrity status, it was difficult for everyone.

"Mrs. [Lucille] Harrison was simply a wonderful woman. She's the reason Shaq is such a warm, fun-loving young man. She was really a nice person to be around during the recruiting process, and she never changed.

"I think, in time, Shaquille will see how important the people around the LSU program really are to him. No one tried to use him. We did everything we could to make it work out for him."

fourteen

The Final Try

Shaquille O'Neal had told friends and teammates that he wanted to turn pro at the end of his sophomore season. By then, Dale Brown had given serious consideration to asking O'Neal to make an early exit, due to mounting problems with his father. However, Brown had a change of heart, Philip Harrison ordered his son to continue his pursuit of a college degree, and Shaq came back.

"Education is the key," Harrison insisted. "I'm really glad he's going back. You've got to keep your priorities in order and keep focused. We've never had any money in 18 years; why all of a sudden now when we've got a little money coming would we jump and go get it? No. Education, that's the main thing."

O'Neal, always the obedient son, said, "My father is the kind of guy who gives you advice, and you do it. It's always best."

Although Brown would always deny it and O'Neal would only hint about it, there was never any real doubt this would be his final season of college ball. After all, he had already achieved the status of being the best player in college basketball.

In fact, Shaq had developed into something of a folk hero. His awesome size and remarkable agility, coupled with his overpowering ability to block shots and dunk, caught the fancy of sports fans all over the nation. There was an unfathomable zeal for Shaquille. Yet not even the most diehard O'Neal fans appreciated and coveted him as much as NBA coaches and general managers did.

"He's an enormously attractive prospect," said Lakers General Manager Jerry West. "He's definitely a player that everyone wants, but the thing I like most about him is that's he's got a great demeanor on the court."

The paq-aging of Shaq had already started. He had shortened his nickname (from Shack to Shaq) to make it more catchy and marketable. Still only 19, he was ready for his Shaq-the-world tour to show off his Sha-kill skills and prove to everyone that he, and not Christian Laettner of national champion Duke, was the Real Deal and the Shaqnificent one.

An impressed Wilt Chamberlain sized up Shaq as "the closest thing to myself that I've seen in college basketball. He's like Wilt Chamberlain reincarnated."

Indeed, the numbers that the Shaq Attack (not yet changed to ShaqAttaq) posted in his first two seasons were on a par with the legendary centers of the game. Chamberlain scored at a 29.9 clip and averaged 18.3 rebounds in his two-year career at Kansas. Kareem Abdul-Jabbar averaged 27.7 points and 16.0 rebounds in his first two years at UCLA, Bill Russell contributed 20.8 points and 19.9 rebounds during his two years at San Francisco, and Bill Walton hit for 20.8 points and averaged 16.2 rebounds in his first two years at UCLA. Right in the pack was Shaq with a 20.3 scoring average and 13.3 rebound rate for two years. O'Neal actually shot much better from the field than Wilt, hitting 60.7 percent compared to Chamberlain's 47.0 percent.

What separated Shaq from the legends was his

team's won-lost record. Walton and Jabbar combined to post an unbelievable record of 119–1 in their first two seasons at UCLA, while Chamberlain and Russell both won 42 of the 50 games in which they played during their first two college seasons (winning percentage of 84.0). Shaq, on the other hand, was way back at 43–19 (69.3 percent).

Former UCLA coach John Wooden, in defense of O'Neal, said Shaq was just as physically gifted as any of the all-time great centers, but did not have the experience as a youth and was still younger than they were when they began their college careers as sophomores.

Having watched O'Neal play in the McDonald's All-American High School Classic, Wooden remarked, "There was no question in my mind that he was going to be a star in college and go on to the pros and have an outstanding career. From a physical standpoint, he had all you could want. I really like the way he ran the floor as a big man. I got to meet him and thought he was an outstanding man in all respects, not just a basketball player. But I would say that out of high school, he was not as far along as Alcindor [Jabbar] or Walton. Certainly, he's strong—probably as strong or stronger than either—but Walton and Alcindor were very maneuverable, you know. Their strength, to me, was not in their size. That's not to say size isn't important. In comparison to other people their size, they were so much quicker, so maneuverable. That's what made their game great."

Wooden also pointed out that Walton and Jabbar had the opportunity to play against tougher competition during their youth, while O'Neal was more isolated during his prolonged stays in Germany while his father served in the Army. Another edge for the early stars was playing freshman basketball and getting to sit back and learn from watching the varsity.

Walton and Jabbar "both are very bright—they have high IQs—and were very wonderful to work with," Wooden added. "They were intelligent, they improved, and they had a strong concept of the game."

Of course, Dale Brown would remind his close friend that Walton and Jabbar also didn't have fathers who told them to dunk all the time and not to worry about anything else.

As for Russell, he was not as far along as O'Neal, according to his freshman coach, Ross Giudice. He said Russell didn't begin to take advantage of his physical ability until his junior season at San Francisco. Giudice also put Shaquille ahead of Chamberlain in terms of early development.

Former Kansas coach Dick Harp described O'Neal as having very similar physical tools as Wilt. "He's big, he's strong, and he can run," Harp commented. "I don't know anyone else in the game who's closer at all, physically, but in terms of physical ability, the ability to run and jump, quickness—no one has surpassed Wilt in those dimensions."

Chamberlain, according to Harp, was more mature than O'Neal in his understanding of the game. Wilt loved the game and was a student of basketball during a time when few players were, Harp said.

Not only was Chamberlain a tremendous basketball player, he was also a member of the track team at Kansas. He ran the quarter mile and competed in the high jump. One time, Wilt helped win a triple overtime game on Friday and came out Saturday to win the Big Eight high jump title.

"I don't think there has ever been anyone as strong or powerful around the boards as Chamberlain," said Wooden.

In reality, O'Neal was by far the most imposing of the big men in terms of size alone. As a junior, he stood 7-1 and weighed 295 pounds. Chamberlain, though certainly the largest center of his era, matched Shaq's height, but played at a mere 225 pounds early in his college career and didn't build himself up to 255 pounds until he was already playing in the NBA.

Walton and Jabbar also were nowhere near the gargantuan size of O'Neal. They were barely over 200 pounds as college juniors. Shaq outweighed all of the current NBA centers as well. Patrick Ewing and David Robinson, as college juniors, were the closest to O'Neal, both weighing in the 240 range. Hakeem Olajuwon had just cracked the 200-pound mark by the time he entered his third college season. Of course, Shaq was younger than any of them at 19.

Yet, even though O'Neal possessed all of the physical attributes needed to not only dominate college basketball, but to be considered one of the top big men in the world at any level, he still was lacking in skills. Everyone in the NBA knew it. All of his coaches saw the flaws, too. But they couldn't do anything about it.

Shaq promised Brown that he was going to work long and hard on his offensive game over the summer. He would come back with a new game. He even joked with local reporters that he would be shooting three-pointers in his junior season.

Teammate Vernel Singleton said O'Neal "is going to go out and basically do the same things. I think from playing with him he's developed some new moves and improved himself."

"He's gotten his moves down much better," said Dale Brown. "We don't want to take away his power game by having him play a Kareem Abdul-Jabbar skyhook game, but we do want him to come with a hook. Also, offensively, he needs to read defenses better."

Enough lip service. Anyone who had seen Shaq in summer pickup games would know that his only new moves were basic power plays to get loose for dunks. He told friends that he had tried to spend time with David Robinson over the summer and work with him on a hook shot. But he said he couldn't find Robinson, so as a result, he didn't find a hook, either.

Walton, having tutored O'Neal in person and then watched his performance throughout his sophomore season, refused to sugarcoat the fact that Shaq had no offensive game, outside a dunk.

"I always come back to one point: You win with skills," emphasized Walton. "Basketball is a thinking man's game. All the guys in the game have great physical tools, and that's something I've tried to impress on Shaquille. It's not just a situation where you just walk out there and push guys around. Look at the guys who have won—and the real test is winning championships. It's Michael Jordan, Magic Johnson, Larry Bird, Isiah Thomas, Dr. J (Julius Erving), Kareem Abdul-Jabbar, Moses Malone. Sure, they've got great bodies, but you win with skills."

What made it even more difficult for Shaq was all the hype he received as the most dominant big man of all time. Many called him the new age of centers, a big man of great proportions with tremendous quickness and agility.

As long as O'Neal could overwhelm the competition by powering over and through them, he had no incentive to diversify his game. He didn't pay attention to the requests of Brown and Walton to add a hook shot or improve his jump shot.

So armed with his dunk-run-block philosophy, Shaq took one more crack at a national title or maybe just a Final Four appearance, anything to get him to the next level.

Entering his junior season, Shaq would get a little more help in terms of talent from the surrounding cast. Maurice Williamson, the academically troubled guard, was back on the team and would ultimately team up with Jamie Brandon, a tremendously talented, yet equally troubled youngster. Brandon, another great prospect out of M. L. King High in Chicago, had originally signed with Illinois, but left there even before starting his freshman year. He sat out one year at LSU and now had to make the transition from his natural position of shooting guard to play the point, simply because there was no one else to play it.

Brandon quickly became disenchanted with the dilemma of trying to please Dale Brown and Shaquille O'Neal. Brown kept telling him to take the open shot, while O'Neal chastised him in the locker room for not passing inside more often. Brandon responded just as Chris Jackson had. Also a quiet, somewhat withdrawn youngster, Brandon lost his confidence, his performance declined, and he threatened to quit the team on several occasions.

"Shaquille really shook up Jamie," an LSU coach said later.

For some reason, Shaq didn't mind freshman Clarence Cesar taking wild jumpers from beyond the three-point line. Cesar got off to an impressive start in the Tigers' exhibition games and the cries of "Hail Cesar" became a familiar chant from the LSU student section. But once the real season started, Cesar would misfire on two of every three shots he attempted. Against lesser opponents, it didn't matter, because Shaq would get the rebound and put it back in anyway. But the Tigers had some tough assignments, even early in the season.

Not only did LSU lose three of its first six games, Shaq and the boys were crushed by a rebuilding UNLV ballclub and swatted by revenge-minded Arizona. Elmore Spencer, the seven-foot center for the Running Rebels, still of Jerry Tarkanian, amazed the nation by clearly outplaying O'Neal.

At Arizona, Ed Stokes and Sean Rooks combined to overshadow O'Neal in the return game of the series. Shaq was so frustrated and angry at the horrible shoving that he shouted at Stokes, "You might win this game, but I'm going to be the first player picked in the draft." Shaq managed only 10 points in a 20-point loss to Arizona.

After LSU blew a big lead to lose to an undersized Louisville club at home, Shaq would have gladly entered the NBA draft on the spot if it were being held in December. The Tigers were 3–3 and the laughingstock of the country.

Even Shaq's grandmother was disgusted with his performance in the first two months of the season. Odessa Chambliss sat back in her living room in Jersey City, New Jersey, and witnessed the debacle against Arizona. She called him to voice her displeasure.

"Shaun," his 59-year-old grandmother (the only person who calls him by his middle name Rashaun) said, "you're playing weak. You'd better toughen up, son."

"I have been playing weak," the giant of college basketball admitted.

His scoring production had dipped from the previous year's 27.6 average to just 19.6 and his rebounding was down to 9.8, a drop of nearly five per game. He had blocked 23 shots, but nearly matched that with 19 turnovers in only six games. His free-throw shooting was anemic at 50 percent (16 of 32).

But what hurt more than anything else was the abysmal 3–3 record that knocked LSU completely out of the national rankings for the first time in Shaq's college career.

"I've been a little bit too nice," said O'Neal. "I'm always shaking hands, tapping somebody on the butt, picking somebody up. I've got to toughen up."

When asked what would make his grandmother happy, Shaq replied, "Intimidating. Dominating, Dunking. Just playing hard-nosed."

Grandma Chambliss obviously learned her basketball strategy from Philip Harrison.

It also became readily apparent that Shaq listened to his grandmother as well as his father. He immediately raised the intensity level of his performance and the Tigers quickly got back on track.

LSU rattled off 11 victories over its next 12 games and suddenly showed the SEC that it could compete with anybody, even a superbly talented team like Arkansas. Nolan Richardson had a veteran ballclub that featured four players who would be drafted later that year: Oliver Miller at center, Todd Day at forward, Lee Mayberry at point guard and Isiah Morris at forward. Two years earlier, that same group of players had led the Razorbacks to the Final Four as sophomores. They were expected to run away with the SEC West title, especially after beating LSU, 101–90, at home in January.

But the Tigers made a race of it. In fact, it was one of the most hotly contested races in SEC history, which was fitting as the league began a new era with the addition of Arkansas and South Carolina forcing a change to two six-team divisions, making the SEC the only super conference in the country.

Other than the loss to Arkansas, Shaq and the Tigers were unstoppable from late December through early February. They buried Northern Arizona, Nicholls State, Texas, Auburn, Alabama, Mississippi State, McNeese State, Ole Miss, Tennessee, Kentucky and Florida.

The furious surge back into the SEC race was capped by a 74–53 annihilation of Kentucky in front of a packed house at the Pete Maravich Assembly Center. O'Neal toyed with the Kentucky double team of Jamal Mashburn and Deron Feldhaus, both in the 6-8 range. His totals of 20 points, 20 rebounds and six blocks in 37 minutes did not come close to describing how he totally controlled the ballgame. Rick Pitino's ballclub was openly afraid to attempt taking the ball anywhere near O'Neal. The lane was off limits to the "Little Blue." Mashburn made the mistake of trying several times to penetrate against Shaq, but his shot was rejected so severely he dared not continue the impossible task.

"You can write us off, but don't forget about us," O'Neal told reporters after the game, echoing the words of Dale Brown.

"I said it would take time," Brown added. "On the road early, I wasn't sure about the combinations, or the rotation. I'm sure it was tough on Shaquille."

Not nearly as tough as Shaq was on the opposition. The Shaqnificent center was back on the cover of national magazines. The headline in *Sports Illustrated* read: "Beware! Shaq Is Back."

Just past the halfway point of the season, the Tigers had improved to 14–4 and O'Neal had soared in the individual rankings. He was first in the country in rebounding at 14.2, third in blocks at 4.7 and 13th in scoring at 24.5.

O'Neal also put an exclamation mark on the Tigers' outstanding comeback by stealing the ball from Kentucky's John Pelphrey and driving the length of the court to lead a 3-on-1 fast break. Instead of passing off, he saw the defender retreat for fear of being crushed by the 300-pound point guard, so Shaq took off from the free-throw line, from 15 feet out, and zoomed through the air, like you know who, to bring down a thunderous dunk. So what if the ball bounced off the back of the rim. His point was made. Shaq was the most feared man in college basketball, again.

Earlier in LSU's winning spurt, O'Neal completed a dunk that was beyond description. No other player in college, or probably even the pros, could have done what Shaq did against McNeese State. It came on a missed shot by Harold Boudreaux of LSU that bounced at least eight feet away from the basket. In one incredible motion, O'Neal sailed through the lane, completely clearing 6-5 McNeese forward Melvin Johnson, grabbed the ball from behind with one hand and swung his mighty right arm across his body to rip the ball through the net. The play would have been a remarkable test of agility for a smaller player like Michael Jordan or Dominique Wilkins. But for the 7-1 O'Neal to be able to make a gorgeous yet thunderous move like that was awe-inspiring. Reporters at the game wrote more about that play than they did the rest of LSU's 115–65 win. They tried to give the dunk a name, thinking they had witnessed something worthy of a legend. Indeed, they had.

Later in the season, O'Neal put on such a superlative show of power basketball in a game at South Carolina that the home crowd began cheering for the visitors' star player. Whenever Shaq slammed, blocked a shot or came crashing down with another rebound, the appreciative South Carolina fans clapped and roared for more. By early in the first half, it became apparent that the Gamecocks had little chance of winning, so the Carolina faithful sat back and savored their first (and what would be their last) up-close look at America's most powerful college player.

"I tell you when I noticed it, it was the first half," Brown said. "We'd built up a pretty good lead, and he went up and blocked a shot, and I saw that whole section stand up and high-five and everything, and I thought, 'This game's over with the crowd.' The crowd was now removed, and the crowd was now looking for entertainment, and they never got back in the game. I've never noticed a crowd turn so fast and to enjoy a game for him."

Like any good superstar center would do, O'Neal obliged the friendly Carolina fans with enough entertainment to last through the remainder of what was an otherwise dismal season in Columbia. Shaq swatted away 11 shots, just one shy of his career best, and LSU ran out in front by as many as 27 points.

Baton Rouge Advocate columnist George Morris wrote after the game, "LSU will go to the NCAA Tournament, where the Tigers will either distinguish themselves or bow out early. Either way, they'll do it with probably the most amazing athlete you'll ever see up close. Take it from the folks in South Carolina."

Another interesting event occurred during O'Neal's junior season. He got a visit from his childhood idol, Julius Erving. Shaq had told Brown how much he admired Dr. J, so Brown relayed the information to LSU athletic director Joe Dean, who had signed up Erving to an endorsement contract during Dean's days as vice president of Converse, the athletic shoe company. Dean contacted an official of the Converse organization and before he could say Shaquille O'Neal, Dr. J was on his way to see the young sensation.

Ironically, Erving had received a similar visit from Bill Russell two decades earlier. Russell, who had just retired from the Boston Celtics, stopped by the University of Massachusetts to offer some tips to its sophomore star about how to become a success.

"As it turned out, I did garner a degree of success in sports," Dr. J said, intentionally underestimating his remarkable achievements in professional basketball.

It was almost as if Russell, the legendary center of perennial world champion Boston, had passed the torch to Dr. J, who would become a world champ himself and help revolutionize the NBA game to its present fast-paced, artful, athletic state. Now it was the Doctor's turn to hand off the torch to Shaq, who appeared destined to become the first dominant center in the league since the days of Russell, Chamberlain and Jabbar.

Erving didn't come to help Shaq's game, as Walton and Jabbar had done. His visit was simply a time to talk about handling the pressures of basketball.

"I've always, at least for the last half of my life, felt like being respected was more important than being famous or being popular—particularly the type of popularity that comes suddenly and can go just as suddenly," Erving said, recounting some of the message he shared with

O'Neal. "You do the things that garner respect in life. That's going to last, hopefully, for a lifetime."

Without question, Dr. J had earned the respect of the sports world, not only for his renowned mastery of basketball, but for what he did outside basketball. Erving completed his degree in management at the University of Massachusetts and eventually bought into co-ownership of the Philadelphia Coca-Cola Bottling Plant. His work with inner-city youth in Philadelphia and other areas of the country has brought him almost as much acclaim as his marvelous basketball career did.

Erving said his trip to Baton Rouge was simply a way of expressing friendship to a young player about to embark on a demanding pro career. He said Russell's visit with him "had a profound effect on my life and my attitude about life more so than about my sports life."

Explaining his commitment to young people, Erving commented, "I sort of obligated myself to do the same thing to other young people if I were to be successful in life," he said. "I shared that story with Shaquille, sort of a way of getting the monkey off my back or maybe obligating him 20 years from now...to sit down with a young person who might be about to go through some of what he would have gone through."

O'Neal beamed with delight as he talked about what Erving's talk meant to him. Shaq, already displaying a special warmth with kids, will undoubtedly be looking for some budding young superstar to share the tradition with, say in the year 2012.

At an informal press conference, O'Neal thanked Dr. J for coming and said, "He's my idol."

The next day when the story circulated nationally, Philip Harrison was infuriated by Shaq's statement that "he's my idol." The next time O'Neal appeared before the media, he was quick to say, "My father is really my idol." So much for Erving's goodwill tour.

Without announcing it, Shaq was making a tour of his own: a farewell visit to SEC towns from South Carolina to Arkansas. With the Tigers chasing down Arkansas, it was the trip to Fayetteville that mattered most. To get into position to challenge the Hogs for the SEC West, LSU had to win four of its final five games. Now O'Neal and company had a chance to send the big guy out in style with an outright SEC title, which would have helped to make up for their horrendous showing in postseason play during his first two seasons. And maybe, just maybe, they could find a way to get to the Final Four in Minneapolis.

LSU dealt with the rowdy crowd in Barnhill Arena and played perhaps its best 20 minutes of basketball in the O'Neal era. The Tigers took a commanding 51–36 lead at halftime. The rest of the game, however, was a comedy of errors as LSU reverted back to its form shown throughout Shaq's freshman season. The Tigers wasted the huge lead, allowing it evaporate into the steamy air of the Barnhill mayhem. The Hogs overtook LSU and began to pull away for what looked like an easy win.

Surprisingly, the Tigers rallied to get into position to win the game and the conference title along with it. With the game tied at 87–87 and the final seconds ticking off the clock, Shaq took a pass on the block, and powered up for a short jump shot. He was knocked clean off his feet, all 300 pounds of him. Yet, amazingly, the three SEC officials kept their whistles silent as the final second ticked off the clock and Barnhill exploded. The championship celebration erupted minutes later when the Hogs completed a 106–92 overtime win.

SEC associate commissioner John Guthrie, who is in charge of the conference's basketball officials, called the next day to apologize to Brown for the blown call. As usual, the mistake by the officials was not publicly acknowledged.

Shaq and his teammates had been given an apology. But Arkansas had claimed the title.

It got worse for O'Neal and Brown at the SEC Tournament the following week in Birmingham. The Tigers opened tourney play by blasting Tennessee. The game was all but over in the first half and LSU kept pouring it on, stretching the lead to 22 points late in the game. No one was sure why O'Neal was still in the runaway game with just minutes to go, when he could have been resting for the semifinals the next day against Kentucky, another likely victim of the Shaq Attack. Of course, his infamous run-in with Tennessee's Carlus Groves led to Shaq's being ejected from that game and suspended the next day, when the Tigers lost to Kentucky.

"I believe Shaquille had good intentions of returning for his senior year," Brown said later. "But he got tired of all the fouls that went uncalled. The Arkansas game was ridiculous. He got mugged and they didn't call a foul. The Carlus Groves incident was the last straw. When he tried to pull Shaquille down, I wasn't going to sit still and watch Groves start something. So I ran out there and got Groves out of the way."

After the Tennessee game, Brown announced at a midnight press conference that he had advised O'Neal to turn pro. The LSU administration later reprimanded Brown for encouraging a player to leave school without finishing his degree work.

"I'd do it again," Brown shot back. "The player's interests have to come first."

Shaq made his last stand as a college player in the NCAA West Regional in Boise, Idaho. It was no coincidence that the NCAA Selection Committee placed LSU in the same bracket with Bobby Knight's Indiana Hoosiers. It marked the third time since the infamous phone-slamming game in the 1987 Midwest Regional championship game that LSU and Indiana were bracketed so that Brown and Knight would face each other in the second round. The first two times, LSU lost in the first round of the tournament and went home without getting a chance to avenge the loss to the Hoosiers.

This time, LSU finally managed to win a first-round game, easily besting BYU, minus Shawn Bradley who was on a church mission. That set the stage for the first meeting between Brown and Knight since the Controversy in Cincinnati that sent LSU home and Indiana to a national championship in New Orleans.

"That's old news," Brown said of the bitter relationship with Knight. "Bob Knight and I have talked, and we have a mutual respect."

While the Knight-Brown controversy might have died down, CBS had another one ready to unleash. Network officials planned to take issue with Brown's performance as a coach, particularly during the O'Neal-Jackson-Roberts era. With those three superstars, forming perhaps the greatest triumvirate of talent ever assembled on a college basketball team, Brown and the Tigers had managed to go 1–4 in SEC Tournament play and 2–3 in NCAA Tournament action (it was about to become 2–4).

The CBS Sports crew had graphics prepared to show what Brown had done with these stars. They also had this highly publicized quote from Knight, dating back to the 1987 game: "I knew we were in trouble until I looked down the bench and saw Dale Brown and then I knew we had a chance."

"CBS was looking to start a controversy," said Brown. "There's no question they were just out to make me look bad. It was a total injustice. That's why I went on national TV two days later to tell the truth. It was an injustice to me, Shaquille and the LSU program. It was tasteless and classless on their part.

"First of all, CBS took something completely out of context in regard to what happened between Bob Knight and me with the telephone incident in Cincinnati. For them to put on the TV screen what Bob Knight had said five years ago, 'That I looked down the bench and saw Dale Brown, and I knew we had a chance to win.' That was a facetious statement. He was just being smart with the media, but CBS wasn't smart enough to figure that out. So it was completely unfair for CBS to use that statement to try and attack me five years later.

"Then [CBS analyst] Bill Walton said it was a mistake to take Shaquille out of the game. Well, Shaquille asked to come out of the game, because he was exhausted from that thin air in Boise. Shaquille came out for 42 seconds, and they scored one 3-point basket during that time. Bill Walton, who has never coached a game in his life, tried to say that was a bad coaching move. Bill also said we should have changed defenses. He didn't see that we played five different defenses in the game.

"When CBS invited me to go to their studio in New York to talk about Bill's comments, my first reaction was that I wouldn't go," Brown continued. "But my daughter kept asking me why I wasn't going to go. I told her that it would just look like I was being vain. She told me, 'Do it for all the other coaches who are being beaten down by those know-it-alls.' She was right, so I went to New York and gave the facts. I explained that Shaquille being out 42 seconds had no bearing on the game. I explained that we changed defenses throughout the game and used five different defenses. Bill Walton just didn't have the basketball knowledge to see the changes. I went there, and as humbly as I could, told them the truth."

Poised to make his first (and last) big splash in the NCAA Tournament, Shaq saved the best all-around performance of his career for his final collegiate game. Indiana's Matt Nover and Alan Henderson were no match for the Shaq. He spun and twisted inside for his usual dunks and power plays, but even more impressively, he stepped outside to sink several jump shots and used the glass to bank in a couple more.

Unfortunately for LSU, Shaq was the show for the Tigers. His teammates couldn't find the range in the light air of Boise. They would eventually miss nine of 11 attempts from three-point range. Point guard Jamie Brandon missed all six of his shot attempts. Nonetheless, Shaq and the Tigers screamed out to the early lead and pushed it into double figures almost before Bob Knight could begin rolling up the sleeves on his bright red sweater. LSU stretched the lead to 14 points when Shaq put up his hand to come out. Brown's policy has always been that when a player asks to come out, he is automatically replaced with a sub, no matter who the player is. Geert Hammink came off the bench to give O'Neal a 42-second breather.

The Shaq-less Tigers failed to score during his absence, but Indiana could come up with just one score, a three-pointer by Damon Bailey, to cut the deficit to 11. What really hurt was the Tigers lost the momentum they had established and got out of rhythm offensively. Indiana came charging back, getting open shot after open shot against Brown's zone defenses.

Indiana pulled within seven points, 45–38, at half-time, having shot a sizzling 53 percent from the field. Shaq was so infuriated by his teammates' horrendous play that he exploded into a fit and had to be pulled away from Jamie Brandon, according to their stunned teammates. The Hoosiers picked up where they left off and sliced away at the lead early in the second half. Brown refused to try a man-to-man defense, even though the Hoosiers were on their way to shooting a sky-high 56 percent in the second half and built a 10-point lead of their own.

Asked why he didn't try a straight man-to-man defense, an incredulous Brown replied, "That would have been the most stupid thing we could have done. I think we had an excellent plan. Indiana made some fine adjustments, but even with that, it was anyone's game with four minutes left."

With a desperation run in the final minutes, LSU did cut a 10-point Indiana lead down to just three at 73–70 with three minutes left. But the Hoosiers had the ball and immediately doubled their lead on a clutch three-pointer by Bailey. Indiana then pulled away for an 89–79 victory, despite an NCAA Tournament record 11 blocked shots by Shaq.

O'Neal finished with a game-high 36, accentuated by his uncharacteristically good shooting, not only on jump shots, but even from his most freightful position, the free-throw line. Somehow he knocked down all 12 of his attempts on foul shots, a career best and a career ender.

"We'll be back," said Brown, always the optimist. "I ain't giving up until we win a national championship."

Shaquille made no such statement. It was obvious to most that he had long since made up his mind to turn pro after his junior season. In truth, he would have left LSU after two years if not for his father's disapproval.

Shaq cried openly in the locker room after the Indiana game.

Throughout the season, O'Neal had either declined to talk about his future or continued to say, "I might be back." Brown played along by remaining optimistic that his star would stick around for a fourth season. But those close to the team knew the decision had already been made.

The two definite signals that Shaq's junior season would be his last were his talk of NBA plans with his teammates and friends and his sudden abundance of cash. No one on the team was sure where the money was coming from, but Shaq sure had a lot of it, and so did his parents. Shaq was always good about signing autographs for children, but during his junior year, he often handed them money as well. "He always had a pocketful of five-dollar bills," said one team member. His parents, meanwhile, stopped driving the family mini-van to Baton Rouge to watch Shaq play. Harrison, his wife and three younger children would fly into town instead.

The most telltale sign of his impending departure was a slip of a tongue by Stanley Roberts. On a trip to Chicago, with the Orlando Magic, no less, Roberts was asked about what his former college teammate was going to do the next season, and Stan blurted out Shaq's intentions to go pro: "I've talked to him often on the phone. He tells me he's coming out this year, regardless of what his father says. He says he's tired of getting beat up, and he doesn't want to take any more chances gambling he won't get injured. I'm surprised he didn't come out last year. But his father wants him to get his degree first."

Roberts's remarks circulated all across the nation. Shaq did his best to squelch the report, saying he had not made up his mind yet. But the truth was out. Most LSU fans, even the diehards, were resigned to the fact that Shaq was on his way to the NBA.

Although his team never lived up to its lofty billing, Shaq earned enough individual awards and trophies to fill a couple of O'Neal-size bookcases. His production was down in almost every category as a junior, but he was arguably the most dominant player in college basketball. He had evened the score with Christian Laettner by outplaying him in a non-conference game during the regular season. When it came time for Player of the Year honors to be given out, O'Neal finished runner-up to Laettner. His final stats of 24.1 points, 14.0 rebounds and 5.2 blocked shots placed him near the top in each category. In fact, he led the nation with 156 blocks in 30 games and finished second in rebounding with 421.

As the LSU team prepared to board its flight home from Boise, Shaq walked up to Brown and wrapped his big arms around the man who had been his coach since he was 13. O'Neal never said good-bye. He didn't have to. Brown knew the career of his most remarkable player in 35 years as a coach was over. He would not miss the frustration of dealing with Shaq's stubborn refusal to build an offensive repertoire and certainly would not miss the headaches of putting up with his obnoxious father. But Brown realized he would never have another player with the raw power of Shaquille, coupled with the fun-loving innocence of a big kid and a smile that made you forget all your problems.

Speaking of Shaq

Jim Childers
LSU basketball assistant and
   Stanley Roberts's high school coach

"Shaquille was very accommodating to everyone at LSU. A lot of people wanted to take up his time—everyone from the fans to the media—but he was very good at taking care of the people. Toward the end of his career here, he got tired of it all and tried to stay away from it. He let us know he didn't want to do it anymore, but that was certainly understandable.

"As a person, he was very loving and thoughtful. He was a lot of fun to be around. He loved to clown around

and joke with you. He also loved to listen to rap music and enjoyed break dancing and things like that.

"Shaquille wasn't really a team leader or a rah-rah type guy. He kept everything to himself. He led through his actions on the court.

"Being such a great competitor, he would get very intense at times. He let his emotions get the best of him sometimes. But he would always regret it if he hurt someone or made them feel bad. With Chris Jackson, you had to be very careful how you talked to him. He was a very sensitive guy. I think he had trouble handling Shaquille's remarks.

"Coach Brown would take Shaquille aside and tell him, 'You need to do more for us. We need you to be more active on defense, block shots and we need you to take good shots.' He always listened to Coach Brown and the other coaches. Like any superstar, he tried to do too much sometimes.

"Obviously, I wasn't as close to Shaquille as I was to Stanley. But I had a very good relationship with Shaq and his whole family. Actually, I was closer to the Harrisons than anyone else on the staff. I was kind of like the liaison between Sgt. Harrison and the athletic department. If there was a problem, I usually went to him and talked about it. We had a pretty good relationship. His youngest son, Jamal, was close to my son, Jay. Jamal would come spend time at our house, and he came to the LSU Basketball Camp in the summer. The sergeant had his problems, but he had a good side, too.

"That first year, the chemistry just wasn't right between Shaquille, Chris and Stanley. Chris had the green light as a freshman to shoot whenever he wanted to, but I think it probably hurt the team the next year. We were still a perimeter team when we could have dominated inside. Chris was a great scorer, but we really needed a playmaker. We started to play great basketball late in the year, but it wasn't easy for everyone to adjust to their roles on the team.

"I didn't realize how much Shaquille really wanted to win until the last game of his career. He never talked much about winning championships or anything like that. But after the loss to Indiana in the NCAA Tournament, he

was very, very disappointed. He showed a new side. I had never seen him like that. He bawled his eyes out and kept crying for a long time. He was really torn up. I think he realized that was his last game and he was distraught about leaving LSU."

fifteen

The Shaquille Appeal

NBA general managers from Miami to Sacramento spent an anxious three weeks waiting to find out if they finally had a crack at signing Shaq. Of course, to get Shaquille O'Neal, they first had to be fortunate enough for him to turn pro, and then they had to be lucky in the NBA Lottery or somehow trade for the rights to him, which would be something akin to convincing Boston to give up the Celtics.

Though most executives in the league anticipated Shaq's early entry into the NBA, no one knew for certain that he would make the jump. And even if he did go pro, would any team have enough money to sign him? It was fully expected that his representatives would negotiate with European teams that might be willing to toss $8–$10 million into a pot to get him for a year. Then he could come back, like many others had done, and negotiate with many NBA teams.

The consensus around the league was that O'Neal was a can't-miss, instant superstar, the magnitude of which had not been seen since Kareem Abdul-Jabbar left UCLA in 1970. Once Shaq was free of the sagging, grabbing zone defenses of college ball, he was expected to display the scoring punch of the real Shaquille.

There were several possibilities as to what his immediate impact would be:

• A superstar player and a dynamic personality, placing him in the select class of Michael Jordan, Larry Bird and Magic Johnson. That, of course, was where everyone in the league, especially Commissioner David Stern, hoped he would fit in.

• A powerful impact center in the same mold as Patrick Ewing, David Robinson and Hakeem Olajuwon. You had to be a superior player to make the cut here, but not necessarily a superstar, and certainly not a super seller for the NBA. Great talent, but not great appeal.

• A very good player who doesn't quite dominate, but still has a certain appeal that puts him in the star class, along with Isiah Thomas and Clyde Drexler. You make the All-Star team, but can't be sure of the Hall of Fame. The impact just isn't there.

• Still a very good player, but with ordinary presence and no lasting power in the league. For whatever reason, perhaps a feeling that they're indeed among the elite, these players don't develop the offensive versatility and all-around games that great players possess. These kinds of players, like Ralph Sampson and Darryl Dawkins, are considered busts.

"He'll be one of our stars in the decade of the '90s," said Hall of Fame center Willis Reed, the New Jersey Nets' president of basketball operations. "He is a franchise center that a team can put all the other pieces around."

Washington Bullets General Manager John Nash said Shaq "has the athletic ability to become a truly great big man of all time."

"Any coach loves to see a guy with his size,

strength and athletic ability, and on top of that he loves to compete and work hard," said Lakers Assistant General Manager Mitch Kupchak. "Then throw in that he is a skilled player, and you really like him."

Knicks vice president Ernie Grunfeld remarked, "You have to pick him because his potential is greater than anybody else's in the draft."

While O'Neal and LSU had not fulfilled their potential, it was clear that the NBA was banking on Shaq's making up for it in the professional ranks and joining the superstar class, if not right away, then certainly within a few years.

Nobody had higher praise for O'Neal's ability than Jerry Reynolds, director of player personnel for the Sacramento Kings, who said, "He's one of the top five centers in the league right now, and he may move up by the end of the week. He's going to make any of the weak sisters better quickly."

Reynolds said it would be unnecessary to scout O'Neal, because everyone in the NBA was already aware of his magnificent ability and even greater potential. Just put his name on the back of the jersey, Reynolds said, and have it ready at the NBA Lottery drawing.

NBA super scout Marty Blake, often critical of college players who enter the draft early, made it clear he thought O'Neal was ready. Blake had said of Shaq's former teammate, Chris Jackson, that the NBA guards would eat him alive if he turned pro as a sophomore. But Blake gave a glowing report on O'Neal.

"He can run the court, he can block shots and he's an awesome physical specimen," Blake stated in his scouting report. "He likes to play, and he is strong. He hasn't been playing for that long, so the offensive refinement will come with experience. And he needs to improve his foul shooting. But he has the ability to be a dominant player."

While Jackson, John Williams, Jerry Reynolds and other LSU players who left college early made their announcements right after the season, O'Neal made the NBA wait for him. Some execs were beginning to wonder about his decision until he called a press conference on

April 3 in his hometown of San Antonio.

Surrounded by family and friends—but no team-mates and no LSU coaches—Shaquille O'Neal cast his vote for the NBA, saying simply that college ball was no longer fun, due to the Carlus Groves-type incidents and day-to-day grind of trying to swat away lightweight opposition who clung to him like flies.

"I am not making this decision out of anger or frustration," Shaq said at the news conference at Fort Sam Houston, the same place where he announced his choice of LSU three years earlier. "I feel that, in my heart, it's time for a change and it's time for me to move on. I've truly enjoyed every aspect of my college years as a basketball player and as a student.

"College basketball just wasn't fun anymore," he continued. "I wish they'd make a rule that guys can't quadruple- and triple-team me, but that won't happen. I got triple-teamed so much I wasn't able to showcase my talents. I'd get bad press and I'd get frustrated. I just wasn't having fun. As I said before, I'm not making this decision out of anger or frustration. But everyone who saw the SEC Tournament, they know an injustice was done. That really wasn't a main factor.

"The main factor was, if I go back to school next year, will I have fun?" he asked. "It's all about fun. My dad told me at a young age, 'If you're not having fun at what you're doing, it's time to do something else.' I said to my-self, 'Shaquille, if you return to LSU, will you have fun?' I sort of looked at last season and I wasn't having that much fun, so I decided to forego my senior year."

The announcement had all the pomp and circum-stance of a military ceremony. It held all the excitement and hope that his press conference three years earlier had brought to LSU. Now every team in the NBA had a chance, albeit remote, to obtain the rights to O'Neal.

Already on hand to begin representing O'Neal was L.A. Gear attorney Leonard Armato. He would not admit to being Shaq's agent and declined to answer questions, saying only that he was there at the request of O'Neal and his family.

For the LSU program and its fans, the occasion marked the official end of the Superstar Era. Everyone who had followed Shaquille for those three glamorous seasons was disappointed to see it end; no one could be disappointed at Shaq's desire to take his game to the next level. After all, that was clearly where he belonged.

Dressed in a snazzy light brown suit, O'Neal flashed his beautiful, childlike smile when asked about the money awaiting him. "I don't really think about it," he said, beaming. "I'm just going to wait and see what happens. It's a lot of money."

The early speculation was that O'Neal would command a long-term contract worth about twice as much as the $19 million Larry Johnson had received as the first player selected in the 1991 draft. The Lottery, scheduled 44 days later on May 17, would determine the lucky winner of the Shaq stakes and the June 24 NBA draft would be a mere formality. Minnesota, Orlando, Dallas, Denver, Washington and Sacramento had the worst records in the NBA at the time of Shaq's announcement, so they had the best shot at picking him up.

"When I was a kid, my dream was to play in the NBA," said the soft-spoken big man, who was hard to picture as a little kid. "Whether I'm the No. 1 pick or the No. 2 pick doesn't matter. And from what I've seen, the No. 1 pick isn't always the best player."

Philip Harrison expressed no doubt that his son would be the first player taken in the draft.

"Of course he will be," Harrison said without hesitation. "Who else would it be?"

Shaq's entry into the NBA didn't come with his parent's complete approval. On the contrary, they encouraged him to return to LSU for his senior season and get a degree. However, he promised his family that he would eventually return to college and complete his work for a degree in business.

"We stress academics in this family and the day he walks across the stage at LSU to get his degree will mean more to me than all the NBA wins he can ever get," said Harrison, who called his son's early entry into the pros "one of the hardest things for me to accept."

Likewise, Lucille Harrison would have preferred to see Shaquille pick up his diploma before picking up a million-dollar paycheck.

"I'd like to see him stay, to be honest with you," she said at the press conference. "But since it was his decision, I'll stand behind him. I asked him to search his soul for the answer. And because this family is his strength, we will stick with him and behind him."

As promised, O'Neal made sure to check with LSU officials about how he could earn the necessary credits left for him to get a bachelor's degree.

Dale Brown had visited the family's home on the military base earlier in the week to offer his advice. Having already stated publicly that Shaq should go pro, Brown stuck with his commitment to what's best for the player, but also pointed out possible advantages and disadvantages of turning pro early. Although O'Neal never said for certain what he would do, Brown left knowing that he had coached Shaq for the final time. He was at the Final Four in Minneapolis when the decision was announced.

O'Neal said he "kind of told Coach Brown how I felt. A couple of people were told that I, my mother, Coach Brown and Leonard Armato had talked about a decision last Sunday. We just wanted to wait a while and rest and enjoy spring break. But somehow, somebody said something and it got all over."

"Shaquille did tell me that he thought this was best for him and his family," said Brown. "He told me he was driving around by himself in San Antonio when he made the decision."

Brown also pointed out he had told the Harrisons that "if he was my son, I'd advise him to go pro."

Later that week, a Minneapolis newspaper story focusing on O'Neal's shoe contract negotiations would cause the relationship between Brown and the Harrison family to crumble. Brown would no longer be a welcome guest in the home of Philip Harrison.

While being interviewed at the Final Four, Brown was asked about Shaq's value in the NBA and endorsements. He mentioned that there was a deal in the works with a shoe company. When asked how much it was worth, Brown answered, "About $10 million for four years." But he would not say which company was offering the deal.

By the time the story hit the press, Brown was quoted as saying O'Neal had accepted a $10 million, four-year contract with L.A. Gear. Actually, Shaq was in the negotiation process with Reebok and Nike. L.A. Gear wasn't even in the picture.

Harrison was infuriated when he read the story in the *San Antonio Express-News,* which picked it up from the Minneapolis paper. He called the paper and called Brown "not a truthful man," along with several other derogatory terms.

"It's a lie, plain and simple," Harrison said in the report, which hit the national press wires and was printed in major papers all over the country. "Before Coach Dale Brown makes any kind of comments on our family's business, he needs to make sure he has all his facts in order."

Even O'Neal took a shot at his former coach, saying, "I'm kind of disappointed because I thought he was the kind of person who wouldn't comment when he didn't have the facts. But I'm not at LSU anymore. I'm looking forward. I'm not looking backward."

Brown was already in Los Angeles and could not be reached to explain what had actually occurred regarding the newspaper account. He was recruiting in the Los Angeles area and was also in town to attend the John Wooden Awards banquet for the Player of the Year. O'Neal and his father were expected to be there as well, since Shaq was a finalist for the award. So a confrontation was imminent.

"What he said in the paper is totally false," Harrison said. "My personal opinion is that Coach Brown should keep his mouth shut. We're just trying to keep the record straight and keep him from running his mouth."

The sergeant continued to blast Brown, saying the whole matter "brings up questions" about the coach's character. Then he dropped the most damaging bombshell when asked if he would tell other parents to send their children to LSU.

"I'll tell them no," Harrison responded. "Because he is not a truthful man, not a truthful man."

Before ending the interview, Harrison took a shot at Brown for reportedly talking about Shaq's decision to turn pro before it was announced at the press conference.

Known for having a hot temper of his own, Brown was irate when he read newspaper accounts of the comments by Harrison and O'Neal. He immediately called Harrison to demand that he retract the statements and issue a public apology. But the sergeant and his son were already on their way to Los Angeles.

Brown didn't get to Harrison's hotel room until it was late at night, because he had been out recruiting. He banged on the door of his room and a groggy Lucille Harrison answered the knocks.

"Lucille, I need to talk to Philip right now," Brown said and stomped into the room.

Harrison, startled by Brown's fury, sat up in the bed, but wouldn't even stand up in front of the screaming coach.

"Philip, what the hell do you think you're doing!" shouted Brown, peering down at Harrison, who began to curl up in a fetal position like a little child afraid he was going to be spanked. "You called me a liar! Philip, do you know what you've done to our program. You've killed our recruiting. Why the hell did you say those things without talking to me? The story is totally false."

As Brown proceeded to explain how he had said nothing about L.A. Gear and had merely mentioned the shoe contract negotiations, Harrison began to say, "I'm sorry, Coach Brown. I'm sorry, Coach Dale Brown. I'll tell the press that it's the damn media's fault."

Brown continued to berate the sergeant, and Harrison kept apologizing and offering to issue a retraction. After several minutes of shouting, Brown finally calmed down enough to call the *San Antonio Express-News,* but of course, there were no writers at the office at that hour. The next day, however, Brown had Harrison call the paper and issue a retraction and an apology to Brown.

During an appearance on Roy Firestone's show on ESPN later that week, Harrison apologized again. His nervous stutter showed he was still shaken up by Brown's reaction.

Harrison said, "I'd like to retract any negative statements I made toward LSU coach Dale Brown and the LSU family. Our family respects and loves Dale Brown a lot and his family."

Firestone reminded Harrison that he and Shaq "owe Dale a lot, too."

"Yes, we do," Harrison said. "Yes, we do."

The Harrison-Brown feud wasn't the only controversy centering around the decision of O'Neal to become a pro. Shaq fueled some controversy of his own. He was openly critical of most of the Lottery teams, he took a shot at his former teammate Stanley Roberts, and he indicated he might not ever play in the NBA at all.

In explaining the way he would call the shots, O'Neal said, "I'm going to look at the team that picks me, look at the players, and if I don't like what I see, I'll explore other options."

Right away, O'Neal expressed disinterest in being selected in the draft by Orlando or Denver. The Magic, of course, had the seven-foot Roberts and Denver featured 7-1 Dikembe Mutombo and Shaq's former teammate, Chris Jackson, whom he didn't get along with either.

"It just didn't work out," O'Neal said of his previous experience playing on a team with two seven-footers.

Shaq wasn't too happy about the prospects of playing for Minnesota, Dallas, Washington or Sacramento, either. He was taking the John Elway approach, using the leverage of the No. 1 draft pick to manipulate the league and get the team of his choice.

While he slammed teams, O'Neal even decided to take a shot at the Houston Rockets for the way they handled a disgruntled Hakeem Olajuwon, who just happened to be represented by Leonard Armato.

"The Rockets have Hakeem and he is one of the best big men in the league, and he's having trouble in Houston," said Shaq.

The only team that O'Neal really seemed to like was the Los Angeles Lakers. "I would love to play for the Lakers," he said. "When I was a kid, I used to watch Kareem play. I always said I wanted to play like Kareem. The Lakers are a nice team, a class organization and they play in a beautiful city."

Of course, it didn't hurt that Armato was based in Los Angeles and would love to have his prize recruit playing in town. Armato had also represented Jabbar and helped him turn around his financial fortunes. The Lakers were also known to be willing to make deals for and pay top money to superstars. General Manager Jerry West had pulled off a remarkable deal to get the rights to Magic Johnson in the 1979 draft.

Overlooking Shaq's negative comments about Orlando, Magic General Manager Pat Williams called his entry into the draft "the most exciting news the league has heard in five years." Williams had no way of knowing that his ballclub was only a month and a half away from coming up the lucky winner in the O'NeaLottery.

"The last marquee big man was David Robinson in 1987," Williams said. "This is a great day for the NBA."

Williams made it obvious that he would take O'Neal with the first choice and thought any other team would be crazy not to take him, even though it was a talent-rich draft. O'Neal's long-time college rival, Christian Laettner, was a senior and would also be available in the draft, as would Georgetown center Alonzo Mourning. O'Neal took great pleasure in the thought of being drafted before Laettner, who had earned all the acclaim and two national titles at Duke and would eventually play for the Dream Team in the Olympics.

The real question in the draft focused on who would be taken after O'Neal. Most experts tabbed Mourning as the likely choice, because he was more physical than Laettner. There was much debate about whether Laettner was capable of making the transition to the physically demanding NBA.

There was no question about Shaq's ability to take the pounding in the NBA. He would immediately be one of the most powerful and strongest centers in the league.

Shaq certainly had no doubts about what he could do at the next level. "Entering the NBA will be a learning experience," he acknowledged, but in the same breath, added, "If I'm not dominant in my first year, the latter half of my NBA career, I will be a force to be reckoned with."

Speaking of Shaq

Matt Guokas
Vice president and former head coach of the Orlando Magic

"I was like most people who wondered why LSU didn't do better with outstanding players like Shaq, Chris Jackson and Stanley Roberts. That was such a great team, but they never played like they were capable of playing. Of course, you have to keep in mind that college basketball is so different from the pros, because of all the zone defenses. I didn't get to see what Shaq could really do because he never had the ball. Chris Jackson did most of the shooting and had the ball most of the time.

"I got to know Chris very well before the 1990 draft. We brought him in for a draft interview and were strongly considering him as our pick (at No. 4). But of course, Denver took him before we could. He's a fine young man. He's very well spoken and had nothing but good things to say about Shaq and Stanley. He said Shaq was really a warrior.

"With all the hoopla and fanfare and expectations thrust upon him—no player has ever had that much, not even Michael Jordan—Shaq has really impressed me with the way he's handled himself. He's remarkable for being only 21 years old. There are already tremendous demands on NBA players, but his are so much greater. I don't know how he does it all and still remains such a fun-loving, easy-going guy.

"Now Shaq had a lot to learn when he came to us and he still does have many things he needs to work on. Training camp was tough on him, but it's tough on every rookie, no matter where you played college ball. Camp was very difficult on Shaq, but he eventually recovered from the long workouts.

"The difference between Wilt Chamberlain, who I played with and against, and Shaq is that Wilt had better developed offensive skills. Wilt got the ball all the time in college. Shaq didn't. Zones make it very tough to develop in college basketball. But Wilt had some good offensive moves when he first came into the league. Shaq still has to learn some.

"Another difference was Wilt's tremendous competitiveness. The true mark of a great player in this league is making everyone else around you better and ultimately winning championships. Shaq has a ways to go there.

"Of course, we still have a ways to go as a team. We need to add some players who can help Shaq. Right now, we're looking for some more good athletes who can go along with Shaq. It really doesn't matter what position they play.

"The great time demands on Shaq detract from what he was able to do as a rookie. We've got to work around his demanding schedule. But it's got to be done. He needs to put in the time to improve his offense. He needs to work on some moves, and of course, he must improve on his free-throw shooting. If he puts in the time, there's no limit to what he can do in this league."

sixteen

The $35 Million Lottery

Lotteries with multi-million-dollar payoffs were popping up all over the country. Louisiana started its own lottery in 1992, the same year the state said farewell to what had been its most celebrated athletic attraction, Shaquille O'Neal.

Now it was O'Neal's turn to play the lottery game. The NBA's O'NeaLottery would make Shaq an instant winner to the tune of approximately $35 million. His asking price would be $5 million per year over five, six or seven years, but he would eventually bring home more than that.

While O'Neal was about to hit the Shaqpot, the real winner would be the team that earned the right to pay him those millions upon millions of dollars. The $35 million investment in Shaq was projected to return dividends of two to three times more. Just as important, the O'Neal deal could turn an NBA cupcake into a championship ballclub within a few years.

"It's going to make May 17 [Lottery Day] a wild

day," Orlando Magic General Manager Pat Williams remarked. "Everyone in the Lottery will be abuzz. If it's Orlando, goody, goody. I think we can make room for him on our roster. He has a marquee name and brings a lot of excitement to the NBA. It's something the NBA needed."

Even though Denver already had one big man in Dikembe Mutombo, Nuggets director of scouting Rob Babcock didn't hesitate in announcing his team's intentions of making Shaq their choice.

"It's a standard for any team to look at a seven-foot, 300-pounder," Babcock said. "Hakeem Olajuwon is like a standard athlete in a bigger size, and Shaquille is like that. It's a very, very rare athlete that has that kind of size and athletic ability.

"He has a long ways to go on the offensive end," Babcock added. "He's a young player, and he has a lot of maturing to do. He'll have to make a lot of adjustments to make it in the NBA. His shooting skills have a long ways to go, but he's got the dunk down."

The Miami Heat, in anticipation of O'Neal's early entry in the draft, had sent Stu Inman, player personnel director, to LSU to watch him practice late in the season. Inman had this evaluation: "He's an extremely bright kid, yet boyish at the same time. He's not ready, but no one at that age is ready for the NBA. He's going to be just a marvelous NBA player. I don't know what he doesn't do well."

During his visit, Inman got a first-hand look at Shaq's fun-loving manner. When Inman walked into the Pete Maravich Assembly Center for practice wearing a Heat sweater, O'Neal quickly noticed him.

"Miami Heat, huh?" Shaq grinned.

"Yes," Inman replied, "and if you're lucky enough, maybe you'll end up with us."

"Alonzo Mourning would have smiled," Inman said later. "Christian Laettner would've given me a blank look. But Shaq broke into this deep laughter. He's a wonderful kid."

Although Inman said it's impossible for a 20-year-old to be ready for the rigors of the NBA, he indicated that Shaq may have an easier time, from an offensive standpoint, than he did in college facing all the gimmick defenses designed to contain him.

"The pro game in many ways will be a little easier for him," Inman remarked. "He'll still get the double-teams, but they won't be able to pack it in on him. And if he gets on a little better team with some good shooters, his passing ability will become a big plus."

Drafting O'Neal "will make some general manager look like a genius, just like Bill Russell did Red Auerbach," Utah Jazz player personnel director Scott Layden offered.

"All of a sudden the Lottery's gotten a lot more attention," said Washington Bullets General Manager John Nash. "He's going to be one of the dominant players in the league beyond the turn of the century. You've got to assume he's going to have as much impact as Patrick Ewing, Hakeem Olajuwon or David Robinson has. He's an awesome talent."

Nash added that O'Neal "has awesome physical strengths and his size alone will make him a dominant player. But he is not just an unusually large player. He has got great jumping ability, good hands and good eye-hand coordination."

Charlotte Hornets coach Alan Bristow predicted O'Neal could lead to a 20 to 30 percent increase in victories for most of the Lottery teams. It could be more than that, Bristow said, if Shaq is highly productive on the offensive end.

"All 27 teams would welcome him," the Hornets coach remarked.

"O'Neal has the same type of potential to become a dominant center in the NBA that Ewing, Robinson and Olajuwon had," Knicks vice president Ernie Grunfeld said. "It might not be in the first year, but to develop into a dominant player, there are no question marks surrounding him."

Some executives in the league speculated that O'Neal could be worth 15 to 20 more wins even as a rookie. The greatest impact ever for a rookie center was Kareem Abdul-Jabbar's emergence with the Milwaukee Bucks, which went from 27 to 56 wins in one season.

The teams most likely to win the Lottery and experience an immediate surge in the win column and the box office were Minnesota, Orlando, Washington and Denver. But at the time O'Neal announced his plans to turn pro, there were still three weeks left in the regular season, enough time for the bottom pecking order to change.

Several teams' general managers said O'Neal's decision would bring unprecedented attention to the Lottery, a system of selecting the draft order for the bottom 11 teams that was put in place in 1985. The team with the worst record would get 11 balls in the Lottery hopper, the second-worst team would get 10, the third-worst nine, and so on through the 11th worst team, which would get only one ball, out of a total of 66. In terms of percentages, the worst team in the league had roughly a 16 percent chance of getting the first choice, while the 11th worst team had only a 1.6 percent chance.

Orlando assistant coach John Gabriel, whose team had one of the best shots at O'Neal even in early April, predicted Shaq would go through an adjustment period, just like most other rookies.

"Ninety-eight percent of rookies go through a rookie orientation period, and he'll be no different," predicted Gabriel. "Nobody is absolved of the learning process in becoming a pro."

However, Gabriel also agreed with many other coaches who said O'Neal would have more freedom in pro ball than he did in college. "It was very, very frustrating to see him play in college," Gabriel recalled. "Teams would put three guys around him when he got the ball, so any way he'd move would be an offensive foul. Every time I saw him he'd have two offensive fouls before halftime."

Concerning the regular reports that O'Neal would demand $5 million a year, even as a rookie, Gabriel was confident he had a way to deal with the potential problem of working O'Neal's salary demands into the $14 million salary cap, which was already being stretched by the Magic.

"I'm probably too dreamy about the whole thing," said Gabriel. "But I'd sit down with Mr. and Mrs. O'Neal

[Harrison] and say, 'Do you want your son to be successful? The only real accolades you get in this game come
when you win it all. And if we haven't got any money left
to build a team around your son, we're not going anywhere.' I know it's his agent's job to make him as wealthy
as he can, but you have to say to him, 'Can you work with
us?' "

If the Magic turned out to be the lucky Lottery
winner on May 17, Gabriel said there "would be no debate
about who we would pick. That'd be a case where you
could take the uniform up there with the name on the
back."

O'Neal and his agent, Leonard Armato, took a self-
imposed mum rule right after Shaq declared his intentions to join the league. As a result, rumors circulated
throughout the country about what was on the future superstar's mind. Many projected that Shaq would demand
to be traded to the Los Angeles Lakers or Clippers, no
matter which team was fortunate enough to win his rights
in the Lottery.

One thing was perfectly clear: O'Neal was going to
be choosy about where he would begin his professional career, even more so than he had been in selecting a college
back in 1988.

Early in May, a report spread throughout the country that Armato had sent a letter to the NBA and the Minnesota Timberwolves stating that O'Neal would not play
in Minneapolis. The T-Wolves had the best shot at O'Neal,
having finished with the league's worst record of 15–67.
The report of Shaq's dislike of Minnesota was first relayed
by a sports agent with connections to Armato. Neither Armato nor O'Neal responded immediately to the report, although Minnesota officials said they had received no such
letter from O'Neal.

Pat Williams, whose Orlando Magic ballclub held
the second position in the Lottery, made it clear that he
would select O'Neal regardless of the player's feelings
about the Magic and the city of Orlando.

"There is certainly an aura about him, but any
comments being made about him now are just hype," said

Williams, who obviously hoped he was right. "It's amazing when you think about it. By no means is he a finished product yet. It's not like he won championships in college."

Another unexpected development in the O'Neal Deal of the Decade was the early talk of multi-million-dollar endorsement contracts, typically reserved for established players. There was little doubt the shoe companies and card dealers believed Shaq would be sensational in the NBA. Rumors had him signing a $1.5 million per year agreement with L.A. Gear for shoes and a similarly priced contract with Classic Trading Cards. That extra income, NBA execs speculated, would make it easier to structure a long-term contract to fit into the league's salary cap requirements and still satisfy O'Neal and his camp of advisors.

In addition to his objections to playing in Minnesota, Shaq had strong reservations about Orlando. The Magic, which finished 21–61 to earn the second position in the Lottery and a 15.2 percent chance of getting the first pick, had one too many seven-footers to please the league's hottest prospect.

Kent Heitholt, sports editor of the *Shreveport Times,* reported correctly that O'Neal and Roberts had bickered and fought throughout their one season together at LSU. Heitholt predicted there was no way they would get along on the same NBA club.

Asked why the Roberts-O'Neal combo had not worked at LSU, Shaq remarked, "Because there's not enough room under the basket for two big men like that." Other players on that LSU team said the real problem was there wasn't enough room for all the egos on that ballclub, particularly Shaq's.

As the days drew closer to the May 17 Lottery, O'Neal maintained his personal vow of silence. He was only the fourth player in the history of the Lottery to be considered a lock for the No. 1 pick. The Lottery debuted in stellar fashion with the hoopla surrounding Patrick Ewing's entry into the league in 1985. Two years later, David Robinson was the talk of the draft and a certain first pick. Likewise, Danny Manning was considered a sure top pick in 1988, although his hype didn't approach that of the previous superstar selections.

The 1992 Lottery focused totally on O'Neal, even though Alonzo Mourning would have been a lock for No. 1 in any other draft since Robinson went out five years earlier. Christian Laettner also could have been a first pick, but in the Shaqpot Draft of '92, he was relegated to possible consideration for the second spot.

Following Minnesota and Orlando as the teams with the most balls in the Lottery hopper were Dallas with nine balls, Denver with eight, Washington seven, Sacramento six, Milwaukee five, Charlotte four, Philadelphia three, Atlanta two and Houston one.

Another recent adjustment to the Lottery guaranteed the team with the worst record at least the fourth spot in the draft. That meant the other 10 teams in the draft could move up into the first three positions, but after that, they would pick in order of their finish in the league standings.

Going into Lottery Day, much of the attention in Orlando centered on what would become of the city's highly popular center, Roberts, in the event that there was magic in the Lottery and the club won the rights to the No. 1 pick, sure to be Shaq. Roberts had just completed a marvelous rookie season and won the hearts of the Magic fans, being selected as the fans' favorite player. A complication was the fact Roberts had signed just a one-year contract and would become a restricted free agent on July 15 and could sign with any team in the league. The Magic would have the right to match whatever offer was made to Roberts, if they could fit it into the cap.

Magic General Manager Pat Williams didn't try to hide the strong possibility that Roberts would become trade bait if Shaq was the team's Lottery prize. "Usually, that comes together on draft night," said Williams. "We don't have to do anything until then."

Gabriel, who had recently been promoted to the Magic's director of player personnel, indicated there could be a possibility of trading the rights to O'Neal or dealing Roberts away.

"You have to look at it both ways," said Gabriel.

"We are enamored with the position and the player [O'Neal]. However, it is a business. We are interested in building this team and we will always do what is in the best interest of the team."

At the same time, Gabriel hinted that the team might try to persuade O'Neal to play alongside Roberts again, given the different demands of the NBA game. "People want to go back to the LSU days, but I think the NBA game is different," explained Gabriel. "We're not sitting here worrying about the dilemma of having two seven-foot centers on our team."

The Lottery finally took place on Sunday, May 17, at halftime of the nationally televised game between the Knicks and the Chicago Bulls. NBA Commissioner David Stern, as usual, had the honor of turning over the cards of the teams indicating the draft order, which had been officially determined earlier by a private drawing of the balls from the hopper by a certified public accountant.

The first team logo turned up in the 11th draft position was Houston, followed by 10th place Atlanta, ninth place Philadelphia, and then came the shocker of the Lottery when Milwaukee turned up in the eighth spot, meaning that Charlotte, with the eighth position going into the drawing, had moved up into the top three. The lucky Hornets were coming off the No. 1 selection of Larry Johnson in the 1991 draft.

"All I could think of was Charlotte had done it again," said Pat Williams later. "I dreaded to think of Shaquille and Larry Johnson on the same front line. I was afraid that was going to happen. I couldn't believe how lucky Charlotte was."

As Stern turned over the next four cards—Sacramento in 7th, Washington in 6th, Denver in 5th and Dallas in 4th—it became apparent that Charlotte was the only team to move up into the first three spots. The No. 1 pick would go to Minnesota, Orlando or Charlotte.

"I didn't enjoy the Lottery at all after Charlotte made it to the final three," recalled Williams. "I couldn't even think about our team getting the No. 1 pick. I was sure it would be Charlotte."

With the tension mounting by the second, Stern went for the card in the No. 3 spot and uncovered the T-Wolves' logo. That left only Orlando and Charlotte. Of course, the odds at that point greatly favored the Magic, which had 10 balls in the hopper as opposed to just four for Charlotte. Nonetheless, Williams said he had a horrible feeling that the day belonged to the Hornets.

However, his suspicions proved wrong as Stern revealed the No. 2 pick to be Charlotte.

"I didn't know how to react," Williams said. "I was just stunned. Naturally, I wanted to rejoice and hug somebody. But who was I going to hug? All the other general managers were upset that they didn't get Shaquille. David Stern had warned all of us not to hug him, because Willis Reed [vice president of the New Jersey Nets] had actually hurt David when he bear-hugged him in 1990 after getting the No. 1 pick for Derrick Coleman. So I just smiled and waited."

Once it became apparent the Magic had won a crack at Shaq, the reaction was not so calm at the team's unofficial Lottery party at an Orlando sports bar. There was wild cheering, high-fives for everyone and lots of hugs. Gabriel embraced Magic head coach Matt Guokas for a long, hard hug. The near hysteria from the Magic staff made it look as if they had actually won the Florida lottery, which had gone as high as $80 million.

"This is thrilling, just exhilarating," exclaimed Guokas.

Gabriel remarked, "We are in complete control" of the draft.

After watching Stern turn over the Magic card, Williams showed off the Orlando jersey with O'Neal and No. 1 on the back of it. "I was no prophet," Williams laughed. "Everybody had a jersey with O'Neal on it. I guess they'll be collector's items."

"We're flying home without an airplane," exuded Williams, the man who would be responsible for bringing this great talent to terms and actually getting him to don a Magic uniform. "This is the most important day in the history of the franchise. We control the draft."

As per instructions from Armato, O'Neal made himself unavailable to the media and issued no statement on the Magic's Lottery victory. But concerns were already mounting that Shaq would not come to the negotiating table with the Magic, a team he had virtually blacklisted from the very day he announced his decision to enter the draft. The central problem was Stanley Roberts's presence in Orlando.

"I played with him in college and that didn't work out," O'Neal said. "I don't think it would work again."

Roberts agreed with his former teammates, saying "We can't do it because Shaquille needs the limelight." So much for college buddies.

As for the financial considerations, Magic owner Rich DeVos, king of the Amway empire, came right out and declared himself willing to meet O'Neal's salary demands. By then, there was talk that he might want more than $5 million per year.

"If we can afford it [within the cap], we'll find a way to get it done," DeVos said on Lottery day. "The amount they're talking about surely doesn't scare us."

"Put two reasonable people in a room together and they ought to be able to come up with something that satisfies both sides," added the team owner. "I presume we'll be able to find a way to sign him."

The only Magic staff member to see Shaq play in person was Gabriel, and he put him in a class with Wilt Chamberlain, Julius Erving, Magic Johnson and Michael Jordan—"players who changed the way the game was played."

"We will be selecting Shaquille," regardless of the salary demands from Armato, said Gabriel.

Guokas said he couldn't imagine not being able to work out a deal to bring O'Neal to Orlando, even if it meant losing Roberts. But the Magic coach expressed a strong desire to put together a Twin Towers concept in Orlando.

"Granted, he's only 20 years old and has a long way to go, but at this point he's got the potential to be up there with the Ewings, Olajuwons and Robinsons," remarked Guokas.

While O'Neal declined to talk about the Lottery, Roberts was clearly dismayed at the prospect of losing his starting position as the Magic's center and being cast into the shadow of O'Neal, as he had been at LSU. Roberts told friends and associates that he definitely wanted out of Orlando if O'Neal signed with the club.

As a restricted free agent, Roberts had to be offered at least a 25 percent raise from the Magic, which would bring his salary to $750,000. But he was asking for considerably more than the minimum increase. His initial demand was $2 million per year.

"I will not accept the minimum raise," Roberts said on Lottery day. "The Magic should be happy to win the Lottery. But me personally? I'm prepared to go on and join another team and make my home elsewhere."

Williams, however, agreed with Guokas as far as wanting to keep Roberts and bring in O'Neal, too.

"Centers are like pitchers in baseball," said Williams. "You never have enough of them."

With that idea in mind, Williams embarked on the precarious assignment of trying to make two big men content and still make the salary cap. It would be the most difficult challenge of his long career in professional sports.

Speaking of Shaq

Brian Hill
Orlando Magic head coach

"When we first started with Shaq, almost everything was new to him: game preparation, walk-throughs, how we defended teams. He had to do so many things that he had never done before, but I think he's done a very good job adjusting. He might have a faraway look in his eyes, but he's still listening and learning.

"Sometimes he's had lapses. He might forget how we're defending the pick-and-roll, or he might forget that we're trapping. But other than that, he's generally in the right place and doing the things that we're asking him to do.

"I think as a staff we all agreed that he was further along with his offensive skills than we thought he would be. He had the footwork and could play with his back to the basket. But we thought he would be further along defensively. That's the area where he's had to learn the most since coming into the league. In college, he was in a situation where he didn't have to prevent opponents from getting low-post position. It didn't matter. He could let them catch the ball in the low post and still go up and block their shots. He never had to put his body on somebody and block them out to get a rebound. He was never in a position where he had to defend the pick-and-roll four, five or six different ways. He just didn't know much about team defense. He spent most of his college career in the middle of a 2–3 zone defense and just had to put his hands up and try to block shots. So I think his biggest adjustment had to come on the defensive end.

"I think he's a fast learner. He's a bright guy and picks things up pretty quickly. I think he's continued to improve as we've gone along and seems to have a better understanding of our offensive and defensive plans.

"But Shaq must learn how to use his body and physical skills. He's got to use them to the utmost. He's made good strides, but he's still got a long ways to go.

"The other players on the team have adapted fine to Shaq. They all know that if we're going to make our move as a franchise, he's going to be the focal point. Everything is going to revolve around him as long as he's with the Orlando Magic. Our guys are all smart guys, and they know he's going to be the focal point.

"Even if we get a player like Chris Webber or Jamal Mashburn, they're going to be complementary players to Shaq. You have to look at the guys available. You wouldn't want to add a power forward who would need to have plays run for him in the low post to be able to score. We *want a power forward who can defend and rebound and block shots. We wouldn't want to run plays for him. Now if we added a small forward, it would be a different story. We could run plays for him outside. But most of the low-post plays would have to be for Shaq.*

"I got to coach Tree Rollins and Moses Malone for four years in Atlanta, but Shaq is the best center I've ever worked with. He's superior to them in his overall skill level, and we're talking about a Hall of Fame center in Malone. Moses is just a very, very hard worker and has a great competitive streak. And Tree Rollins was just a tremendous defender. If Shaq ever gets to become a defender like Rollins, he'll be one of the great centers ever to play the game.

"Shaq is a competitor, but it's hard to tell if he'll be an outstanding competitor. That's something that has to be judged over a long period of time. He went through so much as a rookie in terms of learning the league and handling all the parade of things that have come his way. It took away a lot from what he could do. He'll have a better idea of how to focus on the basketball aspects next year.

"If Shaq wants to become one of the elite centers in the game, he has to have the attitude that he will continue to learn and continue to improve. If he keeps that attitude, there's no question he will be one of the greatest."

seventeen

Deal of a Lifetime

In 26 years of professional sports management, Pat Williams had seen his share of major deals and actually orchestrated some of the biggest moves in sports history. In 1975, Williams was the first general manager in the NBA seriously to consider drafting high school players; he eventually signed Darryl Dawkins to play for the Philadelphia 76ers. A year later, he lured Julius Erving away from the American Basketball Association in a move that many say substantially changed the NBA game. In 1982, he pulled off a sensational trade to bring Moses Malone to Philly, and a year later, the Sixers were the world champions. The very next year, Williams landed Charles Barkley with the fifth pick in the draft, and Sir Charles became one of the game's best and most recognizable players.

But nothing Williams had done with the 76ers, or with the Chicago Bulls before that, came close to the three-month negotiation that amazingly enabled the Orlando Magic to sign Shaquille O'Neal, keep the rights to Stanley

Roberts and still keep a cast of high-paid players around them. Ultimately, Roberts would be traded away in a much-acclaimed three-team deal that sent two first-round draft choices to Orlando and set the stage for the building of another world championship contender, centered around O'Neal.

"As [Charlotte coach] Alan Bristow said this week, 'Whoever wins the Lottery, the village idiot could make the pick,'" Williams recalled in one of the few light-hearted moments during the lengthy negotiations to sign the franchise player. "I appreciate his confidence in me."

Without a doubt, choosing O'Neal was a simple task. However, signing him, keeping Roberts and keeping the other players content would be an order taller than Shaq himself. Williams wondered if he could pull off the most complicated player moves of his career. If he didn't, the critics would rip him to shreds. They were already taking shots at him for his last two No. 1 picks, Brian Williams and Dennis Scott, and rightfully so. Both had been far from the impact players expected with the No. 4 and No. 10 selections in the first round.

If Williams drafted O'Neal and lost him to Europe or a holdout, his future in the league might be in doubt. After all, the Magic was a team on the decline, having won 31 games in 1990–91 and just 21 in 1991–92. Without O'Neal, they wouldn't be expected to win more than 25 in 1992–93. Most executives in the league indicated that Williams, or anyone else, would be unable to sign O'Neal early enough to keep Roberts, who would be getting numerous offer sheets beginning July 15. If Roberts received the anticipated contract of $1.5 million or more per year for three or four years, it would be tough for the Magic to keep him. NBA salary cap rules stipulate that a team can't exceed the salary cap to sign a rookie, hence O'Neal, but can go over the top to match an offer sheet to a restricted free agent. Therefore, the situation was clear: O'Neal had to be signed by early August, so that the club could still match any offer to Roberts. Some general managers figured it would take until November or December before Shaq would come to terms. Others said Williams would be lucky to get his signature as a Christmas present.

Magic owner Richard DeVos gave Williams free rein to try to sign O'Neal soon enough to keep his former teammate, Roberts, whom he didn't like anyway. DeVos would spare no expense to get these two outstanding seven-footers on the roster together.

"People talk all sorts of figures," said DeVos. "If it's something you can afford, you do what you have to do to get it. I presume we can find a way to sign him."

While columnists throughout Florida and the nation were writing that the Magic had to sign O'Neal to save face, Shaq's face was nowhere to be seen. He went into hiding in Los Angeles, where Leonard Armato had set him up an apartment.

The week after the draft, O'Neal finally agreed to issue a statement through Armato. The statement gave some hope for Williams, but stopped well short of a commitment to the Magic. It was obvious O'Neal, per instructions from Armato, was playing coy.

"I am thrilled that Orlando Magic's general manager, Pat Williams, was so excited and sincere about the possibility of having me on the team," O'Neal's statement read. "I was particularly happy to see the people of Orlando so complimentary toward me. I am excited about my upcoming career in the NBA. Soon I will sit down with my family and my attorney to formalize a game plan."

Philip Harrison was tight-lipped about his son's plans. When contacted by the *Orlando Sentinel,* his only comment was, "I have nothing to say. I'm packing so we can leave for Los Angeles."

"Once Shaquille and his family have recovered from the media blitz of the past week, we will sit down and carefully explain to them the various possibilities that exist for someone as coveted and marketable as Shaquille," Armato said. "He thought the things that the Magic said about him were very flattering."

Although Armato told the Florida press that O'Neal liked Orlando and considered it "a beautiful city with hospitable people and experienced basketball management," there was still much talk from the O'Neal camp that he wanted to play in Los Angeles for the Lakers or Clippers and might try to force a trade.

"With Magic Johnson's retirement and Larry Bird nearing the end of his career, there's a little bit of a void in the NBA right now for someone to step in and maybe take the game to an even higher level of popularity," said Armato. "Shaquille could be that person. Certainly, the advantages of playing in a major media center like Los Angeles aren't lost on him."

All the endorsement power of the Shaquille appeal would put him in a position where he could easily forego a season or two of NBA play to get the right situation. Playing a season in Europe would likely force the Magic to trade him to the team of his choice, and he could still make NBA-equivalent money or possibly more overseas. If he sat out one year, he could re-enter the draft. If he opted to sit out two seasons, he could sign with the team of his choice as an unrestricted free agent.

Money would be no obstacle for O'Neal, who had already signed the deal with Classic Trading Cards and was on the verge of accepting a four-year, $20 million contract with Reebok. Nike, Converse and Asics Tiger also made early inquiries into signing him.

Meanwhile, Shaq was turning heads in Los Angeles, dominating the NBA competition in pickup games at UCLA's Pauley Pavilion.

"He has been looking just great," said Pauley Pavilion operations manager Katie Abbott, who had seen many of the all-time greats work out in summer league play. "He's been looking good at just about everything—blocking shots, slam dunking the ball—you name it."

At first, Shaq was going up against former UCLA players like Pooh Richardson and some of the varsity players for the Bruins. But within days, he would begin working out against Magic Johnson and quickly show the future Hall of Famer that he was ready to play with the big boys.

Johnson predicted that with Shaq's signing, the Magic would be instantly transformed from a doormat team to a club capable of contending for the playoffs for the first time in franchise history. "They can be very good," he said. "They should be right there battling for a playoff spot, if everyone is there [the team's veterans]. But I don't think that can happen because with the amount of money he is going to command, somebody has got to go."

Johnson also offered a word of advice to the Magic's future star: Take a lower salary if you want to be part of a championship-caliber team. Magic was the first superstar in the league to take less money to ensure having a cast of talented players around him. The Lakers' long-time star point guard accepted a salary of $2.5 million, well below the price tag for a superstar in the league, so that the Lakers could sign Vlade Divac and keep players like James Worthy, Byron Scott and A. C. Green.

The NBA's salary cap was $12.5 million for the 1991–92 season, but was scheduled to be boosted some 12 percent to $14 million in July. Johnson predicted if Shaq made the bulk of the money on the ballclub, he would have to accept being a virtual one-man team and could forget about challenging for championships.

"He is going to look at what the last guy [Larry Johnson] got last year, and he is going to say, 'Okay, he got three million. I want four or five,'" Johnson projected. "I am not going to condemn him for asking for that, because now that's what's happening. That's the going rate."

At the same time, Pat Williams hoped O'Neal would heed the advice of Johnson and the precedent set by Michael Jordan, who also accepted a below-market salary to guarantee having star teammates like Scottie Pippen and Horace Grant to help the Chicago Bulls remain on top. They had already won two straight world titles and were about to claim a third.

Another bargaining strategy for Williams was to emphasize the enhanced endorsement opportunities for a player on a playoff team. Shaq could sign for $3 to $4 million a year and easily make up the difference in higher endorsement deals if he led the Magic to the top of the Atlantic Division and possibly to the top of the league within a few years. But that could not be done if Shaq was too greedy at the salary table.

Based on the Magic's salary structure, it was obvious the club would have to trade or release some of its higher-paid players or ask them to restructure their contracts to make sacrifices to bring in Shaq. The biggest problem was Dennis Scott, who was scheduled to make $2.4 million for the 1992–93 season, which was way out of line with the limited production he had given the team. Williams would try to trade him away, but could never make a deal for him.

In addition to Scott, veteran power forward Terry Catledge was to be paid $1.6 million and veteran guard Sam Vincent $1.5 million. Starting point guard Scott Skiles was the fourth-highest-paid player on the team at $1.4 million. Former LSU forward Jerry Reynolds, an aging player nagged by injuries, would make $1.4 million as well; giving him a long-term contract was another of Williams's blunders. The team's only other million-dollar player was power forward Brian Williams, due to get $1.01 million for his second year in the league.

The only other Magic players still under contract were: starting shooting guard Nick Anderson, the lone player on the team with a below-market deal at just $800,000; backup center Greg Kite at $900,000, and backup forward Jeff Turner at $700,000.

Joining Roberts as free agents were backup forwards Mark Acres, Sean Higgins and Otis Smith and reserve guards Anthony Bowie and Chris Corchiani.

On contract players alone, the Magic was already committed for almost $12 million and had a mere $2 million left to offer O'Neal and the other free agents.

To pay Shaq, Orlando was expected to release Acres, Smith and Vincent and make minimum raise offers to Roberts, Corchiani and Bowie. The team had until July 1 to make offers to the free agents.

With the rest of the league aware of Orlando's salary structure woes, Williams said he anticipated hearing from some of his colleagues interested in obtaining the rights to O'Neal.

"We are not interested in trading the pick at this point, but we will listen to all the clubs," Williams said.

"There are only a handful of players like this, and you don't trade them."

While NBA rules prohibit teams from signing players before the draft, even obvious No. 1 picks like O'Neal, the league did allow the Magic to conduct salary discussions with him. Williams quickly extended an offer for O'Neal, his family and Armato to visit Orlando and begin the courtship.

In fact, Williams was getting pressure from the media and fans to bring O'Neal to Orlando at any cost. The Magic fans didn't want to miss the opportunity to jump into the big time of NBA basketball and actually begin talking about a championship, rather than discussing where the Magic would finish in the Lottery race.

Yet at the same time, Williams didn't need to be reminded that it would be a disaster if the Magic picked Shaq and failed to sign him or even get something in a trade for him. After all, just down the road from Orlando is Tampa, where the city's NFL club still has egg on its face for drafting Bo Jackson even though he said he would never play for Hugh Culverhouse's penny-pinching team. Bo opted for pro baseball instead of playing for the Bucs and eventually began his football career in Los Angeles playing for the Raiders. A similar debacle could cripple the Magic if Shaq sat out and waited for the chance to play in L.A.

The pressure on Williams and the rest of the Magic organization continued to mount through the long days of May and on into June, leading up to the NBA draft on June 24 in Portland. The fire was fanned as league executives showered Shaquille with praise and made it seem the Magic would be crazy not to get him to sign a contract.

"I see him as a once-in-a-decade type," said Trail Blazers director of player personnel Brad Greensberg. "It's hard to imagine more than one or two guys like him coming out every 10 years. Guys that big, that strong, that athletic, that competitive."

TNT analyst and former Chicago coach Doug Collins rated Shaq "head and shoulders the best player in the draft. He has the strength, speed and quickness, the whole package you'd want. There are a couple of flaws. He has to learn to play in the post and pass out of the double-teams and triple-teams, and at this point, his free-throw shooting is a liability. But coming in, he's on a par with Patrick Ewing at the same stage and probably more advanced than Hakeem Olajuwon and David Robinson. Those guys don't have his strength. They have the speed, quickness, and agility, but not his presence."

"I don't see any drawbacks," Miami Heat owner Billy Cunningham said. "In college, he saw a lot of zones and his supporting cast wasn't good enough. But from what I've seen, he plays for the right reason, which is to win."

NBA super scout Marty Blake added, "I see a great physical player with awesome ability."

Another possible problem facing Williams was the unknown factor of dealing with Leonard Armato. Although Armato represented Kareem Abdul-Jabbar, Hakeem Olajuwon and other players in the league, he was a complete stranger to Williams. In fact, the Magic general manager had never met or even talked to him before the Lottery.

"We had a nice conversation," Williams said of his first phone call to Armato's glitzy Century City office with a view of the Pacific Ocean. Williams didn't have to check with many of his colleagues to learn of Armato's reputation for being a hard bargainer who liked to drive NBA executives to their knees.

Armato, a Brooklyn-born transplant to L.A., was calling all the shots for O'Neal, even though publicly he continued to say he was just "an educator. I will sit down with Shaquille and his parents and try to detail all the options. I will try to present the risks versus certain strategies."

As with his major deals of the past, Armato was totally in control of these negotiations. He would set the ground rules for talks and he would decide if and when Shaq would visit Orlando. He was even calling the shots concerning when and if O'Neal granted interviews with the media. His track record indicated he would throw tantrums with reporters if a phrase or comment was not interpreted or explained to his satisfaction.

Dealing with Armato was expected to make the Shaq negotiations more arduous than they would already have to be. Besides, Armato was already telling confidantes that he encouraged his prize recruit to play in his town of Los Angeles.

Armato, who played college basketball at Southern Cal and the University of the Pacific, got his first taste of professional sports negotiations when he helped form the pro beach volleyball league in 1983. Shortly afterward, he helped restore the financial fortune of Kareem Abdul-Jabbar. Armato hit the front pages again by taking on Olajuwon and immediately earned the label of trouble-making agent in the squabble that most thought would lead to the end of Olajuwon's playing days in Houston.

The Boston Celtics also experienced the wrath of Armato and wound up losing Brian Shaw, yet another of his high-profile clients, who spurned the team's contract offers and took off for a season in Italy. The Celtics charged that Armato actually received a bonus for sending Shaw to Italy.

NBA reporters had called Armato everything from "a snake" to an average agent just looking out for the best interests of his clients. To his credit, Armato had no major squabbles in negotiating deals for Ahmad Rashad, both as a wide receiver and later as a TV analyst.

The calculating agent agreed to let O'Neal make a get-acquainted visit to Orlando the week before the NBA draft. A jubilant crowd of about 200 Magic fans greeted O'Neal at the airport, and the team rolled out the red carpet for the hottest athlete ever to consider playing any sport in the state of Florida.

Accompanied by his father and 12-year-old brother, Shaq visited the Magic's practice facility, Orlando Arena and the Magic Fan-Attic gift shop before meeting with Pat Williams and Matt Guokas.

O'Neal surprised the organization with his comment that he was not overly interested in playing in Los Angeles and considered Orlando to be perfectly acceptable for getting exposure. Shaq explained that far too much was being made of his interest in playing for the Lakers or Clippers.

"The question was 'if you can pick a team, where would you like to play?' And I said L.A.," O'Neal told the Florida media. "They have a major media market out there. My agent said it would be nice to come to Los Angeles, but it's your decision. I think if I can come in here and dominate, then they will find me."

After spending the afternoon with Shaq and his family, team owner Rich DeVos said that this was just the beginning of a long relationship.

"I look upon this as a long-term engagement party," said DeVos. "Today we're announcing an engagement, and we hope we get married pretty quick. I would like to think they would come to believe that we are as interested in him as a person as we are in his basketball ability."

O'Neal's magical welcome to the city of the Magic Kingdom included a billboard along Interstate 4 that read, "Welcome to Orlando, Shaq!" The front-page headline in the *Orlando Sentinel* added, "Welcome to Town, Shaq."

The sure No. 1 draft pick was openly touched by the show of affection from the team, the fans and the city. "Orlando is a beautiful city," he remarked. "This is a real classy organization."

Although described as a pre-draft interview, the visit was more of an effort by everyone associated with the Magic to convince Shaq that he would be happy and successful with the ballclub.

"Our interview process was not too complicated," Williams offered. "We had an exciting day."

"Since the Lottery, there have been all sorts of rumors about Shaquille," added Williams. "We've never had a chance to meet each other, to know each other."

The issue of money and other contract details was not discussed during this get-acquainted event. DeVos, though, said the club would make a very generous offer and try to get O'Neal under contract quickly, obviously so the team would be in position to match an offer sheet extended to Roberts.

Roberts, of course, was not part of the official greeting party, as the team's management was aware of the friction between the two big men whose paths had already crossed.

"There won't be any hiding of issues on our part," DeVos said. "That only drags out the negotiations and creates hard feeling. We'll lay out the issues and work on them."

Though not much was said about it during the initial meeting, Magic officials were very concerned about reports O'Neal did not want to play for an expansion team and would be willing to leave the country to avoid such a fate. Shaq didn't squelch those rumors at all, remaining very evasive on the subject of where he would play next season.

"I'll play anywhere, even Russia," he said with a poker face. "I just want to play."

Asked if he would be satisfied playing in Orlando for the Magic, O'Neal remained noncommittal, as Armato had surely instructed him to be, saying again, "I just want to play."

Certainly, Williams and the other Magic officials were hoping for a somewhat warmer response, but they realized it was primarily a bargaining strategy that was being carried out by perhaps the biggest bargaining chip ever to hit the NBA.

At a planned press conference near the end of his visit, O'Neal was asked about the lofty expectations being tossed his way. He commented, "I'm kind of used to it because when I started high school basketball in San Antonio, I was the biggest thing out there. They always expected good things out of me. So far, I've come to the challenge, but at this level, there are only a few players who come off the college level and onto the NBA level and dominate."

"What are your dreams for the future?" a reporter asked.

"One, to be happy. Two, to have fun. Three, to take care of my family, and four, to win an NBA championship," he replied. "I've won every kind of championship imaginable except college and NBA."

Pat Williams answered the next question for

O'Neal, who was asked if he thought the team was trying to sell itself to him.

"I think this day has been one of getting to know each other," Williams said. "Since the Lottery, there has been an enormous amount of publicity, there have been all sorts of rumors and cross-rumors and we never had a chance to meet each other. We don't know each other, have never really seen the facilities, and that's what today is, a getting-to-know-you day. I think as we go into the draft next week, it certainly makes everybody more comfortable. We're developing a friendship. Knowing of Sgt. and Mrs. Harrison's commitment to family and the values they have, I think far beyond the finances of this is their concern that their son is going to be in the right hands."

Philip Harrison added his thoughts on the day, saying, "People have been really professional, really kind, really generous, and really, really impressive."

O'Neal was also cautious in stating his expectations for his early years in professional basketball. He refused to put himself in the class of the all-time greats, even though most of the league's experts seemed to be reserving him a spot there already.

Concerning the possibility of a long negotiating process, Shaq said he was prepared to be patient. Williams and his associates had to be concerned that O'Neal might stall his contract talks to ensure Roberts's departure from the team, even if it would ultimately hurt the ballclub and Shaq's chances of being on a winning team.

"Patience is the best virtue," remarked O'Neal. "I'm going to be real, real patient. I'm going to make the best business decision possible."

After the first contact with Shaq, both sides laid low and waited for the actual draft day. Even though the draft was a mere formality for Shaq, he brought a group of 32 friends and relatives with him to enjoy the magic moment in Portland. Naturally, Shaq picked up the entire tab of airline tickets, hotel rooms and meals. By then, he had already signed for an estimated $4 million in endorsement earnings and more was sure to come, not to mention the $35 million or more that he was expected to receive from the Magic.

Clever as ever about his demeanor, Shaq shrugged off the significance of the occasion, saying, "It didn't feel like a different day. Today was just a day."

The night before the nationally televised draft, he stayed in his hotel room and relaxed peacefully. No celebrating. Certainly no trouble sleeping on his part.

"I slept good," Shaq smiled. "I watched 'MacGyver.' He made a bomb out of deodorant. Then I went to bed."

Just to make sure he didn't run into any bad luck, he avoided busy city streets. "I didn't want to go outside and get hit by a car," he explained.

On the night of the draft, the top 14 draft prospects gathered in a large conference room under the stands in Memorial Coliseum. Shaq sat at his own table, calmly skimming through a basketball magazine. He stared at a picture of himself calling for the ball. The caption read: "Can Shaq Hack It?"

Not showing any reaction to the slap at him, he turned the page and continued his vigil, waiting to be the first player chosen. Commissioner David Stern, who had earlier hugged O'Neal like the new king of the league that many thought Shaq would become, came into the waiting room and shook hands with each of the players, saving Shaq for last.

"What are you doing today?" Stern joked.

Shaq smiled and sat back down. Stern stayed with him a minute and massaged his huge shoulders as if he were his own son.

One by one, the other players began to filter out of the room and into the arena. Shaq waited until they were all gone before he got up and strolled out to take the spotlight for the Shaq Show.

A packed house in Portland and a half-full arena of Magic fans in Orlando had to wait the full five minutes as Pat Williams teased America by stalling before telling Stern he had selected Shaq. The Magic fans came to their feet and broke into a wild celebration in the O-Rena, while in Portland there was loud applause to welcome the next star into the league.

Wearing a dark green suit, Shaq beamed as he went up to shake hands again with an equally jubilant Stern.

"The pressure's all off now," O'Neal said. "Now there's no question. It's official. I remember on Lottery day when Pat Williams held up my jersey with my name on the back. I felt very proud. They are a good young team."

Not wasting the opportunity to take a slap at Roberts, Shaq added, "All they've lacked is a good center in the middle."

O'Neal predicted a successful future for himself, but didn't say exactly where his future would be played out. He also stopped short of promising a championship.

"Things take time," said Shaq. "But I'll learn the ropes, get my feet wet, and after that, I'm going to be a good player. I think I'll be pretty hard to stop."

Back in Orlando, Magic fan Ned Campbell called Shaq "a franchise player. Orlando's trying to be a big-league town, and if they can land Shaquille O'Neal, they just might make it."

"We're all kind of giddy," Magic promotions and assistant Jodie Pennington said. "Shaq will be idolized here. He already is."

As for the rest of the draft, the Charlotte Hornets surprised no one by taking Georgetown center Alonzo Mourning, and Minnesota followed the expected selection order by taking Duke center Christian Laettner, marking one of the few times he finished behind Shaq. Dallas used its fourth pick in the draft to select Ohio State guard-forward Jimmy Jackson, who would turn out to be the toughest player to sign in the draft.

After the first four picks, considered locks anyway, there were back-to-back surprises. Denver fooled the draft experts by opting for Notre Dame forward-center LaPhonso Ellis, and Washington selected North Carolina State forward Tom Gugliotta.

Sacramento also veered off the expected path of taking Stanford forward Adam Keefe, instead going for a physical guard-forward in Maryland's Walt Williams. The eighth pick sent Arkansas guard Todd Day to Milwaukee as the first of three Hogs taken in the first round of the draft. Arkansas center Oliver Miller was tabbed by Phoenix in the 22nd spot and teammate Lee Mayberry, a point guard, went to Milwaukee at No. 23.

The other interesting developments in the first round included a trade made by the Detroit Pistons that sent backup center William Bedford and their first-round draft pick, UCLA center Don McLean, to the Los Angeles Clippers for center Olden Polynice and two second-round picks.

Other than that, the night belonged to O'Neal and the Magic. But as soon as the draft hoopla ended, the real chore began. Williams and his staff had to find a way to get enough digits on a contract to satisfy O'Neal, and more importantly, the unpredictable Armato. Timeliness was also a key factor as the Magic didn't want to lose the rights to Roberts, even if he didn't want to play with Shaq and O'Neal didn't want to play with him.

Right away the Magic got some good news when O'Neal agreed to leave from Portland to go to Orlando for a weekend of Mickey Mouse and some preliminary contract talks.

O'Neal made an immediate splash in Orlando when he arrived at the airport wearing a pair of Mickey Mouse ears and singing his version of "Shaqie Mouse" in front of another festive crowd of 200 Magic fans, all of whom hoped this would be the trip that would convince the team's top draft pick to become its starting center. This time O'Neal was joined by his entire family and Leonard Armato. Shaq and his family were going to spend a fun weekend at Disney World while Armato planned to continue negotiations with the Magic. Before they split up, though, the whole Shaq contingent stopped for a press conference at the airport.

"We thank you, fans, from the bottom of our hearts for coming out," Williams said. "This is a wonderfully warm reception that you have given to Shaquille and his family. We are really grateful. It shows what kind of basketball enthusiasm there is here in Orlando over this special occasion."

Magic head coach Matt Guokas was also on hand to welcome his new prospect to town. "This just goes to show you the kind of excitement that can be generated when you draft number one and you draft a player the quality of Shaquille O'Neal," said Guokas. "It's certainly going to give the Orlando Magic a presence that we can build around. These have been some tough months where we've had to do a lot of talking and a lot of getting ready. I'll be honest with you, I'm looking forward to the first day of training camp in October when we get all of our team around Shaquille O'Neal."

Guokas went on to call this "a great night for you, the fans of Orlando, and a great night for our franchise."

Once again appreciative of the hoopla, O'Neal thanked the fans for welcoming him and his family to Orlando. Then he made some general remarks before fielding several questions from the press.

"I know I'm capable of playing," Shaq said. "I'm just going to come in and learn the rules. Once I get my feet wet, it's going to be hard to stop me."

The first question from the media concerned the possibility of the Magic winning a championship in his rookie season. Saving his smiles for later, Shaq answered, "Anything can happen. You just need to develop the right chemistry, play hard and play together. Maybe we can, maybe we can't. I'm just going to come in and play hard."

"Will you play a major part in the negotiations?" he was asked.

"I'll probably just leave it up to Leonard and my father, whoever else wants to get involved," O'Neal said. "I probably won't show up."

"Who do you pattern your game after?"

"Myself, myself," he said, smiling this time. "I'll probably look at Patrick Ewing, David Robinson, and Hakeem Olajuwon. They're the three best big men. I'll probably just emulate what they do, plus I'll add a little of my own razzmatazz."

After his brief chat with the media, Shaq was off to

see Mickey Mouse and enjoy his weekend, while Armato and his father discussed options with the Magic management. Actually, Armato had started preliminary talks two days before the draft. Both parties examined all the possible angles of getting an acceptable contract on the table in time to sign Roberts too. The problem was the Magic's near-full salary limit. The team would need to set aside $3 million or more for the first season to get O'Neal. Pat Williams discussed the possibility of a trade, which seemed to ruffle Armato's feathers, so the subject was immediately dropped. Armato was given an opportunity to come up with a proposal that would work for Shaq and somehow fit into the salary cap restrictions. He left town having established a cordial relationship and then began to try to create a package that would work. He sent daily faxes to Williams, and even though he didn't return to Orlando, the negotiation process moved swiftly.

Since time was such a critical factor in regard to keeping Roberts, Magic CEO Dick DeVos didn't try to hide the fact they were ready and willing to make Shaq the richest rookie in the history of all professional sports. "We're ready to move as quickly as he is," said DeVos.

Armato and the Magic execs had some fruitful discussions over the weekend. But ultimately they'd agreed there was no way to put together an acceptable contract for O'Neal until the Magic cleaned house and got rid of some salary suckers.

On July 2, the team made its first attempt at a major move by trading backup center Greg Kite to the Houston Rockets for a couple of second-round draft picks. That would have sliced $900,000 off the club's salary list, but three weeks later, the Rockets nixed the deal after Kite failed the team's physical due to an irregular heart beat. "This is a major piece of adversity," said Williams, who knew it would be only a matter of days before Roberts was offered a contract from one of the several teams interested in him.

Two days later, Williams took a rare day off to go horseback riding with his daughter. When he got back to his car, the car phone was ringing. His wife, Jill, was on the other end of the line, relaying the expected news that Roberts had been signed. The Dallas Mavericks had extended a five-year, $15 million contract.

That same evening Roberts's agent, Oscar Shoenfelt, delivered the offer sheet to Williams's office. Williams, surprised that the agent didn't just send it by overnight mail, stopped by Shoenfelt's hotel room that night.

"Why did you waste your money to fly here with the offer?" he asked the agent.

"It wasn't my money," Shoenfelt answered.

"Then why did you waste Stanley's money?" Williams inquired.

"It wasn't Stanley's money, either," replied the agent.

Williams immediately understood that the Mavericks had sent Shoenfelt as a courier. The Dallas club wanted to establish July 23 as the first day of the 15-day period extended to the Magic to match the offer sheet. That, of course, meant the monumental O'Neal deal had to be closed within two weeks or the Magic would lose the rights to Roberts.

Within days, Williams began a series of a dozen conference calls with Armato and the rest of the Magic executive staff. The hard-bargaining agent, realizing the strength of his position, stressed that his client had to come away from the table with the largest contract in basketball. They continued to discuss trading away current members of the Magic roster and restructuring the contracts of others.

Scott Skiles had already agreed to restructure his contract for a savings to the team of $100,000. The Magic management then turned to aging veteran Jerry Reynolds, who agreed to take a cut in pay for the upcoming season if the team could swing a loan for him. Reynolds owned a successful nightclub in town called Heroes. The Magic got SunBank to rush through a loan for Reynolds, and he agreed to a new contract.

The next restructuring proposals didn't work out. The attorneys for Terry Catledge and Sam Vincent balked at such talk. The same held true for Dennis Scott's agent. He would agree to take less than the 30-percent raise built into his contract only if he were given a longer contract, and the Magic didn't want to do that, considering Scott's injury problems and questionable consistency.

On August 3, there was a major breakthrough. The Milwaukee Bucks agreed to consider taking Vincent off Orlando's hands, and Catledge's attorney had a change of heart, telling Williams, "I don't want to be the one to make you look bad if this deal doesn't work."

The biggest news of the day came from Armato. He agreed to the type of long-term package that the Magic were offering—a six- or seven-year deal worth $35 million or more. The Magic didn't have the money under the cap yet, but Williams was working around the clock to get it.

The next day, more progress was made as Catledge was contacted in Tupelo, Mississippi, and agreed to fly right in to sign a new deal. Then Bucks coach Mike Dunleavy, on his way to the airport heading to the Olympic Games in Barcelona, called to approve a trade of Vincent for the Bucks' Lester Conner. That would free another $600,000 in cap money.

On August 5, the final pieces of the most intricate puzzle in pro sports history were put together. Catledge arrived in town to sign his new contract, and Lester Conner agreed to sign a contract for less money for the upcoming season with a view toward a later hike. That freed up enough funds to complete the O'Neal deal, so Armato flew to Orlando in the afternoon and Shaq flew into town in the evening, along with his family.

Two reporters from the *Orlando Sentinel* got wind of O'Neal's flight into Orlando International Airport and immediately headed to the airport, realizing this was *the* event the whole city had been waiting for. The *Sentinel* reporters were at the gate to meet O'Neal and his family and ask for a comment on the impending close of the contract talks. Shaq just smiled at them and kept walking, despite their requests for a comment. Philip Harrison, too, refused so much as a hello.

"Please, how about a comment?" one of the reporters asked politely as he followed Shaq and his father.

All of a sudden, Harrison swung around and

caught the reporter with his shoulder, knocking him backwards. The sergeant smirked and kept right on walking.

In spite of the tight-lipped approach of Shaq and his father, the *Orlando Sentinel* broke the story of his arrival and the completion of the negotiations. Armato and the Magic management also refused to comment, but another player's agent confirmed that the deal was done.

On August 6, the next-to-last day before the deadline for matching Roberts's Dallas offer, the Magic received Conner's contract and renounced the rights to Sean Higgins, providing just enough room under the cap to fit in Shaq's first-year salary of $3.5 million. Later that day, the official contract was announced as a seven-year, $42-million arrangement, with a peak salary of almost $9 million for the 1998–99 season.

O'Neal signed the contract at 2:15 p.m. in Room 1404 of the Omni Hotel, across the street from the O-Rena. The contract was signed on top of a piano and immediately rushed to the NBA Office in New York.

The next day, the NBA approved the O'Neal deal, enabling the Magic to match the $15-million offer sheet for Roberts and cap an incredible two weeks of whirlwind negotiations, the likes of which had never before been accomplished.

"What the Magic have done basically is shock the world," said Armato, who was given much of the credit for interpreting the salary cap moves. "No one believed they could sign Shaquille. Even I had my doubts. They manipulated the salary cap in unprecedented fashion. It was an incredible feat."

An exhausted, yet overjoyed Williams said, "I don't ever want to hear the word restructure again. It was extremely difficult and complicated, but give our players credit for helping us get this done. It proves that they want to play with a potentially great player like Shaquille O'Neal."

The historic negotiations also marked the earliest signing of a No. 1 pick since the institution of the salary cap in 1983. In fact, it had been six years since the last No. 1 pick had made it to training camp at all.

"I wanted to be in training camp," said O'Neal,

"and I wanted this done as quickly as possible, so I'm very happy. I feel like with the players we have, we're capable of making the playoffs next year if we work together. I like the talent on this ballclub."

For Roberts, it was not such a happy occasion. He had hoped to be heading to Dallas to play with rookie Jimmy Jackson and a rebuilding Maverick club, which could have used him as the star center. Roberts, who had come on strong late in the year for the Magic and solidified himself as the team's starting center, realized his playing time would be greatly reduced with O'Neal around.

"It's LSU all over again," Roberts remarked. "I was second-best to him at LSU, and people are going to consider me second-best to him here. He could have had it all here in Orlando, and I could have had it all in Dallas. I got mixed emotions how this turned out. I don't know what to think."

While the Magic thought it had landed two outstanding young seven-footers in two weeks, Roberts sent word that he wanted out of the Shaq Kingdom.

Speaking of Shaq

Pat Williams
Orlando Magic general manager

"We had to be negotiating Shaq's contract, while we were trying to raise the salary cap level, while we were trying to decide what to do with Stanley Roberts, while we were trying to decide what to do with some of our other veterans. Without question, that was the most difficult challenge in my professional career. There's nothing close to it. Whatever would have been the second-most difficult negotiation, maybe signing Julius Erving or the trade for Moses Mal-

one [with the Philadelphia 76ers], wasn't even close to this.
There's probably never been anything like this done in the
history of sports.

"There were some dark days in July. We had lots of
hurdles to overcome in order to sign Shaq and keep
Stanley Roberts. The salary cap was the biggest obstacle.
We had to create room when it wasn't really there, and of
course, we had enormous time pressure after Dallas signed
Stanley. There were some scary times. We wondered if we
could ever come to terms with Shaq and tie together all the
loose ends. We had to get five contracts restructured with
all those technicalities involved and get it all approved by
the league within 15 days. Imagine all those lawyers involved and getting them all to cooperate. It was really, really tough. I doubt that there has ever been such an intricate negotiation process involving so many players and
personalities. It was very fulfilling to get it all done.

"We needed cooperation from all those players and
all of their agents, particularly Shaquille and his agent,
Leonard Armato. We had to convince Shaq that this was in
his best interest. He had to see the vision of moving early.
There was pressure on them, too. If we matched the offer
for Roberts before we signed Shaq, then there would have
been no money left to sign Shaq. And we fully intended to
match on Roberts. We were not going to just let him walk
away. I think all of those issues came to a head. Fortunately, Shaq and his family and his advisers realized the im-
mediacy of the situation. We were definitely going to match
on Roberts and then try to work something out with Shaq.
We stressed to Shaq and his advisers that we needed to
work as partners. We told them that they were going to get
a good deal, but that there were larger issues involved.
And they understood that. They really worked well with
us. They were terrific. It was a joint effort.

"This was one of the most incredible experiences in
my life, beginning with the Lottery selection. When we got
the first pick, my feeling was shock, disbelief, joy. I was
completely stunned. Actually, I thought it might be Charlotte. They were a developing young team and all of a sudden, it came down to us and Charlotte. I was afraid they

were going to get it. That was the immediate fear. My reaction was: 'This is terrible. They're going to get O'Neal.' But of course, we were the fortunate ones. I leaned over to get a good angle on the team logos as Commissioner Stern turned them over. When I saw the wings of the Hornets in the No. 2 spot, then I knew we had won. So I only had a moment to prepare myself. It was an incredible moment. I tried to be conservative and not show how excited I really was. I didn't know quite what to do.

"Shaq only visited with us once before the draft. He flew over in a private plane with his father and his brother. It was a typical pre-draft interview. We insisted that he have the opportunity to meet us and of course, we wanted to meet him. We did not want him going into the draft in Portland without having met us. We wanted to at least have some idea what his prospective employers were like. He was cordial, but guarded. He seemed very interested and curious, but he contained his feelings very well. They were not going to be gushing with compliments.

"After the draft, we flew them all back to Orlando. The next day was the first time that Shaq stood up and said, 'I want to.play basketball in Orlando.' He had been saying that he just wanted to play in the NBA. But he added that he wanted to play in the NBA and in Orlando. That was met with great enthusiasm and great excitement on the part of our team and fans. Then we got started with the negotiations.

"Once we signed Shaq and matched on Stanley, we weren't sure what we were going to do. We considered Stanley to be an outstanding asset, and we considered trading him, of course. We also thought about playing him with Shaquille and see how that worked out. But we always knew that there would be an option to trade him. Then when that three-way deal came up, we could see it was probably best to move. He had a huge contract. In the worst case, he could get hurt and we'd be stuck with him. There were a lot of bad thoughts going through our minds. There were some good ones, too. We thought we might end up with a better deal later. But we finally decided to grab the chance for two No. 1 draft picks. I guess mainly we

were afraid of that big contract and that Stanley might not be happy playing with Shaquille. There was a lot of that fear.

"We never realized what Shaq would mean to the organization and the community. He's bigger than we could have imagined. It's almost like a rock star. He's known nationally and internationally. There has been a great clamor for him. I don't think anybody could have imagined this. Our main thoughts were on what kind of player he would be and how we would build a team around him. I don't think we quite grasped the enormity of his following and of his corporate value. I think that left us overwhelmed. I don't think there's ever been a young player to get this much fanfare.

"Shaq jumped right in and contributed. There's no question he made a quick transition. He was one of the better players in the league right away. He was among the leaders in four different categories. He jumped us up about 20 wins, which is extremely difficult, so I think you have to give him an extremely high grade for his rookie season. He just turned 21 years of age, so he's got a long ways to go.

"We still need more talent around him. We probably need another guard. We probably need another rebounder. We just have to keep increasing our talent. It gets harder and harder to add talent as you start winning more games. You really only help yourself through your first draft choice, and we're probably going to pick 11th. We could move up—that one ball out of 66 could pop up in the first three picks (of course, it actually did)—but that's not good odds. It's very, very remote. It could happen, but there's not much chance.

"We have four No. 1 picks over the next two years, so these are two very important drafts for us. We've got to add another nice player. But this is not a very deep draft.

"I think Shaq has a very intense desire to be really successful. I think he wants to improve and realizes the amount of work it's going to take. He's physically gifted, but to get to that next level, he's got to work very hard. He really needs to develop an offensive game."

eighteen

Induction to the League

Forty-two million dollars aside, Shaquille O'Neal made a lasting first impression on his new teammates with the Orlando Magic. For one thing, he didn't come to town acting like a rich young superstar. He paid his proper respects to the veterans on the ballclub, first by acknowledging Scott Skiles's NBA record of 30 assists: "Man, I watched you that night on TNT. You were great."

Then the new kid on the block (who had enough money to buy the entire block and soon the franchise, too) showed even more respect in not putting up a fuss when veteran forward Terry Catledge refused to relinquish his rights to No. 33, which Shaq had worn throughout his college and high school basketball career. By virtue of his immediate status on the team, Shaq could have had any number he wanted.

"That's my number," said Catledge, a seven-year veteran and one of the original members of the Magic. "I'm a veteran. He's a rookie. When I was drafted, I wore

No. 23. When I was traded to Washington, somebody else had 23, so I had to take another number. That's the way it works."

Catledge did suggest they discuss the number problem after O'Neal signed and came to camp, but Shaq said that was not necessary.

"I'm going to always be a team player," O'Neal said. "If he doesn't want to give the number up, then I'll find a new number. Numbers don't make players, players make numbers." Shaq told "Cat Daddy" to keep his number; he himself would take No. 32. Chalk up another one for the respectful rookie.

By mid-August, the Magic and the NBA had already started ordering "Shaq Attack" jerseys with No. 32 on them. The authentic jersey would sell for $120 and the replica for $39. Magic executive vice president Jack Swope said the team expected to sell from 10,000 to 20,000 of the jerseys.

Some people around the league speculated that Shaq chose No. 32 because of its superstar lineage. The number was previously worn by Magic Johnson, Julius Erving (in the ABA), O.J. Simpson, Jim Brown, Franco Harris, Marcus Allen, Sandy Koufax, Steve Carlton and, of late, Charles Barkley. "It's the very first number that I wore when I started playing basketball," O'Neal explained.

Finally, Shaq caught his teammates' attention by annihilating Stanley Roberts in summer pickup games. O'Neal made his out-of-shape (as usual) former teammate look like a rookie by rejecting shot after shot. It got so bad that Stan took a quick exit, complaining of a sore leg muscle.

Before getting too involved in Orlando, O'Neal made a trip to Pete Newell's famous big man's camp and was equally impressive against some of the best centers and forwards in the league. Perhaps even more astounding than his showing against top competition was his overall display of power. He damaged all the backboards at the camp, which had seen virtually every outstanding center in the league pass by but had never withstood such a beating.

"Impressive," said Los Angeles Clippers forward Loy Vaught.

"Monster," remarked Kermit Washington, camp director, former NBA center and one-time college rebounding record-holder.

Busy bending rims and backboards and dashing through grueling three-hour workouts, O'Neal declined all interviews at the Newell camp, held on the campus of St. Bernard High School in Playa Del Rey, California, a mile down the road from Loyola Marymount University, the school against which Shaq set a career best of 12 blocked shots during his glorious college career.

For 16 years, Pete Newell had tutored the elite big men in America for a significant fee, usually charged to the players' NBA teams. Dale Brown had tried to send O'Neal to the camp during his college days, but he couldn't work out a way to get it paid for and approved by the NCAA. Hakeem Olajuwon, Bill Walton, Ralph Sampson, Sam Perkins, Stacey King and Ken Norman were just a handful of the NBA pros who prospered under Newell's instructions.

"He's worked as hard as anyone out here," said Newell, impressed that O'Neal, with a $42 million contract, would even bother to show up for extra work. "And he's taken things we've taught him and immediately tried to integrate them into his game."

Former NBA player Stu Lantz, the instructor assigned to the new superstar, laughed when he recalled the way O'Neal bent the rigging for a camera atop one of the backboards. Lantz had been assured by the maintenance crew that the rigging was secure: "There's no way this thing can be brought down," he was told.

"Then Shaquille did it," Lantz said. "He did it Tuesday and he came right back and did it Wednesday. He didn't do it on Thursday. I think Shaquille felt a little sorry for the camera."

Newell, in discussing O'Neal, casually mentioned that the rookie was bigger and stronger than his previous student, Olajuwon. "Hey, it's just the facts," said Newell, when asked if he was serious.

Sam Perkins was standing on the sidelines, well away from the action on the court, when O'Neal spiked a shot attempt by a fellow big man. The ball went flying away like a volleyball and hit Perkins right on the side of his head.

"The guy is huge," Vaught remarked with awe. "I just thank heaven that I'm not a center."

Washington, however, had one concern about young O'Neal. He was worried that his overpowering physical strength might get in the way of his progress in other areas.

"If he learns how to control all that, to not foul," Washington explained, "he'll be the dominant center in the league inside of two years."

Once back in Orlando, O'Neal became an early hit with the local community by pledging to get involved in a number of charitable projects. He even challenged other Florida celebrities to join with him in forming a foundation called "Athletes and Entertainers for Kids." It would be designed to help inner city kids, particularly in the black community, and Shaq wanted to be the first to write a check for the organization.

Hoping to steer clear of the spotlight, at least some of the time, O'Neal said he would take on personal projects that would not have names, but would simply further the goal of helping the less fortunate. He proposed, for example, taking 30 project kids to Disney World and giving them each $100 to spend, or taking a group from a homeless shelter out to eat at a nice restaurant.

"It won't be a media thing," Shaq maintained. "You won't hear about it until it's over. I've been fortunate. I don't need a pat on the back."

As for his own family, O'Neal made plans to buy his parents a new home and refurbish his grandmother's home in New Jersey. He also promised to send a cousin through school at the University of Florida.

Within 15 days of signing his record contract, Shaq became the only big man in Orlando. The Magic, heeding Roberts's request to relocate, came up with a three-team trade that sent Stan off to the Los Angeles Clippers and brought two valuable first-round draft choices to the Magic. The trade was consummated on August 22. The

Clippers received Roberts, New York Knicks troubled point guard Mark Jackson and a second-round draft choice from New York; the Knicks picked up three Clippers, point guard Doc Rivers, shooting guard Bo Kimble and forward Charles Smith; and the Magic received the 1993 and 1994 first-round draft picks from the Knicks.

Suddenly, the Magic had the brightest young star in all of basketball, plus the key draft picks needed to build a strong supporting cast around him. So when the Magic went to training camp in early October, there was no question who would be the focus of all the offensive plans at Stetson University in Deland, Florida, where Matt Guokas and his staff would get Shaq and his teammates ready for a run at the playoffs, something the Magic had not even come close to attempting in their first three years of existence.

Appropriately, the preseason sessions were dubbed "Camp Shaquille." And it was quite a spectacle for the coaches, the veterans and the occasional fans who managed to sneak a peek at the Franchise Man.

Just as he had at Newell's camp, Shaq put on a display of destructive force, ravaging the Edmund Center at Stetson. It took him only three days to leave the rims sagging from the awesome blows of his 300-pound body and muscular arms crashing down on the iron time after time. The Magic gladly footed the bill for repairs to Stetson's equipment and tried to find a new type of rim and support structure to contain him.

Despite his physical prominence, O'Neal made his share of rookie mistakes, and he took time to adjust to the rigors of his first NBA training camp, highlighted by continuous two-a-day practice sessions, the first of young Shaq's career.

A fatigued, somewhat sore O'Neal admitted, "I'm learning the game all over again."

"Any rookie, no matter how good he is, must go through a transition period," Magic coach Matt Guokas said. "Nobody could be ready for an NBA training camp, no matter where you played college basketball or what you've done previously. There's nothing like it.

"Shaquille had a lot to pick up in a short time," Guokas continued. "The terminology was new to him. He wasn't familiar with how to even set a pick or run a pick and roll. So he needed some time to adjust."

To help O'Neal make quicker progress, Guokas assigned veteran Greg Kite and former NBA center Mark McNamara to give him some one-on-one instruction on the finer points of playing center in the league. Kite was impressed with O'Neal's physical talent, but disappointed that the young center wasn't very receptive to advice from veterans who knew the game. Kite was making his fifth stop in nine NBA seasons and had won two world championship rings with the Boston Celtics, so he knew what he was talking about.

When asked if Shaq heeded his advice, Kite answered, "Not really. Sometimes he listened, but most of the time, you got the impression he had his mind made up."

Guokas, though not pleased with O'Neal's early progress, was careful not to make an issue of it. He decided to bring the much-acclaimed rookie along slowly and hope for the best. If he wasn't ready by the start of exhibition play, that would be all right. But with Roberts gone, the Magic had to have Shaq ready to go by the start of the regular season on November 7.

On October 17, O'Neal made his NBA exhibition debut against the Magic's arch rivals, the Miami Heat, an expansion team located 250 miles from Orlando that had come into the league in 1989 along with the Magic. The Heat, however, was coming off a playoff appearance in 1992 and had a huge lead on Orlando as the top franchise in Florida.

As Guokas had feared, O'Neal committed mistake after mistake, but his superior athletic skills and sheer size enabled him to lead the Magic to a 107–102 victory before a hostile crowd in Miami Arena. On the plus side, Shaq contributed 25 points, six rebounds and three blocked shots and basically out-muscled Heat veteran Rony Seikaly, considered one of the better young centers in the league. But in his inexperience he committed nine turnovers, clunked five of his eight free-throw tries and managed to play only 33 minutes, due to foul trouble and fatigue.

Although it was a mixed bag of results, his size, strength and quickness, as compared to Seikaly's, caught the attention of Heat coach Kevin Loughery, who said, "He looked like an unbelievable talent. He's got it all."

O'Neal established his presence in the game right away by swatting away Seikaly's first shot attempt and then causing power forward John Salley to alter his first shot, which sailed over the backboard. The Heat's backup center, Matt Geiger, got four fouls in his first six minutes of trying to match up with the gigantic rookie. Geiger came up with just three points, and Seikaly hit for 12, but only four against O'Neal. As a team, Miami shot just 41.5 percent from the field, largely because the inside was ruled by the rookie.

"It's a whole new world now, Rony," Magic point guard Scott Skiles told Seikaly after Shaq blocked his opening shot.

Miami's double-team defensive strategy confused O'Neal in the early going. He committed six turnovers in the first 16 minutes of play. But gradually he began to pick up the double-team and hit the open man on the wing or throw it back to Skiles at the point.

"He picks things up so quickly," said Skiles. "That's what is impressive, too. Once he figured it out, he was hitting the open man."

Kite, too, praised his fellow center, saying, "There aren't many people in the league who can match up with him."

The next night, though, O'Neal couldn't overcome his erratic play with physical strength and quickness. Facing the Heat again, this time in the Orlando Arena, Shaq did not make a very good showing in his hometown debut. Plagued by foul trouble all night, he produced just 11 points and 11 rebounds before fouling out with six minutes left. Once again, he was turnover-prone and horrendous from the free-throw line. He missed three of four foul shots in his second outing.

Two days later, the Magic headed north for the first time to face the Charlotte Hornets, who were still trying to bring Alonzo Mourning to contract terms. Therefore, Shaq was greeted by the 6-8 tandem of Kenny Gattison and J.R. Reid, who proved no match physically for the 7-1 rookie. Shaq slammed down two early dunks, but then proceeded to miss and miss again on short jumpers and even layups. Bothered by foul trouble for the third straight game, he totaled 22 points and 10 rebounds in only 29 minutes of play.

In his first three exhibition games, Shaq had turned heads with his sometimes frightening, often intimidating display of raw power. But he was giving Guokas and assistant coach Brian Hill more gray hairs with his constant turnover and foul problems. In three games, he had 15 fouls and 19 turnovers. That deficiency would have to be corrected if Shaq was going to make a difference in Orlando right away.

"He is so talented now that without learning anything new, he could be an All-Star every year," Kite remarked. "But if he picks up all the little things, there might not be a limit."

That was a big if, and it was constantly on the minds of his coaches and teammates as Shaq and the Magic went up and down throughout the eight-game exhibition season.

In his fourth appearance, Shaq went up against his old college rival, Christian Laettner, and was embarrassed by the No. 3 pick in the draft. Laettner looked like a polished veteran scoring 25 points and getting 11 rebounds against the taller O'Neal, who was supposed to manhandle him now that they were in the professional game. Shaq did produce 19 points and nine rebounds, but continued to struggle with turnovers and woeful foul shooting.

"Shaq is going to have to learn the discipline of not picking up the cheap, early fouls," Guokas lamented. "He has got to learn how to stay out of foul trouble, so he can stay out on the floor for long periods of time."

By the next-to-last exhibition game, this one in Atlanta, O'Neal was beginning to develop some savvy on the court and get a few more minutes in before suffering with foul trouble. Even though he missed, somehow, on his only two dunk opportunities, he got the best of Hawk centers Jon Koncak and Blair Rasmussen. O'Neal came away from the Omni with 21 points and 19 rebounds. But there was still reason for concern on the offensive end as he missed 15 of his 24 shot attempts from the field and was off the mark on seven of 10 free-throw chances. The Magic won, though, 110–108.

"I'm just trying to play smart and stay out of foul trouble," said a relieved O'Neal. "Like tonight, I just want to keep my composure and not get down on myself after a slow start."

Guokas emphasized that Shaq was doing his job effectively on defense and being aggressive on the boards. As for the offense, "The scoring is going to come in peaks and valleys," Guokas said.

The Magic couldn't have picked a more remote spot to finish up the first exhibition season with Shaq. Orlando ventured to the hinterlands of South Dakota to face the Minnesota Timberwolves at the Rushmore Civic Center in Rapid City. As usual, O'Neal drew a throng of Shaq fanatics both in the arena and at the team's hotel. He obliged the crowd with a strong performance to wrap up the practice schedule, leaving one week for him and his Magic teammates to prepare for the regular-season opener on November 6 at home against the Heat.

There were high expectations placed on the young O'Neal as the No. 1 pick in the draft. He lived up to some of them in the exhibition season. But he fell well short of others, leaving cause for both great hope and serious concern.

Minnesota coach Jimmy Rodgers, whose T-Wolves were the last team to face Shaq before his regular-season debut, said the potential was unlimited for a player with Shaq's physical tools, as long as he learned to make use of them all.

"He's what he's advertised to be," Rodgers said. "Often when you pick No. 1 like that, or in the top five, you think you have a handle on the kid and you think he's going to be something special. Then you get closer and find out he's extra special. He's got everybody excited. He's got a tremendously big upside."

Teammate Scott Skiles, the man most responsible for getting the ball to O'Neal in the post, was in the right place to observe the strengths and weaknesses of the highly touted center.

"I've seen a lot of guys with his kind of reputation," Skiles said. "They come into the league and can either go one of two ways. Shaq could not get any better than he is today and still be a very good player in this league for a long time. Or he could say, 'Hey, I'm going to carry this team.'

"He can start thinking about winning championships. He can start thinking about being one of the best players who ever played the game. He can start thinking about doing all those things and then working very hard to get there. That's what your Magic Johnsons do, your Larry Birds, your Julius Ervings, Michael Jordans. And then there's your Darryl Dawkins.

"Right now, you've got your rookies, they come in, they think they know what it's going to take to play at this level," Skiles continued in his evaluation of Shaq. "And they come in and go through two-a-days for a week. They're already gassed after that because none of them comes in in as good shape as they should because they don't know. Shaq has just unbelievable strength, but if you don't know how to use that to the fullest all the time, what good is having that strength? He's used to not respecting a guy's ability, playing behind him, and then when they throw him the ball, just blocking his shot. What's going to happen here, the guys are going to get position down low, almost under the basket, and he's going to get into foul trouble. They're going to go up, and he's not going to be able to block their shot. But when he realizes he can push them out a little bit, and on the other hand, not let them push him out, he's going to be very hard to handle."

O'Neal had shown a little of everything during the exhibition season, but not a lot of anything. The Magic coaching staff was taking a calm, cautious approach, fully expecting him to develop into a player like Chamberlain or Jabbar, but also knowing he could fizzle like Dawkins or Ralph Sampson.

Speaking of Shaq

Litterial Green
Orlando Magic guard, played against Shaq in college

"Shaquille and I have been friends for three years. His family and my family are very close. So I was extremely happy when the Chicago Bulls traded me to Orlando. It's the opportunity of a lifetime to be playing with the big fella.

"I got to know Shaq from playing against him in college and talking noise to each other during the games. LSU and Georgia were big rivals, and we were the big stars. Before tipoff, he'd walk up to me and say, 'I'm going to get 40 on you tonight.' It was all in fun. It was a competitive thing.

"When we played them for the SEC championship [in 1990], it was the biggest game of my career and probably the biggest game in Georgia history. It was unfortunate for Shaquille and the LSU team because they had played so well in the first half and had a big lead. But it was very fortunate for us. We didn't do anything special. We just went out there and did whatever it took to win, even if it meant scratching and holding and fouling the big guy, which we did. We were going to do whatever it took to win.

"I don't think there will ever be another team assembled like that LSU team with Shaq, Chris Jackson and Stanley Roberts. It just wasn't fair. It didn't make any sense for one team to have three first-rounders like that. They all could have been No. 1 picks. It was just unbelievable.

"In college ball, there was no way to stop Shaq one on one, so you had to put two men around him and just

hope that he passed it out. We didn't want anybody to make him mad and then he would go off for about 40 points.

"Whenever you played them, you just had to be mentally and physically prepared. If you weren't, they'd just come out and blow you off the court.

"I don't know what Shaq did to get ready for the pros, but obviously he's done a great job with all the pressure that's been put on him. It's amazing all the billing that the organization and the league has put on him.

"Shaq is the same player now that he was in college. He's just more mature as a player. As far as his physical attributes, he's exactly the same. He's no better today than he was in college.

"Shaq does his job on the floor. He just goes out there and competes for 48 minutes. He leads by example. That's just the way he operates. Whenever you see a 7-1 guy diving on the floor, it inspires you. He goes out to play hard every night. It doesn't matter if he's playing against Patrick Ewing or Luc Longley. He goes after it every night.

"Money hasn't changed Shaq at all. He's still the same guy he was in college. As a matter of fact, whenever we go out to Bennigan's or Red Lobster, we still fuss over who's going to pay the bill. He's just as cheap today as he was in college."

nineteen

Dynamic Debut

Nothing Shaquille O'Neal accomplished during his exhibition season, not even a highlight film of his finest moments, could have prepared the Orlando fans and followers of the NBA throughout the world for his Shaq-sational debut. When the games really started counting, Shaq proved to be *The Man* that the Magic were counting on him to be.

Up to that point, there had been reason to worry about Shaq and think the NBA's most hyped rookie and the youngest player in the league would take more time than expected to come around. In eight preseason games, he averaged a respectable 17.8 points and 10 rebounds, but many of his points and rebounds came against expansion teams. Even with the lightweight schedule, he looked shaky much of the time, being plagued by foul trouble, turnoveritis, or both. He fouled out of one game in just 18 minutes and exited another with six fouls in just 23 minutes. He averaged over six turnovers a game, including nine in his first outing for the Magic.

While many coaches and executives in the league were tossing praise his way like confetti in a ticker-tape parade, others were throwing up the yellow flag. Magic coaches Matt Guokas and Brian Hill lauded him some days and scratched their heads on other days. Nobody knew what to expect from Shaq early in the season—not even Shaq himself.

"I have no expectations," said Shaq on the eve of his November 7 debut. "I like to experience things for myself. I don't believe in pressure. I don't worry about anything. I'm too young to worry.

"I know there are a lot of expectations for me to become great," O'Neal continued. "If I do become a great center, like Chamberlain or Russell or Kareem, that's good. If not, I'll live a happy life and keep on smiling."

Before the week was over, everyone from Guokas to NBA Commissioner David Stern was smiling about Shaq's smash hit in the league.

Two things worked to Shaq's advantage in his first regular-season game in the NBA. First, the Magic was playing at home in the O-Rena in front of a delirious capacity crowd of 15,151, which would become a familiar sight every time O'Neal stepped on the home floor. Another advantage was playing a familiar foe like Miami, which the Magic had faced twice in exhibition play. Shaq had already manhandled Heat center Rony Seikaly, and there was no reason to believe he wouldn't do it again.

With reporters from all over the nation as well as Japan, Spain, France and South America on hand, O'Neal entered the NBA with a grand display of power basketball, the likes of which the league had not witnessed from a rookie since Chamberlain made his debut in 1959. The only thing that slowed Shaq was himself. He got into early foul trouble and played only 32 minutes before fouling out with 1:32 left. However, before his early departure, he gave the fans and media much to remember, controlling the boards for 18 rebounds and adding 12 points, three blocked shots and two assists. His 18 rebounds were the most for a rookie in his first game since Bill Walton burst on the scene in 1974.

The Heat's Seikaly had 16 points and six rebounds, but didn't try to hide the fact he was out-muscled inside. "You don't realize how talented he is until you play against him," said the Miami center.

The magical rookie stunned the crowd with marvelous back-to-back plays, yanking down a defensive rebound and taking off the length of the court for fastbreak scores that brought the fans to their feet and caused the O-Rena to rock. The first time, he went coast-to-coast for a thunderous slam dunk of his own. Then he decided to play center-point guard on his second full-court flurry, bouncing a no-look pass to teammate Anthony Bowie for an easy layup.

"We had a three-on-one break and I acted like I was going to pass to Dennis Scott," said Shaq, explaining his favorite play of the night. "Then I saw a white jersey out of the side of my eye and I passed to Anthony Bowie for the layup."

When asked if he planned on doubling as a point guard very often, Shaq smiled and said, "If I'm able to do it, I'll do it. I mean it's fun. You know most big guys don't do that."

Not content just to have fun, O'Neal made sure his first game in the league was a victorious occasion. He helped the Magic rally from a 65–55 halftime deficit to take control in the second half and go on to a 110–100 win. His intimidating defensive presence in the middle helped the Magic hold Miami without a field goal for the first eight minutes of the fourth quarter. Orlando outscored its visitors, 29–19, in the final period.

"The big guy's going to be all right," remarked Magic guard Nick Anderson, who was right on target for a game-high 42 points.

"I really didn't know what to expect," said O'Neal. "I'm going to go out and play hard, and if I have a spectacular performance, that's good. But if I don't, I'm not going to get down on myself. The good thing about America is you can always come back tomorrow."

Immediately after concluding his postgame remarks, Shaq had to rush to catch a bus that would carry the team to the airport for a late-night flight on the Magic jet. He got a quick indoctrination to life in the NBA as the Magic had to fly two hours to Washington, D.C., and prepare to face the Bullets the next night in the Capital Centre.

This time O'Neal had to contend with one of most improved young centers in the league, someone he had yet to face. Nonetheless, Shaq went right at Pervis Ellison as if he had been playing against him for years, and he was even more impressive than he had been on opening night.

In helping the Magic shoot out to an early lead, Shaq contributed 16 points in the first half and completely overshadowed Ellison. The second-day rookie made a clutch basket late in the fourth quarter as the Magic came from behind to win 103–96. O'Neal finished with 22 points, 15 rebounds and four blocks. Most impressive was his defensive feat of holding Ellison to single digits. The Bullets' center totaled just eight points and nine rebounds.

Those first two wins set the stage for an incredible conclusion to the Wonderful Week One of the newest NBA star. He had already outplayed two more experienced, albeit young, centers, and the rest of the league was already taking notice.

"He's even more talented than I thought he would be," remarked Magic coach Matt Guokas. "I played with and against Wilt Chamberlain in my day. And he [Shaq] has that same kind of presence. He can do some incredible things."

After a two-day rest, the Magic was back in the O-Rena for back-to-back home games against Charlotte and Washington, which was eager for revenge. The Orlando-Charlotte game would have marked the first matchup of the league's two outstanding rookie centers, but Alonzo Mourning was still holding out for more money. That left the Hornets with 6-8 forward Kenny Gattison to attempt to man the middle against the mammoth O'Neal.

Although it was no contest at center, with Shaq owning his smaller opponent, the Hornets got balanced scoring from the trio of Larry Johnson, Kendall Gill and Johnny Newman and hung in there for a tough road win.

O'Neal delivered 35 points in the first three quarters. But the Hornets' double-teaming defense bothered him so much that he didn't even score in the fourth quarter, which belonged to Charlotte by a 25–17 margin.

The Magic were stung, 112–108, for the team's first loss of the season and first defeat of the O'Neal era. Orlando point guard Scott Skiles said of Shaq, "Double-teams still confused him, but Hakeem Olajuwon hadn't handled double-teams very well until this season. Shaq's within 20, 30 games of figuring that out."

Shaq came back two nights later with a solid performance against the Bullets, who tried in vain to double-team him. While Ellison managed to break through for double-figure scoring against his forceful foe, it wasn't nearly enough to match the production of O'Neal, who came up with his finest all-around showing as a pro. Shaq scored a game-high 31 points and added 21 rebounds and four blocks, compared to 20 points and six rebounds for Ellison.

Supported by Dennis Scott's 27 points and Anderson's 25, O'Neal had no trouble leading the Magic to a 127–100 victory and its first rout of the season. He was now getting the full attention, and complaints, of the opposition.

Washington coach Wes Unseld argued vigorously that the officials were allowing O'Neal to be too physical. "If they let him do what he's doing now, he'll create a whole lot of problems for everybody," said Unseld. "I don't know what they're seeing. I'm seeing off-hand pushing and ducking shoulders into people. He doesn't need to do that. He'll get his points anyway."

It seemed an ironic twist that a Hall of Fame center like Unseld would be arguing that a rookie was being too rough on his veteran center. But what else could he say after Shaq had so thoroughly whipped Ellison, not once, but twice in one week?

The first week of Shaq's arrival on the NBA scene came to an end at the Meadowlands Arena, where the Magic met division rival New Jersey for the first time. Taking the assignment of confronting the red-hot rookie was aging veteran Sam Bowie, who had averaged 28 points a game against Orlando the previous season.

Bowie, the former Kentucky standout, was not up to the test of matching his lean frame against the mountain at center for Orlando. Shaq outscored him, 29–10, and took an even more commanding 15–2 advantage on the boards. But that was not enough as the Magic, who had lost Terry Catledge to a knee injury and Brian Williams to dizzy spells, had no one to contend with Nets All-Star forward Derrick Coleman and surprising small forward Chris Morris. Coleman came through with 30 points and nine rebounds, while Morris was brilliant with 32 points and 13 rebounds.

Anderson did all that he could to complement O'Neal, hitting all 14 of his foul shots and totaling 34 points. But Scott missed eight of 12 shot attempts and added only 10 points for the night. That was not nearly enough as the Nets raced away for a 124–113 win.

Even though Orlando closed out the week on a losing note, its 3–2 record was a solid start to what promised to be a much improved season as compared to the previous year's 21–61 showing.

The biggest difference, of course, was the 7-1, 305-pound man-child who was still not of legal age, but had already caused a rage in the NBA. After one great week, O'Neal led the league in rebounding at 16.4 per game, was tied for fourth in scoring at 25.8, fifth in blocked shots at 3.4 and ninth in field-goal percentage at 57.0.

His amazing debut brought an equally remarkable honor. O'Neal became the first rookie in history to be named NBA Player of the Week in his debut week. This wasn't a rookie award. Shaq had outperformed Michael Jordan, Charles Barkley, Patrick Ewing, David Robinson and the rest of the Dream Team. For the first five games of the year, he was the best player in the world.

Another Dream Teamer, Karl Malone, led the league in scoring for the first week, averaging 31.2 points, but didn't have the all-around dominant showing of the Magic rookie. Other runners-up to Shaq were Barkley, Shawn Kemp of Seattle, Blue Edwards of Milwaukee and

Terry Porter of Portland. Jordan, despite averaging 29.5 points, was not a finalist for Player of the Week, which had been awarded since 1978.

"The only award I really work for is to help make us a winner," said a humble O'Neal. "This is a credit to both our coaches and my teammates who helped me get ready to start the season."

"He may be only 20 years old, but he is a very mature basketball player," Guokas said. "It's a great award for him. But as he learns the game, those numbers are only going to get better."

No doubt O'Neal benefited from an unusually soft schedule for the Magic in the opening week. In its first five games, Orlando encountered just one team (New Jersey) that would eventually have a winning record and make the playoffs. Shaq had also gone through his first five games without going up against one of the top centers in the game. That would soon change, as his first date with Ewing and the bump-and-bruise New York Knicks was right around the corner.

Shaq, though, seemed unconcerned about the more difficult tests to come.

"I want to play against anybody: Ewing, [Hakeem] Olajuwon, [David] Robinson," O'Neal said. "I just want to play because you learn from experience.

"I'm trying to play hard and dominate," he added. "It's still a new game for me, so to speak, and I think when I get my feet wet, I'll really be hard to stop."

Bowie, Ellison and Seikaly would argue that he was already hard to stop. They certainly weren't looking forward to playing against a more polished O'Neal.

NBA officials, meanwhile, were exuberant over the incredible start of the Orlando rookie and were quick to begin promoting their newest superstar. Just when the league needed a successor to Bird and Johnson, O'Neal popped on the scene like magic.

Speaking of Shaq

Dennis Scott
Orlando Magic forward and one of Shaq's "Young Guns"

"We want to take advantage of any opportunity we get to utilize Shaq inside. Whenever we play against a team that doesn't have a big man who can guard him or even come close to stopping him, then we're going to go to our low-post game. If they go to a double-team, we're still going to get the ball down there and we know he's going to pass back out, so we can get some jump shots. Sometimes it's Nick Anderson, sometimes it's Scott Skiles and sometimes it's me. Once we start hitting our jump shots, we're off and running.

"I love having Shaq on the team. It just makes life easier for everybody, because he brings so many things to this team. Before he came, all the pressure was on myself, Nick and Scott Skiles to do all the scoring, but now it's really spread out. A guy like Shaq gets more media attention than the President. You can't help but like it, because it makes it easier on us. We just try to help him out when we can. That's going to help us win.

"Shaq is a Class A guy. He's taken everything in stride. He really knows who he is. He could be a different person, but he's not. He's just one of the guys. His family really raised him well. That's why he's the fine young man that he is.

"I can't say what Shaq likes to do. That's top secret. Basically, we just like to get in our trucks and go riding around. Of course, we like to listen to a lot of music. That's the biggest thing that we do. Just listen to plenty of music. He's got his album coming out and it's going to be a big surprise. Can't say what it's going to be. It's top secret too."

twenty

Beast of the East

As Matt Guokas predicted, his rookie sensation wasn't about to stop with a mere Player of the Week award. Shaquille O'Neal, though still slowed by foul trouble and turnover woes, feasted on the best competition that the NBA's Eastern Conference could throw at him. And before the first half of his rookie season ended, Shaq had outplayed All-NBA center Patrick Ewing to win the starting center's job on the East All-Star team, pounded the badboy Detroit Pistons for 46 points and completely collapsed a basket support in Phoenix, a previously unheard of feat that was witnessed by a national TV audience.

One reporter asked NBA vice president for operations Rod Thorn if the basket-crashing act was staged, perhaps by somehow loosening the bolts to boost TV ratings for the Shaq-Charles Barkley showdown held on Super Bowl Sunday.

"Absolutely not," Thorn answered. "Look, we were as much in shock as everybody else."

Even if it had tried, the NBA couldn't have staged a more sensational start to the Shaq Show. By then, every national magazine and talk show had featured O'Neal or wanted to line him up. He was unquestionably the hottest hit in all of sports.

Commissioner David Stern, the master of professional sports promotions, used Magic Johnson and Larry Bird to create unprecedented notoriety and success for the NBA. Now he beamed with delight at the sight of a new superstar who could keep the league at its all-time high and possibly bring it to the next level as the greatest sports attraction in the world.

"We'll miss Larry and Magic, and there is no question they were more responsible for our growth in the '80s than anything else," said Stern. "But Michael [Jordan] built on what they started, and now Shaquille and Larry Johnson and Kendall Gill and [Tom] Gugliotta will guide us into the next era."

While Stern was careful to include the likes of Johnson and Gill and even another rookie like Gugliotta in the same breath with O'Neal, the rest of the sports world was going Shaq crazy. Basketball junkies everywhere were flocking to the malls and souvenir stands to buy a Magic hat with No. 32 on the back or a Shaq jersey or T-shirt. No, the true basketball fan would never forget Magic and Bird, but the kids and groupie types already had.

"Have you seen Shaq in person yet?" Stern asked a reporter who was doing a story on the young phenom. "He's going to be terrific."

Around the league, opposing coaches shared Stern's sentiments. Many were saying he was already terrific and only going to become more difficult to handle. Even those coaches who had played during the Chamberlain era couldn't recall a young center possessing such a blend of raw power and athleticism.

Philadelphia 76ers coach Doug Moe stated flatly that "you can't hold your ground against him. He's just too big and strong. Kareem, Robinson, Ewing—all those other guys don't have this combination of strength and quickness. Olajuwon, either. I mean, this is a massive man. Once he gets an offensive game..."

Yes, there still remained plenty of room for improvement, despite his exceptional first week of play. His free-throw shooting was still hovering just above the 50-percent mark, and his lack of offensive skills was already causing some to label him merely a dunking machine, who would eventually be contained by double-teams.

Jordan, although respectful of the new challenger for his place as the game's premier player, said the shortcomings of Shaq's offensive ability would catch up with him later in the season.

"He's faking out a lot of people who don't know his game," said Jordan. "But with the level of scouting in this league, he will be facing defensive looks he's never seen. The first time around you surprise them. The second time, they surprise you. That's the way it was for me when I was a rookie."

As the Rookie of the Year in the 1984–85 season, Jordan still averaged 28.2 points per game, third in the league behind Bernard King and Bird.

Now Shaq had to show he could be more than just a one-week hero against sub-par competition. The best centers in basketball were waiting for their first shot against the heralded rookie.

It immediately became apparent that this was going to be a special crop of first-year players in the league. Obviously, O'Neal was the prize attraction and would be joined in the limelight by Alonzo Mourning, who missed the Hornets' first four games while holding out. But through the first week of the season, no fewer than 11 rookies had earned starting roles and 12 were averaging in double figures.

As mentioned by Stern, Gugliotta of the Bullets was the second most pleasant surprise of the draft behind Shaq, at least in the early stages of the season before Mourning got going. The North Carolina State product was averaging a solid 14.0 points, 9.6 rebounds and 3.3 assists while shooting 51 percent from the field. After Gugliotta hit a game-clinching jumper against Boston, veteran center Robert Parish remarked, "He plays with a lot of poise and confidence. He has great court awareness and is aggressive defensively. He has all the tools."

Third pick Christian Laettner got off to strong start for Minnesota, averaging 16.0 points and 8.8 rebounds. The former Duke center was likely to boost his production because he was averaging just 31 minutes a game.

Joining O'Neal, Laettner and Gugliotta as the most celebrated newcomers were Walt Williams of Sacramento, Lloyd Daniels of San Antonio, LaPhonso Ellis of Denver, Clarence Weatherspoon of Philadelphia, Sean Rooks of Dallas, Robert Horry of Houston, Walter Bond of Dallas, Anthony Avent of Milwaukee and Latrell Sprewell of Golden State.

Many observers were already comparing this golden crop to Jordan's rookie class, which also included Charles Barkley, Hakeem Olajuwon, Sam Perkins and Sam Bowie.

In his second week as a pro, O'Neal picked up where he left off and overwhelmed Philadephia's Andrew Lang and Golden State's seven-foot center, Alton Lister. Though still bothered by five fouls, Shaq pummelled Lang for 29 points, 19 rebounds and three blocks and didn't show any brotherly love in his first visit to Philadelphia. The Sixers' center finished with just two points and four rebounds. After a late-night flight home, Shaq and company were back in the O-Rena the very next night to take on the Warriors. Lister wished they had stayed in Philly as O'Neal pounded inside for 29 points, 16 rebounds and three blocks. He also played a season-high 41 minutes and held Lister to a mere four points and four rebounds.

With Shaq so dominating under the basket, Orlando reeled off two more wins to stretch its record to 5–2. That set the stage for a showdown with the New York Knicks, which would match the top two teams in the Atlantic Division and the two premier centers in the Eastern Conference.

The whole country was anxious to see what the great young center could do against the two-time Olympic gold medalist and perennial All-Star pivot man. *Sports Illustrated* went so far as to do a photo essay on O'Neal's first visit to New York. *The New York Times Magazine* had already featured the kid on its cover, and the Arsenio Hall Show had him scheduled for early December.

The Ewing-O'Neal confrontation was to no one's surprise a defensive war that began with the Knicks and their veteran big man holding the upper hand and igniting the sellout crowd in Madison Square Garden. Helped by Shaq's abysmal start, the Knicks vaulted to a 51–37 lead at halftime, and many wondered if the young guy was up to the test. He had already committed five turnovers and missed four foul shots.

But Shaq showed that he was indeed ready for the first major challenge of his pro career. He outscored, outrebounded and clearly overpowered Ewing in the second half. With the help of Nick Anderson's game-high 27 points, the Magic cut the deficit down to single digits and it was anybody's ballgame going into the fourth quarter.

Eventually the experience and defensive pressure of the Knicks took its toll, and the Magic went down to defeat, 92–77. However, it was a personal victory for O'Neal, who had won the first encounter with Ewing.

"He's just so strong. I mean, he is *so* strong," Knicks coach Pat Riley related after the game.

Riley knows his centers, too. He played with Wilt Chamberlain and coached Kareem Abdul-Jabbar with the Lakers, and now he had Ewing on his New York club. As for Shaq, Riley said, "You've got to get him out of the paint. Any time he gets the ball with his head under the rim...Well, you saw what happened." Dunk, dunk, dunk.

Statistically, the difference between O'Neal and Ewing wasn't as pronounced as it could have been. Shaq had 18 points to 15 for his new rival, but missed seven of 11 free-throw chances. He made up for the foul shooting lapse by ruling the boards, totaling 17 rebounds to just nine for the Dream Teamer. In fact, Ewing was not able to get a single offensive rebound in the entire ballgame, thanks to the presence of O'Neal. Shaq even played nine more minutes and committed one less foul than Ewing.

"I tried to come in with the attitude that this was just another game," grinned a satisfied Shaquille. "But I know the fans wanted to see a great center and pretty good center."

And who, inquired the media, was the great center out there in the Garden?

"Patrick," said Shaq, smiling again. "Patrick Ewing, of course."

O'Neal later re-emphasized that he wasn't going to position himself ahead of Ewing, not yet, anyway. "I think I did pretty good against him," he told *Sports Illustrated's* Jack McCallum. "It was a good show. Pat's a great player. I'm a pretty good player."

Shaq, however, wasn't all smiles and compliments. The Knicks' rock-em sock-em defense had annoyed O'Neal throughout the game, and he later voiced his displeasure.

"Guys are trying to punk me," he said, "but they're not going to back me down. I think I held my own."

As for Ewing, he had little to say about being over-shadowed by a youngster who not so long ago was growing up in nearby Newark and went to the Knick games in the Garden with his Dad.

"I just think he's an outstanding player. He works hard; he's agressive," said Ewing, who offered no more praise for the rookie who was already pushing hard for the status of being the best center in the East.

Ewing's teammate, Tony Campbell, shook his head in wonder when discussing the physical ability of O'Neal. Having played on the same team with Jabbar and Ewing, Campbell quickly pointed out the similarities between them and the new guy.

"With his strength and zeal, he'll definitely be in that class," said Campbell. "If not now, then soon. He's going on raw talent. I'd hate to see him when he learns how to play this game."

After a rare three-day break in the Magic schedule, O'Neal had another chance to test himself against one of the league's finest talents, Hakeem Olajuwon. The Houston Rockets came to Orlando riding high on the strength of a six-game winning streak under second-year head coach, Rudy Tomjonavich. The biggest change in the Rockets was that Olajuwon was finally happy, having settled his contractual problems with the club.

Even though it was the day before Thanksgiving, Orlando was buzzing over the prospects of the O'Neal-Olajuwon Showdown. And the Magic fans got their money's worth as their team took charge early, with Shaq forcing the multi-talented Rocket center to stay outside the lane. Orlando built an eight-point lead in the first quarter, but the Rockets eventually pulled even after three periods at 72–72. Scott Skiles and Dennis Scott had season-best performances in scoring 30 and 28 points to complement the outstanding inside play of O'Neal, who altered so many shots and kept the Rockets so far away from the basket that they hit only 41.5 percent from the floor.

While leading the Rockets with 22 points, Olajuwon had one of his worst shooting nights of the young season, missing on 13 of 22 field-goal attempts. He added 13 rebounds and five blocked shots, but that was not enough as Orlando pulled away for a 107–94 upset to snap Houston's long winning streak. O'Neal hit 50 percent of his field-goal tries (six of 12) and totaled 12 points, 13 rebounds and three blocks. He helped his own cause by committing just three fouls and two turnovers, enabling him to play 42 minutes, one more than Olajuwon.

On Thanksgiving Day, O'Neal spent much of his time off fulfilling a pledge he had made prior to signing his $42 million contract. He said he was going to give back to the community, and he did so with something he called "Shaqsgiving." He paid for a Thanksgiving meal for 300 people at an Orlando shelter for the homeless. It had originally been planned for 200, but when the shelter called to ask if it could be expanded for another 100 hungry folks, Shaq quickly agreed and wrote out a $7,000 check.

Not only did he foot the bill, he handed out the meal tickets and helped serve the food himself. Local reporters, who got wind of the event, observed that most of the homeless had no idea of the identity of this big guy handing out all the delicious food.

"Basketball is not everything in life. Doesn't make

a difference if they know me," Shaq told Brian Schmitz of the *Orlando Sentinel.* "As long as they can eat and they're happy.

"Hey, I've eaten on food stamps," continued O'Neal. "I was about six, seven. These people here are just not as fortunate as I am now."

O'Neal, who had originally requested no media coverage of the event, was already making plans to bring thousands of toys to underprivileged children in the Orlando area. Such generosity served to further enhance the glowing image of the NBA's youngest star.

Finishing out the month of November, the Magic benefitted from more impressive play from their center to pick up an easy win on the road at Indiana and a tough home-court decision over the Cleveland Cavaliers. O'Neal shut down the Pacers' Rik Smits and came through with 21 points, 11 rebounds and four blocks of his own in the surprisingly easy 130–116 road win. Then he took advantage of the absence of Cavs All-Star center Brad Daugherty, who was sidelined with an injury, to score 22 points and collect 14 rebounds. Nick Anderson hit the game-winning jumper with 2.8 seconds left to lift the Magic to a 95–93 decision.

As Orlando swung into its second month with Shaq, the club was off to an 8–3 start, the best in franchise history, and there was already talk of making a playoff appearance for the first time and possibly challenging the Knicks for the Atlantic title. O'Neal was already the hit of the league, attracting capacity crowds almost everywhere he dropped his gym bag and laced up with size 20 Reeboks.

"He's got superstar written all over him," Cleveland General Manager Wayne Embry said.

However, the months of December and January and on into the All-Star Break would not be as kind to O'Neal and the Magic as that fun-filled, victory-laden opening month. Shaq was averaging 23.6 points and 15.6 rebounds, which was the best start for any center in the East. It was clear that either Ewing or O'Neal would be the choice to start at center in the All-Star Game. Since the fans were voting on it, Shaq was the odds-on favorite to get the job.

O'Neal opened the month of December with his worst offensive showing of the season. Playing in Seattle on the first of a three-game West Coast trip, he missed seven of 11 field-goal attempts and was off target on six of seven free-throw tries, finishing with just nine points. The SuperSonics, another vastly improved team, used the combination of Shawn Kemp and Michael Cage to contain O'Neal and easily downed the Magic, 116–102.

That set the stage for Shaq's first meeting with former LSU teammate Stanley Roberts and the Los Angeles Clippers, yet another tough opponent. The Clippers' head coach, Larry Brown, said those who had seen O'Neal play in college knew he would be outstanding once he got to the pros.

"He's so motivated, he tries so hard," Brown said. "It doesn't matter if he scores or not. Everybody who saw him knew that when he got to the pros he would be a great player. I love him. I love what he means to this league. He's a nice kid, a great player. I respect guys who come every single day and try to win and bust their butts. He's that."

What O'Neal did best, according to Brown, was force his opponents to change their offensive plan. Even when he didn't block a shot, the other team's players "are aware he is there."

Brown, whose own center, Roberts, was still vastly overweight and unprepared to guard his former teammate by himself, wasn't sure what kind of defensive plan to use against O'Neal. He considered doubling him or trying to force him to stay away from the basket and shoot jumpers.

"The one thing I know is you have to keep him from getting dunks," said Brown.

Even Roberts was complimentary of his old rival, calling O'Neal "everything everybody thought he'd be. I'm looking forward to playing him. We used to talk all the time about getting to the NBA and playing each other."

While Roberts, as expected, didn't fare very well head-to-head with O'Neal, the rest of the Clippers made up the difference and more. Ken Norman led all scorers with 33 points, while former Knick point guard Mark

Jackson contributed 14 points and 13 assists in the Clippers' 122–104 triumph before yet another soldout crowd to watch the new superstar.

Shaq made the most of his first appearance in Los Angeles, where he had said he wanted to play full-time anyway. He led the Magic with 26 points, nine rebounds and four blocks, while limiting his ex-Tiger teammate to 16 points and six rebounds. But it was not enough to avoid a second-straight loss.

"He played really well," Brown said of O'Neal. "He will be the best. He made great post moves and his conditioning is really good. I do not see how other people guard him. He jumps so high, so strong. I am glad we only see him twice."

During his first visit to L.A., O'Neal took a break from basketball to do some rappin' on national TV. He appeared on "The Arsenio Hall Show" with his favorite rap group, Fu Schnickens. The singers had heard about Shaq's fondness of their music and invited him to sing with them, which he gladly did. It was an odd sight as the 7-1 O'Neal, dressed in baggy red clothes, towered above the four-man band as they rapped out the song, "Can We Rock."

Two nights later, the Magic ended the miserable road swing by dropping a 119–104 verdict to Golden State, despite 17 points and 17 rebounds from O'Neal. The club limped home to face the Celtics on December 8 and suffered a similar fate with Shaq outplaying Parish but the team still losing. The next night in Detroit, O'Neal was held to 17 points by the aggressive defense of the Pistons and fouled out in the final minute as the Magic dropped their fifth straight game to fall to 8–8 on the season.

"He's everything they say he is," said Isiah Thomas. "He has all the tools, the total package."

Detroit coach Ron Rothstein said O'Neal "is not a great player now, but he's pretty darn good. When he starts to get a real feel for what this game is about, you know, when he gets two to three years' experience, nobody's going to stop this kid."

Returning to the O-Rena, the Magic hoped to get back on track, but had to contend with Barkley and the red-hot Suns. Although O'Neal outscored (26–18) and out-rebounded (17–11) the Dream Team forward, it was Barkley's club that came away a winner by using a "Foul Shaq" strategy that many opponents would adopt.

Phoenix fouled O'Neal twice in the last seven seconds, and the rookie missed two of four attempts, which allowed the Suns to escape with a 108–107 victory.

"Absolutely, we wanted to foul Shaq," Suns coach Paul Westphal said afterwards. "We'd rather him make two [free throws] from 15 feet than one [field goal] from one inch. The worst he could do is make both and tie the game. If you don't foul him, he's going to the basket."

Remaining as confident as ever, O'Neal said only, "I'm not going to put my head down just because we lost ... We just need to win one to get rolling again."

Indeed, the Magic did in a big way. O'Neal and Dennis Scott, who was starting to become a dangerous weapon with his long-range jumpers, combined for 45 points in a decisive 119–107 win over Philadelphia in the O-Rena. The Magic continued its winning ways with three straight victories over a five-day period, including another 20–20 (point-rebound) effort by O'Neal, this time against the Sacramento Kings.

"Someday I am going to be the man," Shaq said after reigning over the Kings. "I got a lot of tricks in my bag, but I'm still learning the NBA. Right now, I'm just having fun. Wait until I'm a veteran and I start getting veteran calls. That might be interesting."

During the four-game winning streak, Orlando scored an impressive road victory over Atlanta, minus Dominique Wilkins, and capped the streak with a close verdict at home against the Utah Jazz. O'Neal had 28 points and 19 rebounds against the Jazz, but still received a surprising slap in the face from Dream Teamer Karl Malone.

"To me, he is just another player," said Malone, who scored 30 points against the Magic. "He is no different than any other guy I see. That's how I approach this game. I am not in the business of giving people respect. I will leave that to you guys [reporters]. I'm from the old school."

Apparently somewhat disgruntled over the defeat, Malone said, "We didn't come here to play one guy. He played good. He made the shots. But he didn't beat us, that's for sure."

Jazz coach Jerry Sloan, however, credited the Magic with a veteran-like performance and called Orlando a team "that could get to the finals one day."

Miami finally halted the Magic's winning streak as John Salley, subbing for Ronny Seikaly, did a solid job against O'Neal, who finished with 18 points and 11 rebounds. Sally countered with 13 points and 12 rebounds, and Miami rookie Harold Miner came off the bench to score 19 points in just 22 minutes as the Heat held on for a 106–100 win.

With just two games left in 1992, the Magic had the good fortune of beginning its longest homestand of the season, or at least it appeared to be a favorable opportunity. The club would not have to leave home for more than two weeks, including seven consecutive home dates, almost unheard of in the NBA.

Near the end of the string of O-Rena contests, Shaq was scheduled to square off again with Ewing. But before the Magic could get to the Knicks, the team had mysteriously crumbled. After winning the opening game of the homestand with a routine 110–94 triumph over Milwaukee, Orlando dropped three straight to the Lakers, Pistons and Nets by a combined margin of seven points. Each time the young club had a chance to win, but let it slip away in the final minutes.

In the third straight loss, O'Neal did his share with 29 points and 12 rebounds. He scored seven points in the fourth quarter, but fouled out of the game in the last minute. New Jersey won with its outside-inside combo of Drazen Petrovic and Derrick Coleman, who provided 57 points in the 102–99 win that dropped the Magic back to .500 at 13–13.

"Once again, we just kept shooting ourselves in the foot," said Scott, who was four of 12 from the field and scored just 11 points. "We haven't had anyone to really go to when things get tight at the end."

On the same day the Magic lost to the Nets, the early voting for the NBA Eastern Conference All-Star team was announced and showed Shaq with a huge lead over Ewing for the starting center spot.

Shaq showed himself worthy of the All-Star acclaim as he outplayed Ewing in their second matchup and helped the Magic snap the losing streak at home. The January 8 contest was vintage big-time center vs. big-time center. Ewing and the Knicks got off to the early lead and threatened to put the game away in the fourth quarter. But the big kid led the Magic right back into it, stirring the Orlando fans into a frenzy.

In one of his finest all-around performances, O'Neal came through in the clutch, scoring 11 points and grabbing 5 rebounds in the fourth quarter alone. He also blocked three of Ewing's shots and altered many others. The Magic came screaming back to outscore New York, 28–15, in the final period of action. But with Orlando ahead 95–94, the Knicks had a chance for the winning basket and got the ball to their leader. But Ewing was so rattled by O'Neal's imposing play inside that he threw up an off-balance hook or jumper. It was so ugly it was difficult to tell what kind of shot Ewing had attempted. Whatever it was, it clanked off the backboard and didn't come close to the basket, preserving Orlando's first win over the Knicks.

It was also another personal victory for O'Neal. He came away with 22 points, 13 rebounds, five blocks and three assists, while Ewing totaled 21 points, 12 rebounds, one block and one assist. If Shaq needed anything to lock up the starting job for the East, he had just got it.

But there was plenty of basketball left to be played before the All-Star break, and the Magic still wasn't playing very well. Even though O'Neal was superb with 30 points and 20 rebounds, the Magic lost again at home, this time to the same Pacer team that it had beaten in Indianapolis in November.

Orlando closed out a dismal home performance by falling to the defending world champion Chicago Bulls in the first meeting between Michael Jordan and O'Neal.

They posed together for pictures before the game. Then Michael and the Jordanaires used their usual third-quarter explosion to bury the Magic, 122–106. Shaq hit eight of 10 from the field and finished with 19 points and 11 rebounds. Jordan had an off-night, making only nine of 22 shot attempts, but still scoring 23 points.

Having lost five of seven at home, the Orlando club was glad to get out of town and begin a three-game road trip with Shaq's first appearance in the legendary Boston Garden. The *Boston Herald* previewed the game by listing the key to a Celtics victory: Simple, keep the big guy away from the basket. The key to Magic is about as much a mystery as Al Capone's vault. But in Parish, the Celtics have a center who has played O'Neal about as well as any big man this season.

"I didn't feel a soft spot on him," Parish said of O'Neal. "I definitely think he's solid. The main thing is to keep him going. You have to make him work, and move him around. So I have to move him around. He's not a guy you can actually turn and shoot over. So that means the transition game. You make him run, because he's at his best when he's standing there. The other thing is that you have to sacrifice your body and box him out, because he'll win most jumping contests if it comes down to that when you're going for a rebound."

Celtics backup center Joe Kleine compared keeping O'Neal away from his usual power game to shutting down the offensive game of Kareem Abdul-Jabbar.

"You just try to keep him away from the basket," said Kleine. "No dunks or layups. You just make him earn it. You just try to limit him. But that is sort of like saying that the key to stopping Kareem is to guard his hook shot."

While virtually no other center could handle Jabbar's sky hook, at least some of the smarter and more physical big men in the league were managing to slow down O'Neal.

Chris Ford, who played against Jabbar before becoming the Celtics head coach, planned to rotate Parish and Kleine to try to keep a fresh defender on him. O'Neal is "very aggressive, and he moves well," said Ford. "But he still has a lot to learn. He's a force if he's just allowed to plant himself in the middle, though he's always a force for a lot of guys. There's a lot of games where you see him getting 28 points, and 18 or 19 rebounds, and a lot of blocked shots."

The Celtics hoped that their January 15 meeting with the Magic would not be one of those Shaq Attack nights. On the day before the important Atlantic Division matchup, O'Neal said simply, "I'm 7-foot-1, I'm 303, I can run the floor and block shots. I'm just doing my job."

On his first trip to the Hub, Shaq did his job and a whole lot more as he led the Magic to a convincing 113–94 victory. He scored 22 points, grabbed a game-high 12 rebounds and blocked four shots. Boston reporters were quick to point out that O'Neal "shackled" the hometown heroes by changing so many of their shots, leading to a 40-percent shooting performance.

Boston Globe columnist Dan Shaughnessy wrote that the young Magic man brought back unpleasant memories of Chamberlain visits to the Boston Garden. The headline read, "O'Neal won't wilt amid comparisons"; the opening lines read, "There was a young man who was bigger and stronger than almost anybody. News of his arrival in any NBA city was cause to stop everything and watch pro basketball for a night." What every city in the league had done to witness Wilt's debut season was happening again for Shaq. It was happening in Boston, Philly, New York, Los Angeles and seemingly every other major city in America as a nation's sports fans savored the arrival of a new hero. It was fitting that O'Neal had been everything he was supposed to be in his initial visit to Boston, the city that was still trying to get over the loss of Larry the Legend.

Orlando's win over Boston started a weird sequence of wins and losses that created a rocky roller-coaster ride to nowhere. The very next night, Shaq would make his first appearance in Michael's palace, the old Chicago Stadium, and he would be even more outstanding (29 points, 24 rebounds) in stealing the thunder of Jordan's season-high 64-point outburst as the Magic won in overtime, 128–124.

However, the back-to-back wins at Boston and Chicago were followed by back-to-back losses, which were followed by two straight wins, which were followed by two consecutive losses. The Magic finally snapped the bizarre two-wins-two-losses trend by winning three in a row to start the month of February, but then the club slipped right back into the groove by losing two straight.

The high marks for O'Neal during this stretch of twosome outings were 36-point performances against Dallas and Philly, two of the league's worst teams. Naturally, Orlando split those games.

Shaq helped break the club's final two-game losing streak by putting on a memorable show at the Great West Forum in Los Angeles, where he had always wanted to play his pro ball. After coming off a lousy performance in Sacramento, at least by O'Neal standards (18 points, six rebounds, six fouls), he rocked the Lakers and the Forum by pouring in a game-high 31 points and hauling down 14 rebounds in a 110–97 win.

"Every time I have a bad game, I say to myself, 'Next time, you've got to come out and play harder,'" Shaq explained, perhaps shedding some light on the up-and-down swings of the Magic. "I kind of said to myself not to have two bad games in a row."

Laker guard Sedale Threatt summed up the game nicely, "It was way too much Shaq tonight. He has the big dukes. You double-team him, it makes no difference."

With his first appearance at the All-Star Game quickly approaching, O'Neal saved the finest acts of his smash-hit rookie season for the stretch run to Salt Lake City, Utah.

NBC booked the league's new sensation for four straight Sunday's in February, and he came through with flying colors each time. On his network TV debut against Barkley and the Suns, Shaq electrified the Phoenix fans and basketball enthusiasts all over the nation by tearing down the goal standard only three minutes into the game.

Although network executives and NBA administrators were thrilled by the made-for-TV power exhibition, Shaq just shrugged it off as another day at the office. After all, he wanted to rip down the rim, glass and basket standard every time he went up for a dunk, which is just about every time he touched the ball.

"I was just in the right place at the right time," O'Neal said. "I've hit them harder than that before. A lot harder than that. I was a little surprised. But when it started coming down, I started running the other way."

Could the league's strong man be frightened by a basket falling on him? No. "I just didn't want it to hurt my pretty face," he laughed.

Even though arena officials had anticipated the possibility of a Shaq Attack on their goals, it still took 37 minutes to wheel in the replacement backboard, which had already been polished for the occasion. "We knew who was coming to town," said arena coordinator Alvin Adams.

Arena manager Bob Machen explained the standard "just couldn't withstand the strength of his 300 pounds."

While Shaq rated the destructive dunk as only fifth on his all-time list of favorite slams, the officials from NBC placed it right at the top of their list of season highlights. It couldn't have been a better lead-in to the networks telecast of the All-Star Game, which was just two weeks away.

But just in case NBC wasn't satisfied, Shaq was back on the attack only a week later in the third meeting against Ewing and the Knicks. This one went to three wonderful overtimes before the exhausted Magic held on for a 102–100 win over the weary Knicks, who lost Ewing to his sixth foul late in the game. Ewing led all scorers with 34 points, but O'Neal outrebounded him for the third straight time (19–14) and blocked a season-high nine shots to turn the game in Orlando's favor and give the club a 2–1 lead in the series. The game reaffirmed O'Neal's place as the top center in the East, at least for the first half of the season.

Another big-man rivalry had started the game before Orlando faced the Knicks again. It marked the second

Magic-Hornets contest and finally Mourning was able to play. The two top draft picks battled to a virtual standoff, although O'Neal emerged with slightly better individual numbers. He held a 29–27 scoring edge and a 15–14 advantage on the boards and blocked four shots to two for Mourning. But the Hornets won the game at "The Hive" by a 116–107 margin.

In the game after the Knick thriller, the Magic went back on the road to tackle the Pistons in the Palace and got locked in another overtime battle that produced Shaq's most prolific night of the season. He muscled past Olden Polynice and Bill Laimbeer and twisted through double-teams to hit 19 of 25 shot attempts, mostly dunks and layups. In 49 minutes of play, he produced 46 points. Unfortunately, a late lapse at the free-throw line cost him an opportunitry for a 50-point night and cost the Magic a win.

O'Neal made eight of his first 12 foul shots, but the rallying Pistons intentionally fouled him twice in the final minute of regulation. Shaq obliged his hosts by missing four straight attempts at the line, allowing the Pistons to take a 113–111 lead. The rookie saved face by making a tying layup with 5.1 seconds left, and he drew the foul to get a three-point chance that might have won the game in regulation. But he missed the free throw, and the game went into overtime with Detroit eventually earning a 124–120 decision.

"I just missed them," lamented O'Neal. "Maybe it was my fault. I think it is. The next time I get that opportuynity, I'm going to hit those shots."

Nonetheless, his 46-point, 21-rebound performance left an impact on the Pistons and their fans. Detroit forward Terry Mills called his young foe "a great competitor. He said when he was running down the court, 'If I could just make my free throws.' He's starting to come around. I think that will come in time."

In trying to console his young star, Matt Guokas reminded him that he had hit the crucial free throws to beat the Knicks. "Sometimes the bear bites you, and sometimes you bite the bear," said the Magic coach.

There wasn't much time for O'Neal to brood over the missed opportunity as the Magic flew home late that night to get ready to close out the first half of the season at home against Denver. While Shaq's former college teammate, Chris Jackson, outscored him (25–24), O'Neal managed to make four of seven free-throw tries, grabbed 18 rebounds and blocked five shots. Orlando won the game easily, 111–99, to raise its record to 24–23 going into the five-day All-Star Break. There were 35 games left to played, and the Magic was definitely in the playoff race, thanks to the arrival of their first All-Star performer.

Speaking of Shaq

Anthony Bowie
Orlando Magic guard

"Shaq is a guy who likes to have fun, just like most fellas his age. We do lots of things together. We went hunting for wild pigs somewhere just outside Orlando and had a real good time. We went out into the field looking for some of the hogs so we could shoot them. Well, we spotted a family of them, and Shaq decided it would be fun to try to catch one of the little piglets. We were running all over the field, chasing those little things. It was so much fun. You should have seen the big fella out there, trying to catch those little pigs. They were no longer than a foot long, if that, and here's this big seven-foot guy chasing them down and diving after them. We finally caught one, and then we all took pictures with it.

"Basically, we like to listen to music together. He likes a lot of music, and I like a lot of music. When we get on the plane together, we'll sit down and listen to music. Sometimes, we'll make up a new beat. Then someone else will think up a new beat, and we'll put it all together and have a great time singing.

"Shaq is like everyone else out there. He enjoys going to malls and things like that. But he just can't go very often, and when he does go, he has to do it at an off-hour. There are still people who come up to him and mess with him. He doesn't go to the mall unless he really needs something. He doesn't go just to be looking at stuff. He might need some new clothes or another one of those funky-looking hats that he always wears. He'll wear just about anything, as long as he thinks it looks nice.

"I always enjoy being around Shaq. He's a young guy, but he knows how to bring fun to the team. He's young, but he has really added a lot to our team. He's very mature for a 21-year-old, but he still knows how to have fun.

"Shaq knows how to handle all the attention. He doesn't get caught up in the women coming around him all the time. He's mature about that. He's got a lot of good people around him, and they let him know what he should and shouldn't do.

"All the money he makes doesn't really bother me. He has a job to do, and I have a job to do. Of course, his job is different than my job. But we're both playing basketball. He's definitely a franchise player. If I was seven feet, I'd probably be making the same money he is. I'm just happy to see a young fella like him accomplish some of the things that it takes most people a lifetime to accomplish. He's playing the sport he loves and he's making a lot of money doing it.

"I think the sky is the limit for Shaq. He just needs to bear down and really go after it. He could set all types of records and accomplishments. They're all there for him. All he has to do is go get them."

twenty-one

A Star Among Stars

David Robinson stood alone in the baggage claim area of the Salt Lake City airport waiting for a limousine to take him to his hotel. The four-time All-Star and member of the Olympic Dream Team looked down the hall and saw a crowd of personal assistants, family, friends and fans surrounding a tall young man making his first trip to the biggest show of the basketball season. Everywhere Shaquille O'Neal went during the glitzy All-Star weekend, he drew a crowd of autograph seekers and well-wishers, all hailing the arrival of the NBA's phenom center.

The fans of pro basketball singled out O'Neal as the landslide top vote-getter at the center position, even though the NBA made the blunder of misspelling his name on the official ballot. A total of 826,767 fans didn't have any trouble picking out "O'Neil" on the list of Eastern Conference big men. Shaq easily garnered the most votes at the pivot position, outpointing his chief rival and another Dream Teamer, Patrick Ewing, by nearly a quarter of a million votes.

Only Michael Jordan, Scottie Pippen and Charles Barkley picked up more votes of confidence from NBA fans all across the nation, who had been selecting the All-Star starters since 1975.

The last rookie to be voted to the starting lineup of either team was Jordan back in 1985. Since 1970, only two other players—Magic Johnson (1980) and Isiah Thomas (1982)—had been selected to the starting lineup as rookies. All told, the honor had been extended to just 13 other players before O'Neal soared to the top of the balloting results. The other rookies to get there were: Bob Cousy (1951), Ray Felix (1954), Tom Heinsohn (1957), Wilt Chamberlain (1960), Oscar Robertson (1961), Walt Bellamy (1962), Jerry Lucas (1964), Luke Jackson (1965), Rick Barry (1966) and Elvin Hayes (1969).

Although Knicks coach Pat Riley argued that his center should have been the East starter, there were no other complaints from the rest of the league, which welcomed Shaq into stardom.

"Believe me, the rest of the league welcomes him with open arms," said Jordan, who was busy playing golf and happy to have a newcomer deflect the attention from himself. "We just lost two superstars [Johnson and Larry Bird], so we need someone to take up those roles. Shaquille is a respected and proven commodity already."

Not even Riley could dispute that the numbers backed up Shaq's selection. He led Ewing in every important statistic and had outplayed him in at least two of their first three matchups. The Magic also had won two of the three games with the Knicks.

In fact, O'Neal continued to be the only player in the league to rank in the top 10 in four different individual stats. He was second in rebounding at 14.3 and field-goal percentage at .572, third in blocked shots at 3.97 and eighth in scoring at 23.7. Ewing trailed by a wide margin in every stat, except scoring. He was averaging 22.7 points, 12.4 rebounds and 1.93 blocks while shooting .522 percent from the floor.

"Shaq is having a great year," said Ewing, who didn't object to the rookie's starting assignment. "I'm just happy to be selected [as a reserve]. It's always an honor to participate with all these great players."

When asked about the force of the young guy, Ewing replied, "Is he strong? Hell, yes, he's strong. The strongest guy I've ever played against."

"There is no doubt he's going to be a monster," Miami center Rony Seikaly said. "That's an understatement. He palms the ball like a grapefruit. He's as big as Mark Eaton and seven times as quick. And he's only 20. Give me a break."

Chicago Bulls center Bill Cartwright described O'Neal's game like this: "I'd say dunk. Knock people over. Dunk. Knock someone else over. Dunk. Knock some people around. Dunk again. That's about it. Not a bad game to have, either."

Going into the All-Star Weekend, Shaq had indeed proved to be a one-man dunking machine. He had a league-high 182 dunks and counting.

"This kid reminds me of Mike Tyson when Tyson first became champ," said John Battle of the Cavaliers. "Tyson used to win fights before the bell even rang just because he was so intimidating. I look at Shaquille and see the same intimidation."

Even O'Neal himself had to agree that the fans picked the right man to start at center for the East. He would be lining up with Jordan, Thomas, Pippen and Larry Johnson, while the East reserves included Ewing, Daugherty, Dominique Wilkins, Joe Dumars, Larry Nance, Mark Price and Detlef Schrempf.

"I'm not surprised," O'Neal said of the starting honor. "If I was a fan, I'd want to see a 20-year-old who could dunk, run the floor and shoot the turnaround hook. Basketball is a sport, but it's also entertainment. Yeah, if I was a fan, I'd want to see the Shaq, too."

The constant comparison to Chamberlain, who was the All-Star MVP as a rookie, didn't seem to bother O'Neal, either.

"Pressure? Nah," he said. "Pressure is when you go home and you don't know where your next meal is coming from. This is all part of the job and I understand that. You either take it as it comes or you don't deal with it."

If anything, O'Neal was relishing the remarkable opportunity that he had earned through 47 games of hard work and endurance. He had already played more games than he had in any of his three college seasons, and there was still a long, long ways to go before a possible playoff appearance.

For one weekend, though, Shaq just enjoyed being around the great players of the game, many of whom he had watched and admired for much of his youth. Heck, this was his youth.

But now O'Neal wanted to show his worth against an outstanding West squad that featured David Robinson and Hakeem Olajuwon, the two centers who had given him the most trouble to date, due to their superior quickness as seven-footers. Robinson would start for the West, along with Charles Barkley, Karl Malone, John Stockton and Clyde Drexler. Joining Olajuwon as the reserves were Tim Hardaway, Sean Elliott, Shawn Kemp, Danny Manning, Dan Majerle, Terry Porter and Mitch Richmond.

A major point of concern for O'Neal would be how the other East stars would react to all the notoriety and acclaim being cast at him. There was talk that they might freeze him out of the offense, as the East team had done to Jordan in 1985. The main culprit had been Thomas, who joined other disgruntled veterans in keeping the ball away from the new superstar. Jordan took only nine shots and scored just seven points in the ballgame. He and Thomas had been enemies ever since.

"I don't think you'll see what happened to me happen to Shaquille," Jordan said. "People already respect his game. His star status is assured. I just hope he treats the game with respect and dignity and comes out playing hard."

But before O'Neal could get to the court of the Delta Center for Sunday's game, he had to deal with two days of media and fan fanaticism. He said on his first day in town that he was already eager for the day to end, so he could have some peace and quiet for a change. His first day of All-Star festivities had been carefully planned by the Magic, which had offered to fly him in on the team jet.

He turned that down, saying, "Naaah, I'm not that big yet." But he was getting close, no doubt.

Everyone from NBA officials to his own family wanted to spend time with him or requested that he make an appearance for them. He met again with members of Fu Schnickens to talk about the rap show they were scheduled to do at the NBA Stay in School Jam on Saturday morning.

Shaq passed on a chance to practice with his favorite musical group, saying rap "was like riding a bike. Once you learn, you don't forget."

However, Riley and the East coaching staff did insist that Shaq attend the team's Saturday afternoon practice and press conference. He fielded more than his share of questions and then took off to see the magnificent Rocky Mountain countryside.

As usual, O'Neal toyed with the media, saying that he wanted to go sliding down one of the ski slopes on an inner tube. His contract with the Magic prohibited him from skiing, skydiving or motorcycle riding, but had no clause about using an inner tube on the slopes. Shaq held back a smile as he explained, "There's nothing in there about tubing. That and bungee jumping. That's something else I'd like to try."

In reality, Shaq passed on the snow tubing and instead spent much of his free time hanging out with Paula Abdul. They were the main attraction at the Stay in School Jam and also chatted before and after the event.

Later in the day, O'Neal seemed unfazed by the news that his All-Star jersey was the top prize at an NBA charity auction. His game shirt sold for $55,000, while the next highest bid was $25,000 for Jordan's. Shaq shrugged it off and went back to his hotel suite for a short nap, followed by a return trip to the Delta Center to do a live interview on TNT.

When introduced that night to the Utah fans, O'Neal drew the loudest and longest ovation outside the two local players, Malone and Stockton. Surprisingly, the rookie center admitted he was going to be "a little" nervous on Sunday.

Jordan, though, said that was only natural. "There's always a problem when you try to live up to the fans' expectations," M.J. remarked. "That's not smart. You just have to try and live up to your own."

But every All-Star, former NBA star and coach attending the celebrity weekend kept lauding the young guy with more and more praise. It was clear that the youngest player in the league had the highest expectations cast squarely upon his broad shoulders.

Connie Hawkins, one of the pioneers of the modern NBA game, said, "Once he really learns how to play the game, he is going to be the greatest player ever. Would I take the ball to the basket against him? Look, I took the ball to the hole against anybody. I took to the hole against Wilt. But Shaq's a great player. All he needs is a couple more shots."

"If I was a coach, that is the one rookie I would like to have on my team," said Zelmo Beaty. "In a few years, you are probably going to see him become one of the greatest centers ever to play in the NBA. The only way to defend that guy is to keep the ball out of his hands. Once he has got the ball, he's too big to do anything with."

Maurice Lucas, a wide-body himself, called the young giant "an awesome talent. He is so much bigger than the other players he is playing against. He has no fear. I definitely think the guy is in line to be a legend."

Now for the real test. The talk of the town had to prove to his peers, and most importantly to himself, that he was worthy of all the acclaim. The only way to do that was to hold his own against the Dream Teamers and all the other elite players in the league.

On All-Star Sunday, Shaq came to play and immediately showed everyone in Delta Center and basketball fans all over the world that he was indeed the "Real Deal."

With everyone's pride on the line, the All-Star event quickly developed into a body-banging grudge match, creating perhaps the most physical game ever played on a weekend that's supposed to be a break for the pros. Shaq obviously felt right at home with the heavy contact under the basket, even though he was knocked down by Charles Barkley once in the first half and floored by Hakeem Olajuwon one time in the second half.

An intense Shaq started out with a flurry of points. He hit three free throws and would eventually hit six of nine from the line. Then he caught Robinson off guard by stepping outside to knock down a 15-foot jump shot, something he rarely even attempted during the first half of the season.

O'Neal, naturally, added a thunderous dunk to cause a roar of applause from the appreciative Utah fans, who obviously wanted the West to win. Having played 14 of the 24 first-half minutes, the Magic rookie had 13 points at halftime and was clearly one of the contenders for the coveted MVP award. Only Chamberlain and Robertson had ever won the top honor as a rookie.

However, O'Neal disappeared in the second half, sitting on the bench for a stretch of 16 minutes. While million of basketball fans waited anxiously for the prize center to return to the hard-fought ballgame, East coach Pat Riley kept him on the rookie's seat on the bench, instead using his own player, Ewing, for most of the second half.

The East's starting center played the first six minutes of the third quarter before being pulled for Ewing. Incredibly, O'Neal was not put back in the game until there were less than two minutes to go in regulation. He scored only one point in the second half to finish his first All-Star outing with 14 points and seven rebounds in 25 minutes.

To make matters worse for Shaq, the East lost the game, 135–132 in overtime.

"No, I wasn't upset," said O'Neal about the snub. "I was just glad to be out there having fun."

But pressed on the point of the long bench ride, he revealed more of his disappointment in the highly questionable move by Riley, saying, "I was anxious to get in. I was wondering, 'When am I going to get back in?' I guess Pat Riley wanted more experience down the stretch."

Although Shaq refused to criticize the Knicks coach, his father gladly obliged. Philip Harrison, who had earlier caused an uproar of his own with the Delta Center's security force, lashed out at Riley for benching his son.

"Of course I was [upset]," Harrison fumed. "And everyone knows why he was doing it."

Riley was highly defensive of the way he used his centers. In addition to O'Neal and Ewing, he said, Daugherty had to get some playing time as well.

"I wanted to get everyone enough minutes and then take a look at what was going on in the fourth quarter," Riley said. "I wasn't counting the number of minutes people were sitting out. I was counting the number of minutes that everybody got. That was more important."

Larry Johnson, another young starter for the East, saw even less playing time than Shaq. He was given only 16 minutes of action in the 53-minute overtime contest and scored just four points.

The other controversy of the day centered around Harrison, who put on quite a show himself. Before the game, he got mad because he didn't have enough tickets for his 14 guests, so he went on a rampage that sent security guards scurrying all over the Delta Center in a vain effort to control him.

Basically, Harrison ignored the pleas of the Delta Center security staff to stay out of areas off-limits to the public. The Army sergeant barged past every guard who tried to stop him and went anywhere he chose.

Alerted to the ongoing problem, NBA officials advised the security staff to be extremely cautious with the sergeant, who had already caused repeated trouble with security guards in Orlando and other NBA cities.

"We don't want a confrontation with him," a senior security officer told *Orlando Sentinel* reporter Barry Cooper, who wrote that NBA officials know as much about Shaq's Dad as they do about the young center.

Aware of the leverage inherent in being a superstar's father, Harrison admitted that he took advantage of his status and didn't let anyone tell him what to do.

"Yes, I am very aggressive. I have to be," Harrison said after the All-Star incident. "But I don't care what people say about me. Those people don't pay me. Those people don't feed my family. I am totally committed to my children and my family, and everything I do is for them."

Harrison went on to say, "I'm living through my son, Shaquille, playing in the All-Star Game, being on the All-Star team, being in the NBA."

His eldest son had given him something to be proud of in his first appearance against his peers, even if it hadn't been as long as Harrison or Shaq would have liked.

O'Neal left a lasting impressing on his teammates and opponents alike. For those who weren't already convinced he was for real, they were now.

"He's tough. He's big. He has strength," Olajuwon said. "He can play against anybody."

Speaking of Shaq

Wes Unseld
Washington Bullets coach and Hall of Fame center

"We have to gimmick defensively against Shaquille, which is no good. There's not a lot we can do against Shaquille, except try to double him all the time.

"When Orlando needs a basket, there's little doubt where they're going to go. When we try to double them or something, he kicks it out to somebody for the jump shot. We don't have a lot of options against a team like the Magic.

"The reason we have to double-team Shaquille is not so much that he's going to score, it's just that he gets our people in foul trouble. When he powers in, he usually picks up a foul on somebody. We don't have enough big people to spare. If I lose one big guy to foul trouble, I've got a substitution problem.

"I think you have to go back to Wilt Chamberlain to find somebody as big and strong as Shaquille. But whenever we played against Wilt, we always had somebody who

could match him. We don't have that right now when we play Shaquille.

"Shaquille is a very talented center, no doubt about it. The thing that I've noticed is not so much his talent, but the way he picks things up. It looks like he learns from every game. He has improved every time we've faced him.

"He has really learned to recognize what people are doing to him defensively. He knows now how to pick up the double-teams and take advantage of it. He wasn't doing that early in the year.

"I don't believe in comparing players. It's unfair to Shaquille, and it's unfair to some of the other centers who've played this game. I played against some guys like him—Chamberlain, Bob Lanier, Nate Thurmond, Walt Bellamy. They were all big and strong, just like Shaquille. There have been lots of big guys in this league, but there haven't been many great ones."

twenty-two

Still a Big Hit

As Shaquille O'Neal embarked on the second half of his rookie season, the fans and the media continued to shower attention upon him. But some serious questions had to be answered as well.

Some in the Magic organization and in the media wondered out loud if Shaq would "hit the wall" in the final stages of the long, grueling NBA season. Others questioned whether he was ready to hit the big time and lead his club into the playoffs. Another question that surfaced in late March was: Would he keep hitting opponents?

The only sure thing was that O'Neal would remain the hit of the season and continue to capture the hearts of NBA fans all over the world. He would also finally hit the 21-year-old mark, still a tender age for having established himself as a superstar.

"Shaquille is a good player, and he has made an impact, but really hasn't won anything, nor has his team won anything yet," cautioned Michael Jordan. "He certainly has the potential to be one of the all-time greats, though."

Jordan had duly noted that no player in the NBA is considered to be one of the greats until he transforms his team into a great ballclub that actually wins playoff games and championships.

After starting with so much hope, the magic was wearing off the Orlando club, which had back-to-back disappointing efforts going 10–16 in the months of December and January. The Magic still had a shot at slipping into the playoffs, but even if the team earned a berth, it would likely have to face the Chicago Bulls or New York Knicks in the first round. Orlando, at 24–23, held the eighth position in the Eastern Conference going into the final two-and-a-half months of the season.

By this stage, O'Neal had already played in 56 NBA games (eight exhibitions, 47 regular-season games and one All-Star event), which was almost as many games as he had played in his last two seasons at LSU. And there were still at least 35 games left to play. The standard in the NBA was that most rookies who started out like gangbusters would tail off in the second half of the season. The perfect example was Denver's Dikembe Mutombo, who just the previous year had been marvelous for three months, but due to injury and fatigue, was not much of a factor in the final three months.

As early as January, reporters began asking O'Neal what he thought about the NBA wall theory. As could be expected, he shrugged it off and made light of the subject.

"Hit the wall? If you're coming to ask me if I hit the wall, I haven't," Shaq responded. "I've never been too tired. If I am, I'll just go get a B-12 shot. Take some vitamin A. Eat a salad. I'm 20, not 30. I have young lungs, young legs."

Listening to his young teammate talk was veteran point guard Scott Skiles, who advised him that the wall theory was often accurate.

"I've seen rookies hit the wall," Skiles said. "It happens."

With his interest piqued, Shaq glanced down at his playmaker and asked, "They just get tired, Scott?"

"They reach a point where they have to turn it up after 30, 50 games," Skiles explained. "Some regroup, the others go into the tank. It's mostly mental."

Magic coach Matt Guokas was carefully monitoring the playing time and demands of his rookie star and continued to ask him how he was feeling. Guokas had also talked to Paul Westhead, who had coached Mutombo as a rookie. The Nuggets' big man averaged 17.1 points and 12.3 rebounds through the first four months of the season. But his production tailed off to 10.1 points and 8.9 rebounds in the last two months of the season. Westhead told Guokas part of the problem was the team just didn't play very well together.

Guokas hoped that all the attention being given to Shaq's condition wouldn't somehow make him feel tired, both physically and mentally.

As it turned out, all the worrying was for nothing. O'Neal never felt the effects of the long season; at least his stats didn't show it. He remained the leading scorer, rebounder, and shot blocker and defender on the ballclub. He also continued to be the only player in the NBA to be ranked in the top 10 in four different stats. His scoring average, which was expected to dip, remained over 23 points per game, a clear indicator of his superior conditioning and personal resolve.

Unfortunately, the rest of the team wasn't holding up as well. Dennis Scott missed much of February and March with a strained Achilles tendon. Scott Skiles would sustain a separated shoulder, but continue to play. Brian Williams would go to Injured List with a broken hand. He and Terry Catledge, the team's top two power forwards, managed to play in just 21 games each.

Guokas, however, pulled everything together in a fine coaching performance and kept the Magic within striking distance of that eighth and final playoff spot in the East and a possible winning season.

Coming off the All-Star Break, Shaq and the Walking Wounded stayed home to face the defending Western Conference champion Portland Trail Blazers. And for the second time, the Magic knocked off the Blazers with yet another solid effort from O'Neal, who did it all, scoring a game-high 28 points and adding 14 rebounds, five blocks and three assists in the 125–107 triumph.

Jordan and the Bulls returned to town for their third meeting with Orlando. This one was a classic show-down between the league's premier player and the young sensation who was hot on his trail. Even though it was not a vintage shooting night for Jordan, he still led all scorers with 35 points. But O'Neal paced the Magic in a valiant comeback bid. He delivered 30 points and 19 rebounds as the Bulls slipped away with a 108–106 win.

Hitting the road later that night, Orlando traveled to Washington and picked up its third victory over Wes Unseld's Bullets. As expected, Shaq had his way against Pervis Ellison again, totaling 28 points and 11 rebounds in a 92–91 decision. That set the stage for yet another na-tionally televised confrontation for the hottest attraction in the league.

One week after All-Star Sunday, Shaq was back home in the O-Rena to defend his territory against David Robinson and the San Antonio Spurs. NBC was rewarded with still another amazing performance by the Magic's marvel. The statistical edge went to Robinson, who daz-zled the fans with his quick baseline moves. Shaq, though, came through with his typically exciting display of power in the pivot. There were no broken goals or three overtime periods, but it was still a thrilling game. The Spurs, led by Robinson's 23 points and 16 rebounds, edged the Magic, 94–90. Shaq answered with 19 points and 13 rebounds. Both big guys had three blocked shots.

Later that night, sports fans across the nation got some bonus coverage of the Shaquille Appeal. ESPN, in an unprecedented move, devoted the full hour of its award-winning "Outside the Lines" show to a documentary enti-tled "Shaq's Sudden Impact."

ESPN anchorman Bob Ley explained that the cable network "started out with the intention of doing a special on the great rookie class in the NBA this year. But the focus quickly went to Shaq because he's such a phenome-nal story."

The show covered Shaq's family and background in great detail and devoted only a little time to his on-the-court basket-breaking and other such acts. The show also depicted the tremendous impact that the rookie star had on the Magic and the rest of the league.

Through the first four months of the season, the Magic had a winning record of 26–25 and was holding on to the eighth playoff berth. But mounting injury problems in March and April would cause the club to drop below .500 and put the Magic in position to scramble to get back into playoff contention.

In the first week of March, O'Neal had back-to-back sub-20 scoring nights, which fueled the fires of the "Hit the Wall" worries. The Magic also lost three of their first five games in the month, which put a slight damper on the occasion of Shaq's 21st birthday, celebrated at his Isleworth mansion with a few close friends, including teammate Dennis Scott.

"I'm going to buy myself a boat and a car," said Shaq, who added that he was going to Toys-R-Us to pick up some new playthings as well.

As for including Scott in his birthday celebration, Shaq said, "Hey, you know I'm going to have my man, 3-D, around." By then, O'Neal had developed a close friendship with several of his teammates. He spent most of his free time by himself, but when he wanted his buddies around, he usually called Scott, Nick Anderson or Litterial Green. Shaq nicknamed the trio of himself, Scott and Anderson the "Knuckleheads" and the "Young Guns."

"I'm not going to let anyone mess up his head," Scott said of his tallest pal. "As long as I'm his friend, I'm going to make sure he's all right. This is one superstar who's not going to get screwed up."

O'Neal called Scott "the older brother I never had, someone I can talk to. He's someone I can trust."

When necessary, Scott didn't hold back from putting the rookie in his place. He was also understanding enough to know when not to criticize his teammate.

"I tell it like it is," Scott explained. "I don't give him lip service. When he's good on the court, I tell him. When he's bad, I tell him he stinks. I think he appreciates the honesty. He wants people to act normal around him."

What O'Neal really would have liked was to get Scott back into the starting lineup. Despite a yeoman's effort from Anthony Bowie, another of Shaq's chums, the Magic were hurting without the outside threat of 3-D.

In the final meeting of the year with the Knicks, O'Neal was smothered by Patrick Ewing and Charles Smith, who didn't have to worry about looking out for Scott and could help double down on the big guy. Shaq had perhaps his worst showing against Pat Riley's ballclub. He scored 23 points, but had only nine rebounds, a season low against the Knicks, and fouled out in the final two minutes of regulation.

Ewing, on the other hand, stayed out of foul trouble and had his finest showing against Shaq. He delivered 37 points and 17 rebounds and was the driving force in a 109–107 overtime win that split the season's series at 2–2 and dropped the Magic back to 28–28 on the season.

Although Orlando bounced back to beat Indiana, behind a 25-point, 11-rebound effort from its superstar, the Magic continued to nose-dive through March. A road loss to Atlanta signaled the start of a five-game losing streak that would send the Magic tumbling to 29–33, marking the first time all season that the club had been four games below .500.

Robinson and the Spurs struck the final blow during the Magic's week-long skid. The "Admiral" outquicked his young adversary again, hitting for 30 points and getting seven rebounds and four assists. O'Neal was well below his normal level of play, producing just 15 points and 13 rebounds in a 96–93 loss.

O'Neal also had to face Hakeem Olajuwon during the long losing streak. He had better success against the Rockets' center, but still couldn't lead the Magic to victory on the road. Shaq out-rebounded Hakeem, 17–15, but the scoring edge went to Olajuwon, 20–16. Houston, meanwhile, came from behind to win the game, 94–93.

That defeat came on the heels of a particularly dismal showing in Orlando, where the Magic were easily beaten by the Seattle SuperSonics. Several of the Sonics mentioned that the Magic looked like a weary ballclub that might be fading.

"They looked tired," Seattle point guard Gary Payton said. "They didn't have anything left in their legs. If they missed a shot, they didn't want to chase it."

As always, Shaq denied any possibility of hitting the proverbial wall.

"I don't feel it bothering me," he said. "No, brother, not at all."

The day after the club's second loss to San Antonio, the Magic finally found a way to get back on the winning track. The answer to the losing woes came in Denver, where O'Neal overcame foul trouble to score 22 points and collect eight rebounds in only 29 minutes of play. Nick Anderson and Donald Royal provided the long-range firepower, combining for 57 points in a 114–108 win over the Nuggets, whose top scorer, Chris Jackson, was held to 18 points.

Orlando closed out the miserable month of March on a positive note by winning three of its final four games. All three victories—against Miami, New Jersey and Detroit—were in the O-Rena, where the team continued to win about two-thirds of its games. Its lone road trip, to Chicago, resulted in another loss.

The team's final game of March not only marked the end of a rough stretch, it also started a potential problem for the Shaq sensation and the young star's pristine image.

Frustrated by a 2-for-11 shooting night, O'Neal unleashed his pent-up anger at Detroit Pistons guard Alvin Robertson, who was holding Shaq back from attacking Bill Laimbeer. It was clear that Laimbeer, infamous for his cheap shots, baited the rookie center by taunting him and finally delivering a wrap-around, intentional foul to send him to the free-throw line.

O'Neal had enough of Robertson's bear hug, so Shaq threw an overhand right and struck his smaller foe in the head. That meant immediate ejection from the game and a one-game suspension.

"The replays all show the fight from the waist up," said O'Neal. "They don't show what happened below the belt. He hit me in the groin, so I hit him back. And I'd do the same thing if it happens again."

When told that Shaq had charged him with taking a cheap shot, Robertson scoffed and said, "Shaq's the new ambassador of the league so he can pretty much do whatever he wants. He's the heir apparent, but it's a joke that he says I hit him. I never hit him."

No one else seemed to believe it, either. Some reporters speculated that O'Neal had been advised to contrive some type of excuse to protect his spotless, multi-million dollar image. But nobody accepted it.

"As for Shaq's contention Robertson hit him below the belt, which supposedly prompted the punch to Alvin's head, I don't buy it," wrote *USA Today* columnist Peter Vecsey. "I saw a push in the small of the back, that's the extent of the contact from his end."

There was a collective gasp heard on Madison Avenue, where the corporate execs using Shaq as a marketing tool were frightened they had picked the wrong man.

"These incidents are just fleeting," said BBDO chairman Phillip Dusenberry, who was working out the final aspects of O'Neal's deal with Pepsi. "For the most part, I don't think clients are disturbed."

Magic coach Matt Guokas, who called himself exasperated by the incident, worried out loud that the problem with Shaq's temper could fester down the stretch.

"You would like to think that we learned our lesson last night, and now it will never happen again," Guokas said. "But I know we'll go out and somebody will bump him, and it'll be the same thing all over again."

Obviously, Guokas was concerned about Shaq's complete lack of remorse for fighting and hurting his own team.

After receiving a fine of $10,250 and loss of one game's pay—$36,585—Shaq laughed it off, saying, "The money thing doesn't bother me. With my contract, I'll still have a little bit left. Missing a game is what hurts."

While the Magic managed to hang on to beat Detroit, the loss of Shaq was critical with a showdown on tap with Alonzo Mourning and the Charlotte Hornets. The Magic, 33–34, had a chance to overtake the Hornets, 35–35, for eighth place in the East.

However, without Shaq, there was no magic in the O-Rena. Mourning took advantage of his absence to dominate Greg Kite and Tom Tolbert, scoring a game-high 30 points in a 102–93 victory for the Hornets.

Even with Shaq back and Scott healthy again, the Magic lost two more games to stretch their losing streak to three. They didn't even come close to beating Indiana or Miami.

On the day of the Indiana game, Shaq and Scott took a side trip to the Indiana Youth Center, the prison that held former heavyweight champion Mike Tyson. Nobody was sure why O'Neal was going to visit the boxing great who had been convicted of rape. It certainly wasn't anything to help his damaged image. Peculiarly, the Tyson visit was announced by the Magic in a press release. O'Neal, though, would not say a word about it.

Tyson had refused visits from other athletes and celebrities, but for some reason, agreed to see the two young Magic players.

"It was a pleasure meeting the guy," said Scott. "He is doing great. I hope that he gets out soon."

Scott went on to say that Tyson "definitely has charisma and a fine work ethic."

Interestingly, Tyson spent his days handing out basketballs in the prison gym and keeping the equipment clean and orderly. He was being paid about a buck per day for his work ethic.

According to the Magic public relations staff, O'Neal set up the prison visit with Tyson all by himself. But he refused to tell anyone on the club, other than Scott, why he was going.

After the rough road trip, Shaq and the Magic came home to beat a weak Philadelphia team by 26 points for the club's second-largest margin of victory in the season. Then Orlando went to the "Hive" in Charlotte, seeking some revenge at the expense of the Hornets. It also marked the first national televised matchup of O'Neal and Mourning, and TNT got its money's worth this time.

O'Neal was brilliant on both ends of the court. He showed some rare offensive moves that Mourning couldn't stop. In the first half, Mourning apparently had his foe trapped on the baseline, but Shaq simply spun around for a 360-degree slam. In the second half, Mourning and Larry Johnson tried to cut off the driving O'Neal, but Shaq simply split them and powered in for another dunk. He finished his night's work with 29 points, 10 rebounds and three blocks, compared to Mourning's 21–8–0, and the Magic earned a 109–96 win.

The Magic, with Shaq outplaying another rival, Christian Laettner, picked up another road win, beating Minnesota, 95–92. O'Neal provided 29 points and nine rebounds, while Laettner had 20 points and nine rebounds. Shaq also swatted down six shots.

But Orlando couldn't keep winning and slipped into a mid-April skid that left only a flicker of playoff hope left. The Magic split a home-and-away series with Milwaukee but lost back-to-back road games to Philadelphia and Cleveland. That left the club with a 13–17 record after the All-Star Break and its overall record of 37–40 left the Magic in 10th place in the East.

Speaking of Shaq

Jeff Turner
Orlando Magic forward

"For us to improve as a team, Shaquille has got to become a better free-throw shooter. I think that comes strictly from repetition and hard work. He's gone to the line more than anybody on our team, and that's a big part of it.

"Many of the great scorers in this league weren't good free-throw shooters when they first came into the

league. You look at guys like Karl Malone and Dominique Wilkins—they didn't shoot very well from the line at first, but they worked hard and made that part of their game. That's why they're such great scorers today.

"I would like to see the big fella pick up a couple of moves. I think he needs to work on his low-post game. We've seen all year that he can go up strong and dunk on anybody. But when we've played against a big, strong shot-blocker guy, who can push him out of the lane, then he has trouble. Look at a guy like Patrick Ewing. He's developed some great moves. He can spin to the middle for a hook or he can turn to the baseline for a turnaround jump shot. If you've got two or three weapons, it just makes it easier to score and makes it more difficult to defend against your team.

"This year, we weren't really looking for Shaq to hit the turnaround jumper or a long hook, because he really doesn't have that right now. Right now, he's not asked to shoot anything from beyond six to eight feet, but we're going to need that from him later on. The opponents are going to get bigger and stronger, and they're going to try to push him away from the basket. So he's going to need to do some other things to help us.

"Shaq is our bread and butter, so whenever we're able to post him up inside, then we're going to go to that first. We've got to get whatever we can out of him.

"All year long, Shaq has done an excellent job on the boards. That's the best thing that he's done for us. He's been effective as a rebounder. He has also learned to pick up the double-teams and kick it back out to us for the jump shots, so that helps."

twenty-three

The Final Week

As the Magic brought down the curtain on their first season with Shaquille O'Neal, the injury-riddled, inconsistent club pulled it all together to take one last-gasp dive for the play-off finish line. It was a dramatic conclusion to a whirlwind season that caught the fancy of the league and its fans.

Not about to go out without a splash, Shaq saved one last phenomenal feat for the final week when he completely tore down a goal at the Meadowlands Arena in New Jersey. His second basket-smashing blow came on the next-to-last day of the regular season and simply added the last remarkable story to the legend of the league's freshest superstar.

However, the Magic's focus during Week 25 of the long, tough NBA season was on pulling off the improbable mission of passing up Detroit and Indiana, or Detroit and Atlanta, or Indiana and Detroit to slip into eighth-place in the East and earn the right to face the top-seeded New York Knicks in the first round of the playoffs.

Orlando had long since surpassed the old franchise record of 31 wins. Now there was a chance for the team's first winning, or at least non-losing, record, and more importantly, the first playoff appearance.

Of course, NBA and network officials were hoping for a magical conclusion to O'Neal's marvelous rookie season and a dream matchup of Shaq and Patrick Ewing to start the playoffs.

Entering the last week, Orlando was in 10th place in the East with a 37–40 record. Atlanta (40–38) was in seventh place, just barely ahead of Indiana (39–38), and Detroit (38–40) stood alone in ninth place.

Both Orlando and Indiana had a chance to improve their positions on Sunday, April 18. The Pacers, however, had a much easier assignment facing Milwaukee at home than did the Magic, which had to play host to the Boston Celtics, who were battling with New Jersey and Charlotte for the 4–5–6 slots in the East.

At the outset, Boston picked up where it left off the previous afternoon during a convincing win at Miami. Aging Celtic center Robert Parish was holding his own against O'Neal, while Reggie Lewis and Xavier McDaniel were getting most of the points. The Celtics jumped out to a 20–12 lead in the first quarter, despite six points and six rebounds from O'Neal. But the Magic made a move shortly after Greg Kite came on to give Shaq a rest. Jeff Turner and Tom Tolbert hit key baskets to help the Magic pull within 24–21 at the end of the quarter.

With Shaq back to start the second quarter, Orlando quickly tied the game on a 3-point jumper from Turner. Backup forward Donald Royal got the hot hand and scored nine of the Magic's 33 points in the quarter. The highlight was Shaq's power slam over Parish that sent the ball bounding off the head of the 39-year-old Celtic warrior. Surprisingly, O'Neal, who had hit just 40 percent of his foul shots in the previous four games, made four straight free throws to send Orlando to a comfortable 54–43 halftime lead.

"The amazing thing about Shaq is he's not even playing that well and he still has 14 points and 12 rebounds," Magic shooting coach Buzz Braman remarked at halftime. "Shaq can give you 26 points and 18 rebounds on a bad night. Incredible!"

Meanwhile, Celtic Hall of Famer Tom Heinsohn, now a TV analyst for the club, was complaining at half-time about the team's difficult schedule of back-to-back road games in a period of 21 hours.

"You're supposed to have at least 24 hours between games," Heinsohn said. "That's a league rule. They played at 3:30 yesterday in Miami and now they're playing at 12:30 today. That's the league for you."

Heinsohn went on to say that the Celtics often played consecutive night-afternoon games when he was playing with the club. And of course, the team didn't have chartered flights back then, he noted.

Tired or not, the Celtics made a quick run at Orlando to start the second half, but Shaq cut them off at the pass with two straight alley-oop dunks that caused an explosion of cheering in the packed O-Rena. O'Neal helped extend the lead back to 71–61 before taking his usual late third-quarter rest. Scott Skiles hit a 3-pointer to stretch the margin to 13, but Boston pulled within 10, 77–67, at the end of the quarter.

Even though Shaq came back to the lineup to start the fourth quarter, the Magic had trouble getting any offensive flow, and the Celtics were just as ragged. Boston finally made a mini-run in the final five minutes. Point guard Dee Brown drove the lane and drew a touch foul from O'Neal, his fifth. With 3:44 left, Brown made one of two free throws to make it 84–79 and anyone's game.

Boston, due to a series of turnovers and poor shot selection caused by Shaq's 7-1 presence, did not score a single point the rest of the way. Orlando's only points in the last three and a half minutes came on Skiles' two free throws.

In the Magic locker room, a frustrated Dennis Scott yelled, "I'm glad we don't play any more 12:30 games. That game was horrible."

It would rank as one of the all-time ugly games in Celtics' history. In fact, the Celts' 79 points was the fewest ever scored against the Magic in its four-year history. Another milestone for the Shaqnificent rookie season.

Later in the day, Indiana knocked off Milwaukee to move into a seventh-place tie with Atlanta, both at 40–38. Orlando was tied with Detroit at 38–40. All four teams had just four games left.

If Orlando were to finish tied for eighth place with Indiana, the Pacers would get the nod, due to complicated playoff tie-breaker formula used by the NBA. The Magic, though, would win a possible tie-breaker with Atlanta. So it was clear to the Magic club and its fans that they should pull for Indiana to beat Atlanta in a vitally important road game on Tuesday.

The Magic, meanwhile, had the good fortune of facing Washington in the O-Rena on Tuesday, having already beaten the Bullets three straight times. Coach Wes Unseld probably considered dressing up himself, after losing starting center Pervis Ellison and backup big man Charles Jones to injuries.

Washington wound up starting former Magic center Mark Acres against O'Neal, and it was no contest right from the opening tipoff. Shaq won the tip, sprinted down court, took a pass from Skiles and spun past Acres as if he were standing still. Harvey Grant stopped a sure dunk by hammering Shaq, who clunked both foul shots. But Scott got the loose ball and sank a 20-footer to get the Magic off and gunning.

With Nick Anderson hitting long jumpers and Shaq slamming at every opportunity, the Magic raced out to a 30–17 first-quarter lead and was on its way to a certain victory.

Shaq added another one for the highlight film early in the second quarter when he swatted down a shot attempt by Doug Overton, got loose on the fast break and fed Scott with a beautiful no-look pass that resulted in a layup. Shaq's third dunk of the half stretched the cushion to 20, 39–19, with 9:38 left. Some sloppy play by the Magic allowed the Bullets to creep back within the range of respectability, trimming the deficit to 49–40 at halftime.

In the first two periods, Shaq took advantage of

constant double-teaming to feed Anderson, Scott and Anthony Bowie for jumpers. O'Neal had four assists in the half to go along with nine points, 10 rebounds and two blocks.

Bullets rookie forward Tom Gugliotta led his ballclub with 10 points and three rebounds, but his effectiveness was reduced by the absence of Ellison.

Prior to the game, there had been an interesting discussion among media covering the game about O'Neal and Gugliotta. *Washington Post* reporters David Aldridge and Bill Brubacher were trying to put together their NBA All-Rookie team, with the help of *Sports Illustrated* basketball writer Jack McCallum. The consensus was that O'Neal, Alonzo Mourning, Christian Laettner and Gugliotta were locks to make the first team, but the fifth spot was up for grabs among Latrell Sprewell, Robert Horry and Anthony Pealer.

There was also debate about whether O'Neal would be seriously challenged for Rookie of the Year. Shaq had won the Rookie of the Month honor for the first four months, but Mourning held the title in March and had a good shot at winning April as well. Aldridge said he would vote for Shaq, but wouldn't be surprised to see some first-place votes for Mourning. His colleagues agreed with him.

Later that night, Aldridge would ask O'Neal to name his All-Rookie team. Shaq excluded himself and tabbed Mourning, Laettner, Gugliotta, Horry and Harold Miner.

Shaq and the Magic went back to their low-post offense to begin the second half and soon stretched their lead back to a safer margin. O'Neal overwhelmed Acres in the quarter, pulling down eight rebounds, scoring six points and adding yet another assist. It took Orlando less than four minutes to build another 20-point cushion. The score was 82–66 at the end of the period.

The fourth quarter was not without its fireworks as Shaq was called for flagrantly hammering Gugliotta with his body, resulting in a two-shot foul and possession to Washington. It didn't make much difference, though, as the Magic cruised home to a 105–86 victory and waited for some good news in the Indiana-Atlanta game.

Unfortunately for the Magic, the Hawks came back to recapture the lead they had been holding for most of the night and ended up beating Indiana. With three games left, Atlanta was in seventh place at 41–38, Indiana in eighth at 40–39, Orlando in ninth at 39–40, and Detroit in 10th at 38–41 after a loss at Cleveland.

The next night, Atlanta got the luck of the draw by getting to play the hobbled Bullets in Washington, and the Hawks won again, improving to 42–38 and thereby clinching a playoff berth. Orlando, however, lost a chance to gain ground on Indiana, which lost to red-hot Cleveland.

Rematched with the Celtics, this time in the Boston Garden, the Magic played its worst game of the season. The Celtics, apparently inspired by their abysmal showing in Orlando three days earlier, came out firing away to take a huge 66–42 first-half lead, despite 15 points from Shaq and 13 from Scott Skiles.

The Magic never found a way to mount a serious challenge in the second half as Sherman Douglas (24 points, 11 assists) had a field day, along with McDaniel with 19 points. O'Neal countered with 20 points and 10 rebounds, but needed to have a 40-plus scoring night to make this one close. Boston soared to a 126–98 victory, handing the Magic its largest margin of defeat for the season.

In the morning, the *Orlando Sentinel* headline read: "Magic on brink of elimination." Indiana, 40–40, was in eighth place, just one game in the standings ahead of Orlando, 39–41. But due to the NBA's tie-breaking procedure, the Pacers would win a possible tie-breaker with the Magic and were, in effect, two games ahead. Simply put, the Magic had to win its final two games—at New Jersey on Friday and Atlanta at home Saturday—while Indiana had to lose its last two—at Detroit Friday and Miami at home Saturday. The Pistons, 38–42, still had an outside shot at getting the eighth spot. In addition to playing host to Indiana, they would close out their season at New Jersey Sunday.

The NBA tie-breaker system begins with head-to-head competition: Orlando and Indiana split their four games. The next step is divisional record: Those two teams aren't in the same division, so that doesn't count. The third step is conference record: they were both on pace to finish 27–29 in the East. The fourth step is winning percentage against playoff teams in the conference: they were both on pace to finish 13–17 against playoff teams in the East. The fifth step is point differential in head-to-head games: Indiana outscored the Magic by seven points in their four games.

On Friday, Shaq and the Magic entered the final 26 hours of its regular season, hoping to find a way to extend the year into the playoffs. They did their part with an implausible comeback against playoff-bound New Jersey.

Shaq stole the show in the early going by thrilling even the Nets' fans with his second basket-destroying dunk. This thunder slam came with 3:00 left in the first quarter and his incredible force pulled down the entire backboard and support system. Shaq was fortunate not to get hurt as his head was grazed by the tumbling shot clock. It was a splendid display of Shaq-sational power. The maintenance crew took 47 minutes to bring in a new goal.

Orlando pulled within 31–27 at the end of the opening quarter, and then Nick Anderson, scoreless to that point, caught fire and set a team record with 20 points on seven of nine shooting in the second quarter, slicing the Nets' lead to 58–57 at the half.

Slick Nick was nearly as impressive in the third quarter when he sank six of 10 attempts, but the Nets' Bernard King, Cliff Robinson, Derrick Coleman and Drazen Petrovic were all on their way to 20-point nights, helping the Nets push the lead to 94–87 going into the final quarter.

While O'Neal, perhaps still stunned by his he-man heroics, was having a terrible time, hitting only three of 10 shot attempts for the night, Anderson remained unconscious. He seemingly couldn't miss in the fourth quarter and eventually shot the Magic into the lead by draining a 10-foot runner to make it 114–113 with 37.0 seconds left. The Magic, despite only 10 points and five rebounds from

Shaq, pulled out a 119–116 win and remained alive in playoff chase as Detroit knocked off Indiana.

Heading into Saturday's regular-season finale for both teams, Orlando and Indiana were tied for eighth place at 40–41, with Detroit on their heals at 39–42. A win by Orlando over Atlanta or Indiana over Miami would eliminate Detroit. For the Magic to make the playoffs, it needed a win over Atlanta and a Miami upset at Indiana, which wasn't likely to happen because Heat center Rony Seikaly was injured and would not play.

Nonetheless, for the first time ever, playoff fever struck Orlando full blast. Every talk show in town was packed with calls about Shaq and the Magic men. Every fan in Central Florida was hoping for a 41st win by their team and some help from the rival Heat against Indiana. As could be expected, there wasn't a ticket to the O-Rena to be found anywhere in Orlando, and wishful ticket seekers began lining the streets three hours before game time.

The Magic, though weary from a late-night flight home from New Jersey and from the arduous six-month season, gladly rose to the occasion against the Hawks, who hoped to edge out Charlotte for the sixth spot in the East, thereby missing out on having to play Chicago in the first round.

Dominique Wilkins, a lock to win Comeback Player of the Year, hit a three-pointer early to help the Hawks bounce out to a 12–2 lead, but coach Matt Guokas settled down his club during a timeout, and the Magic came roaring back. The hometown heroes ignited the O-Rena by pouring it on during a remarkable 32–5 streak that extended into the second quarter.

Using its post offense, the Magic worked the ball inside to O'Neal, who either muscled past Jon Kocak or passed back out to Anderson, Scott or Skiles. Shaq picked up a three-point play just before the end of the first quarter and finished the period with 11 points and 11 rebounds, pushing Orlando in front, 26–17.

Early in the second quarter, Shaq fed Scott for a three-pointer and then took a pass from Skiles for an alley-oop slam. On the next possession, Shaq returned the favor to Skiles with a nice assist on yet another three-point shot, this boosting Orlando's lead to 34–17. Wilkins and Mookie Blaylock led a mini-run by the Hawks as they pulled within 48–37 at halftime. But the first-half show belonged to Shaq with 17 points, 13 rebounds and three assists. Wilkins, well guarded by Anderson, hit just six of 15 shot attempts and had 15 points.

An Anderson runner boosted the Magic's margin back to 15 points early in the third quarter. Then Scott finally hit a baseline jumper to get the difference back to 20, 68–48.

At the 2:42 mark, O'Neal slipped free for a break-away slam that caused the basket to shake back and forth. This time, it didn't come down, but the Magic fans still showered him with waves of cheers. The lead was 75–59 going into the final quarter of the regular season.

Midway through the fourth, word began to spread throughout the O-Rena that the Heat was beating Indiana and the Magic could be headed to the playoffs. The timing seemed almost too good to be true as the Magic had played some of its best basketball during the final week of the season. O'Neal continued to be the main force in the offense and defense, but was really picking up the double-teams and becoming more proficient at setting up Anderson and Scott on the wings. And Skiles, despite the shoulder injury, was starting to hit three-pointers again. The club was also getting reliable minutes from power forwards Tom Tolbert and Jeff Turner and reserves Donald Royal, Anthony Bowie, Litterial Green and Greg Kite.

Orlando was well on its way to victory with a 94–79 cushion when team officials gave public address announcer Paul Porter approval to reveal the halftime score in Indianapolis: Heat 57, Pacers 50. The Magic fans, already exuberant over the wonderful season-ending showing, became delirious over the news.

O'Neal scored his 31st point on a free throw that completed a three-point power play and sent the Magic ahead 97–79 with 2:07 left. He went to the line one more time, but missed twice in a fitting finish to a tough year at the foul line. Guokas pulled his young star with 1:12 left, and O-Rena fans came to their feet for a final standing ovation. The Magic closed out the 104–85 victory and waited anxiously for the Pacers' game to end.

For about an hour, the Magic held eighth place all by itself with a 41–41 record. However, a heart-breaking tie-breaker would eventually cost the club a coveted play-off berth as Indiana rallied to beat Miami, 94–88, and win its 41st game as well.

Speaking of Shaq

Xavier McDaniel
Boston Celtics forward

"Shaq is already a very good player in the league. He's very strong and very physical. As soon as he starts getting down some moves, he's going to be a great player in this league. No one in the NBA has been that big and that mobile since Wilt Chamberlain. We had Kareem Abdul-Jabbar, Patrick Ewing, Hakeem Olajuwon and those guys, but they're only about 240 or 250 pounds. This guy is over 300 pounds and he runs the floor like a forward.

"If Shaq had post moves like Kevin McHale, he would really be unstoppable. He would completely dominate this league. Nobody could stop him. But sometimes with the double-teams and the traps, he needs to have a drop step and a nice face-up move. Once he gets that, I can't imagine how you're going to stop him. Kevin McHale proved that you score a lot of points with those kind of low-point moves. You give a player so many looks that it just eats at a guy.

"From day one, Shaq has improved, but he's basically using power moves. Of course, there's no room for him to use finesse because he's so strong.

"Anytime you play against a powerful seven-footer

who can block shots, you have to do some different things. It changes the way the game is played. You shoot more jump shots, and you don't try to drive to the hole as much. Therefore, it's a lot tougher to score. He changes the game.

"Shaq is really hard to compare to anyone else. I don't like to compare players anyway. How are you going to determine who's the best center or the best player ever? That's really impossible to do. Basketball changes from decade to decade. There are so many bigger, stronger players in the league. I think it's unfair to say he's one of the greatest players ever. You can't say what he would have done against Chamberlain or Jabbar. An injury could knock all that hope out. So any statement you could make wouldn't be accurate. Look at Ralph Sampson. Everyone thought he was going to be one of the all-time great centers. He made the All-Star Game several years and then he got hurt. All of a sudden, people said he was a flop. So I don't think it's fair to compare players."

twenty-four

It's Magic

As expected, Shaquille O'Neal was a runaway choice for the NBA Rookie of the Year honor. He would also finish seventh in the voting for the league's top honor of Most Valuable Player. No other rookie even got a vote. He was also proclaimed by The Associated Press as the most celebrated player to enter the NBA in a generation. But the day after Shaq's selection as the league's top rookie, national columnists took shots at him, writing that he didn't win anything in college and questioning whether he had the drive to do it in the NBA.

What shocked the sports world, however, was the magical draw of the NBA Lottery. By finishing with the 11th worst record in the league, the Orlando Magic was given a token one ball in the Lottery hopper that held 66. The odds of the Magic even moving up to one of the first three spots didn't seem worth calculating.

When NBA Commissioner David Stern opened the envelope for the 11th position in the draft, Magic General

Manager Pat Williams and a national television audience of basketball fans were stunned to see the Detroit Pistons' logo, meaning the Magic had jumped at least into the top three positions, marking the first time in Lottery history that the team with the best record among the 11 non-play-off teams actually moved up.

The drama built to a crescendo by the time Stern got to the final three picks, and the only teams left were Orlando, Philadelphia and Golden State. The Warriors came up the lucky losers in the third spot, which would probably bring them a premier player like Jamal Mashburn, Calbert Cheaney, Anfernee Hardaway or Rodney Rogers. That left the Magic and 76ers as the teams that would get the first two picks, probably good for either 7-6 center Shawn Bradley or 6-9 power forward Chris Webber, two of the sensational underclassmen to make this a fairly strong draft class.

Once again, the Magic defied the odds as Stern turned over Philly's logo in the second spot. He made it official by opening the magical envelope for the first pick. By then, Williams was already flipping out.

"What can I say—it's magic," Williams gasped. "We went from No. 11 to No. 1."

Going into the Lottery, Williams had projected his team's chances of winning the top pick as being "tantamount to World War II breaking out, with Switzerland winning."

When I had asked Williams who he would take with the first pick, he told me straight out that it would have to be Bradley, because there's such a premium on big men in the league. However, he really didn't think it would be his club that would have the first choice anyway.

What were the odds of one team winning the Lottery two years in a row? Particularly a team that had a break-even 41–41 record the second year? They were incalculable.

The flabbergasted executive had been spending all of his time trying to figure who would be a good choice at the 11th position in the draft. The team's two major needs were power forward and point guard. Since Williams made the determination it would be tough to get a quality power forward in the middle of the draft, he had focused most of his attention on point guards, namely Bobby Hurley of Duke and Sam Cassales of Florida State.

"Right now I have no idea," Williams said of the draft possibilities. "We were thinking that we'd be picking 11th, so we're suddenly thinking about the top, the Bradleys, the Webbers, the Mashburns."

While some national writers speculated the Magic may want to go with a Twin Towers of Shaq and Bradley, everyone who had followed O'Neal knew that would be highly inadvisable and very unlikely to happen.

"Our power forward position needs to be solidified, stabilized," said Williams, pointing out his foremost need.

Veteran Terry Catledge started out the 1992–93 season as the club's starting power forward, but went down quickly to prolonged injury problems. Second-year player Brian Williams never stepped up like the club had hoped he would and eventually joined Catledge on the injured list. Tom Tolbert was picked up after being released by Golden State and ended up starting at the position for much of the season. He was backed up by Jeff Turner, Greg Kite and Donald Royal. None of them averaged more than 8.3 points.

While Williams was considering the possibilities at power forward, Philly and Golden State officials were itching to get a shot at Bradley, who had reportedly grown to 7-7 and gained 40 pounds during his two-year Mormon church mission.

"Shaq's a pure center, so I don't know where Bradley fits," Philly General Manager Jim Lynman said, hoping that the Magic would pass on the big man. "It's going to be a very intriguing process for us over the next couple of weeks as we start to examine which player we're going to take."

Golden State coach Don Nelson coveted the chance to get Bradley on his ballclub. Nelson had not been fortunate to have a true center since he coached Bob Lanier with the Milwaukee Bucks. It was clear the Warriors would be willing to consider trading up to get Bradley, which created even more options for Williams and the

Magic. The club let everyone in the league know that it was willing to deal away injury-prone Dennis Scott, which would free up enough money under the salary cap to sign one of the top three picks.

"We'd certainly like to get bigger," Nelson said. "We're not disappointed at No. 3. That opens a lot of doors to make a trade. We like seven players and we'll have the opportunity to draft all but two."

The most unlucky team in the Lottery was once again the Dallas Mavericks, which came close to setting an NBA record for the fewest wins in one season. But the Mavericks, with 11 balls in the hopper, didn't claim any of the first three spots and had to settle for the fourth choice. Following the Mavs were Minnesota, Washington, Sacramento, Milwaukee, Denver, Miami and Detroit.

For O'Neal, it had already been a very successful post-season, even if his team wasn't in the playoffs. In early May, he picked up 96 of the 98 votes from a nationwide panel of sportswriters and broadcasters in the Rookie of the Year selection. His chief nemesis, Alonzo Mourning of Charlotte, got the other two votes and took second place in the balloting.

Hailed as the next great center to play in the NBA, Shaq led an outstanding rookie class in every major statistical category for a big man: 23.4 points per game, 13.9 rebounds, 3.53 blocks and .562 field-goal percentage. But Mourning was not far behind and had actually outperformed Shaq down the stretch.

"I hope I can get an NBA championship trophy to go along with it," O'Neal said, "so that when I retire and have children, I can tell my son, 'I was bad.'"

As for his overall showing, Shaq said, "I was just doing what I was supposed to do. At 7-1, 303, you're supposed to go out there, dunk, rebound and battle. It was just doing my job."

While he didn't put a dent in any of Wilt Chamberlain's rookie records, he had become the first rookie in more than a decade to take down more than 1,000 rebounds. He also had seven games with at least 20 points and 20 rebounds.

Mourning joined O'Neal as the only unanimous selections on the NBA All-Rookie team, which was announced a week after the Rookie of the Year award. They were joined on the first team by Christian Laettner of Minnesota, Tom Gugliotta of Washington and LaPhonso Ellis of Denver.

The All-Rookie team was selected by the coaches. Their second team included Walt Williams of Sacramento, Robert Horry of Houston, Latrell Sprewell of Golden State, Clarence Weatherspoon of Philadelphia and Richard Dumas of Phoenix. Other rookies who received votes were Harold Miner of Miami, Anthony Peeler of the Lakers, Todd Day of Milwaukee, Adam Keefe of Atlanta, Jimmy Jackson of Dallas, Bryant Stith of Denver, Sean Rooks of Dallas, Anthony Avent of Milwaukee, Lloyd Daniels of San Antonio and Doug Christie of the Lakers.

Coaches and executives throughout the league were still calling Shaq the league's next super center, although there were a few more reservations, due to his lack of offensive improvement through the course of his rookie season.

"I can't imagine there's anybody in the league who doesn't think he'll be an absolutely great player," said Sacramento Kings director of player personnel Jerry Reynolds. "There hasn't been anybody coming into the league who caused this kind of stir in a long time, maybe since [Kareem] Abdul-Jabbar."

No doubt, Shaq was the most celebrated rookie since Michael Jordan won top rookie honors in 1985. After Jordan, the Rookie of the Year winners included Patrick Ewing, Chuck Person, Mark Jackson, Mitch Richmond, David Robinson, Derrick Coleman and Larry Johnson.

Robinson was the only one of the group to post numbers anywhere close to what Shaq had. But even Robinson didn't impress his peers and dominate inside like the Magic rookie.

O'Neal helped the Magic make the biggest improvement in the league, going from 21–61 to 41–41. With a little more help, he hoped to be on a championship contender before long.

Interestingly, Shaq's highlight of the season was not the big wins over the New York Knicks or the Chicago Bulls, and not even the fantastic finish that put the Magic in position to make the playoffs for the first time. Instead, he pointed to an individual accomplishment.

"When I ripped the backboard down on my head," he said, referring to his basket-smashing dunks in Phoenix and New Jersey.

His teammates hoped O'Neal would put more significance on winning the important ballgames and challenging for division, conference and league titles.

It didn't help that Shaq's summer schedule was completely booked before his rookie season even finished. He would be spending much of the summer in Los Angeles filming the movie, "Blue Chip" with Nick Nolte. Commercials, videos and a European tour for Reebok would fill up the rest of his off-season.

"Every time I get a good business opportunity I'm going to take it," he said. "Those deals don't come along every day."

Shaq's intrigue with making more and more millions and his emphasis on individual goals was already catching the attention of the national media. Some writers were comparing him to Chamberlain who got all the individual records, but most often played second fiddle to Bill Russell when it came to world championships, the true mark of a great player in the league.

Mourning, who was brilliant in the playoffs, showed that he may be the next Russell. Certainly, Alonzo benefitted from playing on a more well rounded team than his arch rival in Orlando. He had a great forward at his side in Larry Johnson and a superb guard in his backcourt by the name of Kendall Gill.

But it was Mourning who led the Charlotte Hornets to their stunning upset of Russell's old team, the Boston Celtics. 'Zo added the finishing touch by sinking an off-balance 21-foot jumper at the buzzer to clinch the series victory. Shaq, of course, couldn't even sink an eight-footer during his rookie season.

The Hornets' young center was even more spectacular in going head-to-head with Patrick Ewing in the second round of the playoffs. Overall, Mourning outplayed his fellow Georgetown alumnus, using his edge in quickness and vast offensive skills to keep the Hornets in the game. The Knicks finally subdued the feisty Charlotte ballclub in Game 6.

While Mourning's stats for the season (21.0 points, 10.3 rebounds and 3.47 blocks) were slightly behind Shaq's, they didn't account for the fact he missed all of training camp and sat out the first four games of the regular season, thereby having to play himself into the lineup.

After the All-Star Break, Mourning outscored Shaq (23.6 to 23.2). But more importantly, he raised his game to a higher level during the Hornets' stretch run to the playoffs, something O'Neal was not able to do.

In the final 13 regular-season games, Mourning took charge of the Hornets' playoff hopes all by himself. He stepped up his game to average 26.3 points, 11 rebounds and shot 57.5 percent from the field. Shaq, on the other hand, skidded down the stretch, averaging 20.1 points in the final eight games and shooting less than 50 percent from the floor.

So who's the best young center in the game?

"Alonzo is so great, the world doesn't know it yet," Bullets General Manager John Nash said. "If I had to pick one player, I guess I'd pick Shaq because of his potential. But Alonzo brings more to the table at this point."

The O'Neal-Mourning matchup is certain to be one of the hottest rivalries in basketball for years to come. The Magic and Hornets could easily be the dominant teams in the Eastern Conference in the 1990s.

Shaq was certainly helped when the Magic selected power forward Chris Webber with the No. 1 pick and proceeded to trade him to Golden State for No. 3 pick Anfernee Hardaway, a superb point guard from Memphis State. Not only did the Magic get a floor leader to run the Shaq-oriented offense, but Pat Williams pulled off a remarkable deal by getting Hardaway, who has been compared to Magic Johnson, and three first-round draft choices from the Warriors. Beginning next year, the Magic will have two first-round picks every other season through the year 2000, putting the once-floundering organization virtually in a can't-miss situation. Another draft day development had Brian Hill taking over as head coach and Matt Guokas moving into the front office.

But ultimately, the Magic will go as far as Shaq carries the club. His impact on the NBA will be determined largely by his own desire to improve his individual skills and be part of a championship team. He holds all the cards. If he takes charge of his own life and takes full advantage of his unlimited potential, he will assure himself a place among the all-time greats. If not, he will have only himself to blame.

Index

ALSO AVAILABLE FROM BONUS

FIGHTING TIGERS BASKETBALL
Great LSU Teams, Players, and Traditions

From Bob Pettit to Pistol Pete Maravich to Dale Brown and Shaquille O'Neal, LSU has developed a rich tradition of star players, coaches and teams. In *Fighting Tigers Basketball*, every great player, coach, and event is described in vivid detail, accompanied by more than 150 action photos. Here is the definitive pictorial history of Louisiana State University basketball.

Bruce Hunter and Joe Planas

ISBN 0-929387-60-0
210 pages, $24.95 cloth

160 East Illinois Street
Chicago, Illinois 60611